Akbar Papers in African Psychology

Na' im Akbar

MIND

PRODUCTIONS

© Mind Productions & Associates, Inc.
324 N. Copeland Street
Tallahassee, FL 32304
Phone 850-222-1764 • Fax 850-224-5331
www.naimakbar.com

First Printing: January 2004

Cover Design: Marie A. Roberts

Published by Mind Productions & Associates, Inc.
Tallahassee, Florida 32304

Library of Congress Control No: 2003104592
ISBN: 0935257098 (paperback)
ISBN: 0935257101 (cloth)

Printed in the United States of America

Dedication

In *Memory* of my dear friend
And distinguished colleague:

DuBois Phillip McGee, Ph.D.

(March 22,1942-June 29, 1999)

TABLE OF CONTENTS

PREFACE	Alvin Turner	i
FOREWORD	Jerome Schiele	iii
INTRODUCTION		ix
I. The Opening		1
A. Voodoo or IQ: An Introduction to African Psychology		3
II. The Afrocentric Paradigm		
(Overview)		27
A. Paradigms of African American Research		32
B. Evolution of Human Psychology for African Americans		55
III. Concepts of African Personality		
(Overview)		89
A. African Roots of Black Personality		93
B. Cultural Expressions of African Personality		107
C. Rhythmic Patterns of Black Personality		123
D. African Metapsychology of Human Personality		135
IV. African American Mental Health		
(Overview)		155
A. Mental Disorders of African Americans		160
B. Awareness: Key to Black Mental Health		179
V. Nile Valley Origins of the Science of the Mind		
(Overview)		195
A. Nile Valley Origins of the Science of the Mind		199
VI. Epilogue		
(Overview)		217
A. Afrocentricity: The Challenge of Implementation		221
BIBLIOGRAPHY		225
ACKNOWLEDGEMENTS		231
INDEX		233
ABOUT THE AUTHOR		237

Preface

This book allows us to bear witness to the many men, women, and children who have been denied a voice in our tragic history and simultaneously provides language, vocabulary, and the structure for the development of new ideas and concepts related to the transformation of human beings. Na'im's concepts both include and transcend race, culture, and ethnicity. He facilitates our understanding of the continuing psycho-spiritual confusion which describes many African-Americans in this country.

Psychologists know that one of the more devastating characteristics of complex post-traumatic stress disorder is an alteration in systems of meaning, but we have been reluctant to establish the linkage between the historical trauma of slavery and present psychological and sociological phenomena. Na'im's unique perspective moves us to explore a vision of humanity that is not reduced by suffering but is rather enhanced by it. His creative voice is transcribed onto these pages and propels us into a journey of seeking truth, personal honesty, and a transcendence of reality.

This book should be required reading for all African-American people and anyone who is exploring the mind as a process leading to continuous transformation rather than a fixed place. Reading this book makes us feel like we want to say "Amen" or "Tell the truth, brother" reminding us of the call and response exhibited in countless African-American churches on Sunday mornings.

Those readers who have had the good fortune to hear this brother speak will be truly blessed with the opportunity to re-experience his words and his wisdom. He affirms and validates us, he teaches, motivates us, and loves us for who we can be as well as for who we are. Na'im is a passionate writer and speaker who touches all of our senses when we read or listen to him. His words carry metaphorical images, which awaken, incite, and reposition readers to experience the deepest aspects of ourselves. His words invoke spiritual consciousness, which increase our capacity to be more human, more loving of all of life, and more conscious of our own potentialities.

i

Finally, Na'im is a national and international treasure. This book provides the reader an opportunity to more completely know him and to understand and appreciate his vision of us as human beings on this earth.

Alvin Turner, Ph.D.

FOREWORD

I first met Dr. Na'im Akbar in 1974 when I was only 13. Known then as Dr. Luther Weems, I met him in two roles: 1) as my only sibling and elder brother's psychology professor at Morehouse College, and 2) as an assistant minister in the Atlanta, Georgia Nation of Islam temple. Since my brother joined the Nation around the same time as did Dr. Weems, my parents and I traveled to Atlanta in 1974 on a fact-finding mission to see what this "Muslim thing" was all about. I use the phrase "Muslim thing" because I believe that during that time, as it is today in the post 9/11 world, most Americans who are Christian view Islam with considerable suspicion. That suspicion also was relevant to my parents since my father was a Baptist preacher and my mother was a sincere and devoted minister's wife. So, my first meeting of Dr. Akbar was during a time of significant, personal family conflict, a conflict between a son's desire to boldly embrace a different theology he believed was right for him and deeply concerned parents who internalized my brother's choice as a rejection of them.

During our visit to Atlanta, I did not realize then that I would be exposed to one of my first formal lectures in what was the inception of African psychology. This occurred when my parents and I visited the Atlanta Nation of Islam (NOI) temple to personally experience a NOI worship service. After being searched by FOI (Fruit of Islam) security guards and then seated in an all male section of the temple, I was surprised to see that Dr. Akbar was the featured speaker. Those who recently have been introduced to the dynamic oratory skills of Na'im Akbar should have seen him in those days. Relatively unknown and with the advantage of youth, his delivery was much more provocative back then. The speech he gave that night was consistent with the Hon. Elijah Muhammad's precepts, but his training as a clinical psychologist, and his proficiency in arousing and inspiring the all black audience, gave his speech added appeal. His speech, which was imbued with the exceptional skill of appealing to the audience's reason and emotion, was well received that night. The vast number of persons who stood up after the speech and who proceeded to join the NOI that night demonstrated Akbar's effectiveness.

In retrospect, Akbar's speech delineated some essential themes of what we now know as African psychology. As conceptualized by its leading proponent, the origin of African psychology can be said to be the result of a remarkable confluence of Akbar's affiliation with the theology of Hon. Elijah Muhammad and his training as a Ph.D. level clinical psychologist. Akbar's training in analyzing and healing the human mind merged well with the Hon. Elijah Muhammad's focus on how slavery had polluted the minds of African Americans. The confluence of Akbar's academic training with the precepts of the Hon. Elijah Muhammad was quite apparent that night, and as I reflect on that occasion, three (3) themes of African psychology were conveyed.

The first was that African and European people were significantly different. They were different in origin, culture, and political/economic status. In origin, I learned that African people were the first people, and because of this, they were the original people on earth to grapple with the problems and potential of being human. Being the first to experience the human dilemma made black people very special. They were special not only because of their success at constructing societies and advancing social organization, but also because of their relationship with God. This special God-human relationship was said to give black people additional potential in drawing on God inspired wisdom and ingenuity. It created a unique opportunity for black people to tap into the knowledge of God and to optimally develop what can be referred to as a "God Consciousness."

African and European people were also said to be different culturally. Whereas the culture of European people was characterized as materialistic, competitive, and xenophobic, the culture of African people was described as spiritual, cooperative, and xenophillic. These distinctions engendered divergent cultural styles that dictated the kinds of societies and civilizations that emerged in Europe and in Africa. More than just shaping societies in the general sense, these worldviews (the term that would be used by African psychologists to describe a group's cultural perspective) shaped the character of social relationships and the norms and mores that governed them. What emerged in these two, distinct worldviews, or what Diop (1978) called "cradles," were different ideas about normal human behavior and aspirations.

I also understood African and European people to be different in political/economic status or in their relationship and access to power. This power differential was ascribed to the experience of the transatlantic slave trade that privileged people of European ancestry and simultaneously stigmatized and brutalized African people. Although this power differential was manifested quite obviously in the divergent treatment of African and European people, it also was expressed in the debilitating narratives that people of European descent constructed about people of African descent. Particularly grounded in the writings and speeches of religious leaders and scholars and social philosophers, these narratives created what Martin and Martin (2002) call "religious mythomania," that is, the creation of myths and distortions to support Eurocentric domination using religious (i.e., biblical) justifications. The material power that Europeans had over African people allowed them to systematically impose their mythomania so that no American social institution would be untouched. The hallmark of this mythomania would be the gospel of inherent black inferiority and innate white supremacy. This gospel would be the springboard to launch and reproduce intergenerational racial oppression that would perpetually render African people vulnerable to political, economic, and physical violence.

The second theme of African psychology that I obtained from Akbar's speech was that the power opportunity Europeans had to generate and replicate mythomania had deleterious mental consequences for them and for people of African descent. I understood from Akbar's lecture that people of European descent suffered, in clinical psychological terms, from a form of ego inflation while people of African descent experienced ego deflation. It was further noted that distortions of superiority – experienced by European people – were just as mentally and humanly debilitating as were distortions of inferiority. Although African psychology considers the mental falsifications that confine the positive potentiality of people of European descent a critical social problem, its primary goal is to address the misrepresentations of inferiority that confront and cripple so many people of African descent.

From Akbar's speech, I further noted that the root of African people's distortions of inferiority was the transatlantic slave trade and the institution of European/European-American slavery. Although many African American scholars and others focus solely on slavery as an institution of labor exploitation, African psychology focuses on slavery's sociocultural and psychocultural outcomes for African people. The emphasis on slavery's inimical effects on African people's psychosocial development was given much attention that night by Dr. Akbar. Much attention was devoted to underscoring the relationship between African people's psychic development under slavery and their (our) contemporary socioeconomic and cultural dependency on people of European descent. Because we continue to experience the "plantation ghost," Akbar argued, African people continue to act as if we were dependent slaves with little or no will to construct an independent African, socioeconomic and cultural reality. Slavery had destroyed our will to think and behave independently of European American norms and mores, and, as Malcolm X asserted in the early 1960s, had left black people in an appalling state of 20th century (and yes now 21st century) enslavement. Slavery's worst legacy, there-fore, was a mental one, and for people of African descent to advance politically and economically, we had to honestly confront and over-come the quagmire of low cultural self-esteem, or what Akbar and other early African psychologists simply called "self-hatred," a ha-tred of ourselves as Africans.

Another point about that I obtained that night, and that would really crystallize later in my life, was that black self-hatred was not peculiar to diasporic Africans in North America. It also occurred among continental Africans, a point that often is overlooked by scholars of contemporary racial oppression. Although continental Africans did not experience the particular calamity of physical bondage, they did, however, endure the equally horrific condition of colonization. European colonization, just as North American slavery, sought to dehumanize Africans by vilifying and disavowing their history, tradi-tions, and being. Both forms of domination worked organically to produce a similar desired outcome, and that was the suppression of the African's will to be free. African psychology attempts to free the African by affirming, celebrating, and codifying those traditions upon which free and thriving African civilizations had been built.

Because these traditions were so critical to our liberation, the third and last theme that I remember about that night was the need for African people to become familiar with and conscious of these traditions and to associate them with the legacy of Africa, not exclusively with the legacy of slavery. Although many people of African descent in North America acknowledge that black people have traditions that are distinct from those of European Americans, they frequently attribute these traditions to our experience as slaves. African psychology contends that this viewpoint is not only erroneous, but that it severely limits the psychosocial and psychohistorical development of African Americans to 1619 Jamestown, Virginia as our historical starting point. By confining our development to 1619 colonial America, diasporic Africans in the United States fall into the shameful trap of believing that all that we are is a response to Eurocentric domination. Although an acknowledgement of the nefarious and indelible effects of Eurocentric domination is clearly within the purview of African psychology, concluding that this form of oppression is the lone contributing factor shaping the psychocultural ethos of black people is not. Thus, a critical African centered assumption – indeed a reality – is that the psychocultural and sociocultural ethos of diasporic Africans in North America is a result of a clear yet complex confluence of the cultural legacy of West Africa and the tragedy of terroristic and European-American sponsored captivity. As stated by Wade Nobles (1974), another founding African centered psychologist, African Americans are of "African root and American fruit."

Once African people consciously recognize Africa as the root of their psychosocial and sociocultural ethos, African psychology contends that they will be motivated to explore, integrate, and perpetuate the traditions of this ethos systematically. Systematically implies using the traditions of Africa as a foundation to construct institutions and organizations that serve and advance the interests of black people and others who wholeheartedly accept the right of all human beings – including black people – to be self-determinative.

However, a group cannot be self-determinative if it views its sociocultural traditions as mere slight variations of a group who benefits from its lack of self-determination. Although identifying similarities between and among cultural groups is not inherently problematic, it can be when one group imposes and institutionalizes its cultural way as the universal model. This implies that a discussion of cultural similarities and differences between groups must be viewed within a context of power relations. African psychology assumes that because the cultural particularity of African people has been systematically suppressed, denied, and vilified by Eurocentric domination, it is extremely important for people of African descent to acquire a fundamental recognition of and respect for the African origins of contemporary African/African-American behavior and cultural distinction. Encouraging this recognition and respect is the promise of African psychology, and the papers presented in this volume represent this promise's earliest expressions.

Jerome H. Schiele, D.S.W.
Norfolk State University
Norfolk, Virginia

References

Diop, C.A. (1978). *The Cultural Unity of Black Africa: The domains of patriarchy and matriarchy in classical antiquity.* Chicago: Third World Press.

Martin, E.P., & Martin, J.M. (2002). *Spirituality and the Black Helping Tradition in Social Work.* Washington, D.C.: National Association of Social Workers.

Nobles, W.W. (1974). African root and American fruit: The Black family. *Journal of Social and Behavioral Sciences*, 20, 66-75.

INTRODUCTION

There will, of course, be those who will pick up this book and with incredulous curiosity ask: "What is African Psychology?" My reply would be: "African Psychology is not a thing, but a place—a view, a perspective, a way of observing." African Psychology does not claim to be an exclusive body of knowledge, though a body of knowledge has and will continue to be generated from the place. It is a perspective that is lodged in the historical primacy of the human view from the land that is known as Africa. It is not limited to a geographical place, neither a particular ethnicity nor an identifiable ideology. It is the view that led to the very dawning of human consciousness and it is the substratum of all that is uniquely human on this planet. It carries the vestiges of humanity's view from the infancy of our being. It is rooted in the prototypes of Ancient Nile Valley Civilization and was probably spawned in the garden we know as the mythological Eden. African Psychology is the perspective of the world's vestigial science when its separation from mythology and religion was not yet imagined. African Psychology is the primal view of humanity's perception of her own humanity and the criteria that she etched into the foundation of civilized life on this planet.

African Psychology is also a more recent view. It is a deconstruction of a view that has mechanized humanity, robbed it of its consciousness, taking away its soul and has ultimately driven it out of its mind. It is a deconstruction of the conceptualizations that have lost the key to the Divine spark that makes humans human. It is a deconstruction of an ethic that has permitted humans to make servants and captives of their sisters and brothers and claim scientific legitimacy of the crime. It is a deconstruction of a worldview that has intentionally robbed most parts of the human family of their divinely given right to know and define their humanity in the context of their legacy and particular cultural experience. It is a deconstruction of the conditions that have created a hegemony that has systematically robbed generations of their volition and their autonomous will to be somebody. African Psychology is the view of the oppressed, but it is also the view of the humanly liberated.

African Psychology is a reconstruction of the world's Truth about the nature and potential of the human being. It is a reconstruction of the certainty of the human being's resiliency and capacity to be restored to the celestial heights from which we emerged. It is the restoration of all that is correct and noble in the human spirit while being cognizant of its potential for downfall. African psychology is that perspective that sees all humans as fundamentally spirit and therefore not subject to the gradations of worth and value that characterized the more distorted vision that bred racism, sexism, materialism, classism and all of the other "isms" that diminished the human spirit. It is a reconstruction of the scaffolding that permitted the earliest constructions of human possibility that permitted the human being to soar far beyond the limits of the physical illusions of our being. It is the reconstruction of the view of human beings that will once again permit us to create and harvest the bounty of compassion, peace, dignity, balance and harmony that the early idealists projected in their symbols of Ma'at, Pyramids, Sphinxes, Ankhs and imagined in the dramas of Heru, Auset, Ausir, Adam, Eve and so many others who were human only in persona but spiritual creatures who were on a journey back home.

Rhetorically, this is what African Psychology is because, as these papers will reveal, it's much too large for science as we have come to know it and far too precise for art as we have come to practice it. It is superstition and it is supra-rational; it is religion and it is science; it is profound and it is folly; it is precise yet it is elusive. It is a place that we have discovered as those who lost our way and have found a map to get back home.

The papers in this volume represent my unique contribution to the conceptualization of this place or perspective that we have identified as "African Psychology." The lead paper in this collection, *"Voodoo or IQ: An Introduction to African Psychology,"* is a selection co-authored by the founding voices in this discipline that has come to be known as African Psychology. First published in 1974, the paper captured the concepts that had been introduced originally in joint presentations by the authors at the annual meetings of the Association of

Black Psychologists in 1972-74.

Syed Khatib, (then known as Cedric Clark) and D. Phillip McGee were colleagues in the Department of Psychology at Stanford University, where their graduate student, Wade Nobles was completing his Ph.D. in the early 1970's. McGee had spent three years completing the research for his Ph.D. at the University of Michigan where we met as graduate students in psychology. The early conversations that Phil McGee and I had initiated during our 1967-70 associations in Ann Arbor were paralleled and extended with the conversations that began to be formalized when McGee met Clark and Nobles at Stanford. The four of us made our first joint presentation on African Psychology at the 1971 meeting of the National Association of Black Psychologists in Detroit. We found a kindred spirit in our recognition that we needed to think differently about the psychology of Black people. There was already a clear recognition among Black Psychologists that there was the need to focus on the unique issues affecting Black people.

The birth of the National Association of Black Psychologists in 1968 was bred from recognition of the inadequacy of the profession of psychology in America to address the social and psychological issues of Black people. The formation of the Association and its conferences provided a forum to begin to ask even more in-depth questions about understanding the psychology of Black people.

The ideas that we brought to the Association regarding the need for a new paradigm in our study of Black people were initially met with considerable skepticism on the part of the seasoned psychologists who had established the organization. The fundamental assumption that we put forth as this cadre of "African Psychologists" was that Black people were fundamentally *African*. We argued that it was important to understand Black people within the conceptual framework of our cultural origins rather than being preoccupied with our current condition and circumstances. Of course, such a broad-range conception of causation represented a radical idea to Western Psychology and to those who had been trained within the confines of the European-American approach to psychology. Though we had been trained under the same set of assumptions, as young Ph.D.'s entering the field of psychology we had a degree of flexibility that our more seasoned colleagues initially found difficult to accept.

It was an important time, in the world, however and there was a dawning of consciousness and identity unlike any other era in the history of African people in America. Simultaneously, poets, artists, scientists, politicians and African people all over the world were identifying themselves in ways that we never had in our post-slavery and post-colonial thinking. The idea that there was another norm and another older and broader context in which we could understand our humanity had taken root in African American thought.

The confrontations, achievements and new discoveries of the 1960's had engendered a new level of pride and self-acceptance that permitted us to look at ourselves independent of our European American captors and former slave masters. The Association of Black Psychologists was spawned from a caucus that formed within the American Psychological Association, the premier professional organization for the field and practice of psychology in America. The APA was the unquestioned accrediting and legitimizing body for establishing what was legitimate in the research, teaching and practice of psychology. Without exception, every Black psychologists at this (1970's) point in history had been trained and awarded degrees only on the basis of their demonstrated mastery of the fundamental assumptions defined by this body of almost exclusively white, male, Judeo-Christian psychologists. The generation of these novel ideas about the psychology of African people came from minds without parentage in traditional mainstream psychology. These new and innovative ideas were born out of a social and political climate of protest, deconstruction and restoration of a lost consciousness that permitted us to access a genetic memory that had been long gone. It is as if there was a revelatory intervention from Divine and Ancestral forces that permitted this new paradigm to emerge. The fact that these ideas were startling to our more mature colleagues was not surprising since they had devoted many more years to seeking justification for the limited tools they had been given to understand our people as various forms of deviant Europeans. The agenda of social science as well as politics was to seek inclusion into the Eurocentric world and way of understanding. As new scholars in the field, we only had at stake, the work that we had put forth to acquire the European-American academic degrees. We had neither reputation nor experience at stake so we could comfortably desert the paradigmatic ship of Western psychology.

Because of the times that created the context for the birth of these ideas, the opposition was limited. The fact that the Association of Black Psychologists was a new organism permitted it to embrace a new set of assumptions without a great deal of protest based on history, tradition or former guidelines. This African centered paradigm came to the Association on the heels of its birth and as the organization grew to form an identity, the conception of Black people in this innovative and empowering way found a comfortable fit with this body that had identified itself as the official authorized body to define the psychology of Black people. The African centered paradigm became an intellectual "emancipation proclamation" of the liberation of Black thought from its shackled state as enslaved and colonized victims of the Western assumption of white supremacy and European American cultural and intellectual hegemony.

Cedric Clark came to this gathering out of a Communications background. He had a clear understanding of language, definitions and a firm personal grasp of the philosophy of science and knowledge. His grasp of epistemology as a universal scholarly process helped him to uncover the definitional problems that were so essential in re-thinking a scientific study and objectives of a Black Psychology. He was able to critique the limitations of Western definitions and formulate the assignment of genuine Black Scholars to engage in authentic "Black Studies," as opposed to the "Study of Black people." In our seminal presentations as well as the opening article in this volume, Clark's major contribution was to clarify the issue of definition and to engage in the construction of a paradigm that grew from an authentic definition of Black people. All of the subsequent ingredients of an appropriate paradigm followed from this carefully conceived definition of who were the subjects of study and what was to be the subject matter.

Wade Nobles, as an Experimental Social Psychologist, continued with his formulation of the correct parameters of understanding the subjects (Black people) and our particular portal in understanding humanity as a whole. His classic and seminal paper, "African Philosophy: Foundations for a Black Psychology," published initially in the first volume of the Reginald Jones (1972) collection that defined and delineated Black Psychology, served as the major catalyst for identifying the social and cultural context of Black people as fundamentally Africans. He identified the cultural matrix that laid the foundation for looking to an African worldview as the ethos of Black people throughout the Diaspora. He brought this perspective to the African Psychology project. His special contribution to the dawning evolution of this thought was the importance of the social ontology, "*I am because we are,*" as the unit for understanding African people. He initiated the inquiry into the social nexus of the family that has become the hallmark of his major research and theory over the last thirty years. The major principles of what has emerged as his major work in this field were laid out in this seminal piece of *"An Introduction to African Psychology."*

Phil McGee who was an experimental psychologist by training with particular interest in physiological psychology became a natural spokesman for the biological basis of African consciousness. The melanin pigment effectively lent itself to identifying both the uniqueness of the manifestation of the Black person as well as the transpersonal characteristics of the African consciousness. In similar fashion as we described for Nobles' major work, the study and teaching about melanin was the focus of Phil McGee's major scholarly study for the majority of his scientific career. The significance of melanin as a relevant concept in the study of Black Psychology had its premiere with the work of Dr. Frances Cress Welsing who pioneered the study of melanin deficiency as a foundation for the practice of white supremacy. The conceptualization of Melanin as being considerably more than just skin color was first introduced in this article and opened the door for McGee's research and that of many other scholars in subsequent years.

In retrospect, it is rather evident that this article not only introduced the basic parameters of the African Psychology paradigm that has generated a full generation of theory and research based in this frame of reference, but it also provided a prophetic vision into the work of four of the major voices in the formulation of this paradigm. My interest in understanding the well-functioning African personality as well as the flaws of its dysfunction has certainly become the primary focus of my work over the last three decades. The nature of the Black personality and the centrality of self-knowledge as the basic function for a healthy personality has been the hallmark of my work in this field. The papers that follow as well as my other books, not included in this volume continue to elaborate this description of the Black personality, the consequences of disrupting healthy consciousness and the power of self-knowledge to restore order to a disordered personality. Neither of us knew that the ideas that we formulated in this early but very concise presentation was an overview and a prelude for our entire career as psychologists.

In 1975, this premiere article by the same name *"Voodoo or IQ: An Introduction to African Psychology"* was reprinted in a pamphlet series by the Chicago based Institute of Positive Education. The article later appeared in another seminal collection of papers entitled *Reflections on Black Psychology* edited by Smith, Burlew, Mosley and Whitney (1979). By this time the writers had identified ourselves as the founding members of the "Society for the Study of African Sciences" (SSAS) Though the organization never obtained a formal chartering, informally, it did introduce a society of scholarship that blossomed into the vanguard of progressive Black thought in the final quarter of the 20th century. The extensive research, writings and scholarship of Dr. Molefi Asante were pivotal in developing and exposing this notion of "Afrocentric" thought and offering it to the broader arena of nationalist Black scholarship. Dr. Asante in his first volume *Afrocentricity: The Theory of Social Change* (1980), credits the Black Psychologists as the pioneers in the formulation of this paradigm.

In the mid to late 1970's, there was a Black Community Mental Health program directed by Louis Ramey at that time, a member of the staff of the Southern Regional Education Board in Atlanta. Lou Ramey offered great support to the emergence of these ideas and used the resources of his project to bring together a series of presentations and collaboration with a group of young Black Psychologists from across the country. It was at these conference workshops that interactions with Joseph Baldwin (a/k/a Kobi Kambon), Bobby Wright, Nancy Harris Marshall, Gerald Jackson, Frances Cress

Welsing and Luther Weems (a/k/a Na'im Akbar) began to occur on a regular basis. Frances Cress Welsing, Nathan Hare, Robert Williams and many others participated in these conferences and concentrated in many areas of psychology, not necessarily identified with the Afrocentric paradigm. There were a number of students active in this group who subsequently earned graduate degrees and became major contributors in a variety of areas of Black Psychology. Some of these students were Charlyn Harper-Bolton (Brown), Bernard Schiele (a/k/a Adib Shakir), Harold Braithwaite, Kevin Taylor, Anees Fardan, Harun Black and many others. The discussions that took place in these workshops and conferences over the course of about five years did much to stimulate the dialogue about African Psychology and the beginning formalization of the language and concepts that would constitute this paradigm.

Another important influence that underlies the development of my thinking and the ideas that are put forth in this collection of papers was my exposure and study of the philosophy of the Honorable Elijah Muhammad. Cedric Clark became a member of the Nation of Islam in 1970-71. I found myself quite fascinated by Clark's understanding and sharing of the concepts and meaning of the teachings of Elijah Muhammad. As I began to study the ideas of the Nation of Islam much more closely and to listen to the instruction of these teachings from Minister Louis Farrakhan and other representatives of Elijah Muhammad, I embraced the basic tenets of this significant social movement and found my ideas strongly impacted by the ideas that came from this very radical redefinition of the Black mind. Elijah Muhammad's ideas fit so very well into the basic format of the new paradigm that we had already argued for and had begun to formulate. The social/spiritual system that I found in the Nation of Islam offered substance as well as demonstration of the power of this paradigm to alter and cultivate effective and affirmative Black life. As a psychologist, I was concerned from the outset with the effective alteration of Black behavior into more constructive and positive expressions. My desire was to be a healer of Black people and to offer this model of self-healing as a prototype for any disoriented group of humanity.

The Nation of Islam was doing miraculous work in altering the behaviors of chronically self-destructive groups of substance abusers, criminal types, social "misfits" and a full range of conditions that I had already come to understand as reflective of the self-alienation that had characterized the socially stigmatized and former American slaves. I didn't know what the answer was, with the limited tools that I had been given with my training in Western Psychology, but I knew that Elijah Muhammad had hit upon something that was making a real difference. It was generating impressively productive behavior from the least productive elements of American society.

Some of the least skilled of the American population were engaged in the most impressive institutional developments such as independent schools, businesses, journalism and most of all an ethos that was psychologically liberating and healing. People were learning to love themselves again, to believe in their capability and to rejoin the global community of humankind without seeing themselves as just the rejects of American society. The desire to discover the identity of the mechanism of the Nation of Islam that was accomplishing these remarkable feats was extremely compelling for me.

Despite the loss of a large degree of my "scientific objectivity" by embracing the ideas of Elijah Muhammad, I continued to explore the underlying psychological significance of these ideas that were having such a profound impact on the lives of those people (including myself) who accepted the ideas and discipline of the Nation of Islam as a way to live their lives. I watched the significant changes in my personal life that freed me of many emotional handicaps that had impeded the effective self-mastery of my life in so many ways prior to the acceptance of these ideas. I was able to see empirical evidence of the power of self-knowledge that has come to be a focal concept of my conceptualization of human psychology. I have subsequently discovered that the idea of "man know thyself," was a concept with origins in ancient Egyptian thought that far preceded my exposure to the concept through the teachings of Elijah Muhammad. Despite the contemporary and culturally appropriate phrasings of how Elijah Muhammad taught Truth, I found that the most important ideas of the Nation were ideas rooted in the Universal Truth of all of the World's master teachers and prophets. Though we embraced those teachings as if he had invented truth, the universality of the meaning beneath the metaphors simply gave us a culturally relevant introduction to Universal Truth.

These ideas are woven into the conceptualizations of African Psychology as I have written about it, not as a subtle device to proselytize, but as an interpretation of the disguised universal principles that are presented in a culturally relevant and focused way in the teachings of Elijah Muhammad. Truth must have relevance beyond a specific instance or we must question whether it is really Truth. Certainly, the early conceptualizations that are found in the opening paper, *"Introduction to African Psychology,"* reflect the influence of Elijah Muhammad on both Cedric Clark and my contributions to this piece. It was clearly our interpretation of Elijah Muhammad and not a straightforward presentation of how the ideas were being communicated within the Nation of Islam. Wade Nobles and Phil McGee were certainly aware and very much impressed with the work of Elijah Muhammad and his ideas. They were very much supportive of Cedric Clark's early conversion as Cedric X (eventually Syed Khatib) and my later conversion as Luther X (eventually Na'im Akbar). Neither McGee nor Nobles fully embraced (or "joined") Elijah Muhammad as we did, but they shared our excitement about the impact of Elijah Muhammad's influence and they embraced many of the ideas that we brought from our influence by the Nation.

They had no argument with the consistency of many of Elijah Muhammad's ideas with the paradigm that we were trying to formulate in African Psychology. All of the papers in this volume carry the imprint of the thinking that I felt to be consistent with my best understanding of the ideas of Elijah Muhammad. I did not see myself as being either an interpreter or a representative of his philosophy. I was committed to understanding the positive influence of his ideas as a key for healing the disturbed psyches of Black people. My distortions were my own and the particular rendering of his ideas in my writings about our psychology must be my responsibility as well.

In addition to the founding members of SSAS described at length above, by the mid 1980's several other Black psychologists had adopted the Afrocentric paradigm and had begun publishing a variety of papers dealing with conceptualizing and even beginning investigative research of the paradigm. Names such as Joseph Baldwin (a/k/a/ Kobi Kambon), Asa Hilliard, Linda James Myers, Gerald Jackson,

Edwin Nichols, Vernon Dixon, Lewis King, Daudi Azibo, Thomas Parham and others had become associated with the African psychology paradigm and many of their early papers expanded and reinforced the emerging definition of this new perspective of inquiry. Subsequent books by Kambon and Azibo did much to organize and present a systematic formulation of these basic concepts of an African-centered psychology.

The papers in this volume represent the first half of my career as a psychologist, a period that spans from 1971 until 1986. My work was primarily conceptual based on my belief that we could not begin to effectively address our psychological issues until our definitions were clear. It was also evident to those of us involved in this work that we could not solve our problems utilizing the same concepts that had been used to put us into the situation that we were in. The norms of Eurocentric psychology were replete with the bias and hegemony of white supremacy. There was no way that African people could reconstruct our reality utilizing these norms. In many ways, this early part of my career was a clearing operation of the cluttered fields of scientific inquiry that had characterized the study of African and African American behavior. This work was essentially deconstructive and it opened the door for my work of the last twenty years that has been primarily reconstructive work in the form of a series of short books intended to be user friendly with the objective of helping African people to better understand ourselves and what must be done to reconstruct our lives.

This volume is intended to summarize in a single setting the evolution of my thinking during these early years. Though the basic conclusions remain as valid, certainly some of the emphasis and some of the stridency of these early statements have moderated over time. I believe that it is very important that future generations of scholars of African American mental functioning should appreciate the context of the thinking that evolved from these critiques and conclusions. Not only does an appreciation for this early deconstructive work keep the context clear, but it keeps the weeds clear from the development of future ideas that may obscure the ontological distinction between African and non-African people. This is my contribution to a tradition of African thought that has worked to reconstruct the valid representation of the unique human contribution of the African experience. I place myself in the tradition of Pan Africanist, nationalist and other Black scholars who have valued the special and unique perspective that Africa has given to the world.

Na'im Akbar
Summer 2003
Tallahassee, Florida

The Opening

Voodoo or IQ: An Introduction to African Psychology (1975)

By
Syed Khatib, D. Phillip McGee, Wade Nobles, and
Na'im Akbar

Definition and Rationale

African Psychology is the recognition and practice of a body
of knowledge, which is fundamentally different in origin, content, and direction than that recognized and practiced by Euro-
American psychologists. The differences between African Psychology and Euro-American Psychology reflect the differences
between Black people and white people or, in terms of basic culture, between Africans and Europeans.

It is one of those many anomalies of the Euro-American (or
white, Western) scientific tradition that, while differences between Blacks and whites are recognized enough to warrant the
systematic study of such and the formulation of unique public
policies concerning each, these same differences are not recognized enough to preclude measurements with common instruments nor are they recognized enough to warrant the formulation of distinct disciplinary orientations devoted toward their
explanation. This anomaly is due, in part, to the peculiar nature
of social and psychological inquiry. Unlike the physical sciences,
the behavioral sciences have yet to agree on uniform standards
by which behavior can be appropriately judged. Also unlike the

3

physical sciences, the behavioral sciences employ concepts, which are derived not from universally agreed-upon criteria, but from the peculiar cultural experience of the scientists themselves.

These are, of course, issues with which the better Euro-American behavioral scientists are quite aware; they are thus often embarrassed by the attempts of some of their colleagues (e.g., Jensen) to liken concepts such as "intelligence" to physical concepts such as "electricity"—with the argument that, since nobody knows what such phenomena "really are," it is quite appropriate to adopt "operational definitions" which serve utilitarian ends if not "truth".

The embarrassment of these better-trained scientists has not yet, however, been articulated in a form which would effectively counter the actions taken, under the name of science, by their less well-endowed colleagues. Part of the reason for this might be attributed to the fact that while the better-trained scientists might find serious fault with the logic and methods of their better-known colleagues, they are in basic agreement with some of the utilitarian ends sought. It is this "common agreement concerning ends" which, in sensitive areas such as racial intelligence, has permitted legitimate scientific and philosophical issues to be translated as issues concerning "freedom of speech" or "civil rights".

Responsible white scientists are, for example, quite familiar with Thomas Kuhn's reminder that every revolution carries with it a concomitant revolution in the scientific enterprise. And many of these scientists would probably recognize that we are now living in the midst of a social revolution one characterized by a substantial change in race relations, not only in America but throughout the world.

Such changes in social relationships are invariably accompanied by changes in the mental or conceptual sphere — a point which Marx and Mannheim pointed out long before Kuhn presented it to his scientific colleagues. These changes in the conceptual sphere call into question some of the basic assumptions under which scientists, like all other participants in a given culture, operate.

Some changes, however, are not easily absorbed into the scientific world — a fact that even those only nominally familiar with the history of scientific revolutions are cognizant of.

But, in deference to the probability that most readers are ignorant of scientific history, we can note that just as most 14th century scientists found it difficult to cease viewing the earth as the center of the *physical* universe so too do many of today's (behavioral) scientists find it difficult to cease viewing the Caucasian race or European culture as the center of the *social* universe.

It is for this reason that Euro-American psychology adopts, as the conceptual and behavioral standard, the characteristics of a minority (less than 10%) of the world's population. Indeed, if history were to be any judge at all, it would be a most remarkable occurrence if the participants in Euro-American hegemony would recognize and accept conceptual changes, which would undermine their privileged positions *vis-à-vis* others. This is particularly true for those participants whose very occupations are intimately involved with the maintenance of an established conceptual universe; i.e. educators, scientists, and politicians. These issues can perhaps be heightened if we cite an example of how the conceptual universe in modern America has changed concomitantly with changing racial relationships.

This conceptual universe was once bound by the issues of "integration vs. segregation". These conceptual parameters guided most of the scientific thinking and research in the area of race relations: moreover, public policies were adopted within this frame of reference. This frame of reference (or what Kuhn refers to as a "paradigm") has been all but shattered for most Blacks; indeed, it is questionable whether in fact this ever was the way most Blacks viewed the world — particularly if Black scholars (as distinct from Black "spokesmen") accurately reflected the thinking of the majority of Black people. The writings of the novelist-essayist James Baldwin are particularly relevant in this connection. Baldwin, over a decade ago, asked a question which struck a deep, responsive chord in the minds of many Blacks but was almost completely baffling to most whites. His question was: "Who wants to integrate into a burning house?" This question, it should be emphasized, was asked long before the release of the Pentagon papers, the crimes of Watergate and their cover-up, the energy crises, and all other phenomena which, today, make the question perhaps less baffling to whites. There is an important lesson that can be learned from this example, that is, that Black people see things about white people, which white people do not see about themselves. A cynic might observe that this is because whites spend more time looking at Blacks than they do looking at themselves — an observation which is perhaps less comforting to the scientific community because it is perhaps more relevant to it.

It is because of this difference in perception that the conceptual universes and their resultant paradigms differ for white people and Black people. This difference eventually manifests itself in the kinds of questions people ask in the area of racial relations. While many whites question whether integration or segregation is best for America, many Blacks question whether America is best for Black people.

The conceptual paradigm governing the former question is bounded by an "integration vs. segregation" dichotomy whereas the conceptual paradigm governing the latter is bounded by a "liberation vs. control" dichotomy. The differences between the two paradigms are important for any peaceful settlement of the racial issue. The Euro-American "integration vs. segregation" paradigm carries an important common dimension, *viz.,* control by whites — whereas the liberation vs. control" addresses itself directly to what many Blacks believe *is* the critical issue: self-control or other-control. The failure of Euro-American psychology to recognize and/or appreciate this alternative paradigm is what leads many thinking Black students to dismiss much contemporary research as "irrelevant."

White scientists, if they are truly interested in science (as distinct from politics) should not assume that just because George Gallup has not asked Blacks whether or not they want to integrate in white society that, therefore, they do; nor should these scientists assume that just because some Black politicians and social scientists promote schemes such as "compensatory education" or "affirmative action" that, therefore, the majority of Black people believe themselves to be in need of compensation and affirmation. These programs and policies reflect political decisions based on social expediency; they do not necessarily reflect Black public opinion nor, for that matter, sound scientific thinking.

In brief, then, African Psychology recognizes, perhaps more so than Euro-American psychology, that the way in which a question is asked predetermines the range of possible answers. If the question is asked in terms of "integration vs. segregation" the answer perforce excludes "separation." If the question is asked in terms of "Which is more important in determining Black intellectual inferiority, genes or environment?" the answer perforce excludes the possibility that

Blacks are not intellectually inferior. And, relatedly, if the question is asked "Are Blacks equal in intelligence to whites?" the answer perforce excludes the possibility that Blacks are *superior* in intelligence to whites.

Because of this recognition that scientific questions are, at the same time, often political and social answers, African Psychology is quite sensitive to problems concerning the history and philosophy of science itself. It thus views itself as not only different from Euro-American Psychology, but as superior to it in the same sense that philosophy is superior to science in that the latter is valid only if certain assumptions of the former are accepted.

The Content Emphasis of African Psychology

So much, then, for the "Why?" of African psychology; let us turn our attention to the "What?" bearing in mind that its content differences are a result of its conceptual or paradigm differences.

Before proceeding with this discussion of content, we should first acknowledge – deference to alternative paradigms — the essential *radical* nature of African Psychology. It is radical not so much in the political sense, but in a scientific and philosophical sense; i.e., it is "radical" because it addresses itself first and foremost to the roots (radicals) of human thought. For, we believe, only when such roots are exposed and examined critically can a solid foundation be constructed for the subsequent investigation of specific psychological phenomena.

Consistent with this content-concern of "root" questions, African Psychology attempts to understand:

1. Which is the Original Race, The Caucasian or The African?

Many Euro-American psychologists, no doubt, would consider this question a theological one at best and irrelevant at worse. Such apparent unconcern with questions of origin is rather peculiar, given the great current concern with the role of genetic factors in human behavior. Clearly, if one is to be consistent with any genetic thesis, one must surely give at least nominal attention to the nature of the first human gene pool — for it is from this original gene pool that all contemporary genes were derived. If, then, we are to be concerned about the genetic transmission of human intelligence, we must admit only one of two possibilities: either the white race is evolutionary prior to the Black, in which case whatever intelligence (or lack thereof) Blacks have has been inherited from whites; *or* the Black race is evolutionary prior to white, in which case the reverse would be true. (We should perhaps note, again in deference to alternative paradigms, that either position would effectively nullify the conclusions of some modern-day genetic intelligence theorists).

We should perhaps note in this connection that many Euro-American and Euro-American-trained psychologists tend to minimize the significances of this issue of origins. So they adopt a neo-Darwinian perspective and assert that there has been an evolutionary improvement in the species such that the Caucasian race represents the highest end of the evolutionary scale. This perspective equates *technological* superiority with *intellectual* and *moral* superiority

African Psychology, with full and grateful acknowledgment to the Messenger of Allah, the Honorable Elijah Muhammad — who was the first to raise and answer this question of origins —

works on the assumption that the African race is evolutionarily prior to the Caucasian race and, therefore, is the original source of whatever genetic factors account for contemporary white and Black behavior in the world. African Psychology thus attributes the decline of Black civilizations not to genetic weaknesses but to a spiritual decay which left in its wake, however, a high testimonial to its original intellectual supremacy in the form of stone monuments spread across Africa — monuments which reflect a mastery of mathematics, geometry, physics, and all other sciences known to man. The construction of the African pyramids has, to this day, baffled Western scientists to such an extent that the most recent explanation is that they were built, not by the Africans themselves, but by alien space creatures!

While African Psychology accepts as a "given" that the original race was African and not European, it does attempt to validate this on grounds other than assumption or authority. Why these other sources of validation are necessary for African Psychology and not Euro-American psychology says more about the dynamics of racism in the Western world than it does about anything else. So ingrained is this racism in America's educational institutions that many geography books, even today, separate Egypt from Africa — to foster the idea that the Egyptian civilization was built by non-Africans. Hollywood has played a major role in insuring the perception of Africans as uncivilized.

Because of the way in which the mass media and educational institutions have attempted to present the world as white, African Psychology recognizes its need to validate some of its own assumptions — at least to the extent that it is possible to validate assumptions with empirical research. This validation is done not so much to convince whites (a task which we have recognized as virtually impossible) as to convince Blacks — particularly Blacks who receive their education in white institutions. Indeed, this particular educational constituency is very important in the eyes of African Psychology, for it is precisely this group of people who often come to be recognized by established white institutions as "leaders" of other Black people. Such people become "spokesmen" even though (or perhaps because) they lack the most essential educational ingredient of all: knowledge of self. The importance of this element of knowledge is discussed in later paragraphs.

The point we wish to stress as important in this context is that however much we might deplore it, it is still a fact that many Black people in America will continue to be educated by whites and, this being the case, it is only natural for such people to develop a conception of self as inferior to whites. This negative self-conception extends itself to other Blacks and, as a result, such people are more likely to be influenced by what whites have to say about them rather than by what their own people have to say. Indeed, such a tendency is frequently associated with "success" and "intelligence" in American society.

Because of this, African Psychology recognizes the necessity of supporting its assumptions by referring to research published within the Euro-American tradition. Thus, in support of our assumption that the original race was African not European, we call attention to the research of Professor Louis Leakey, a British anthropologist. Shortly after Leakey's death a few years ago, his son, Dr. Richard Leakey made an archeological finding which completely revolutionized scientific thinking concerning the origin of man. He found remnants of early man in East Africa dating back some three million years.

While Black Muslim scholars know that this date is wrong in an absolute sense (the origins of man date back much, much farther than this), Leakey's finding is correct in a relative sense — i.e., in the sense that it clearly establishes the biological precedent of the African relative to the European.

Moreover, we know from the science of biology that it is biologically impossible for whites to produce offspring of color, whereas it is quite possible for Blacks to produce white offspring. Thus, as far as African Psychology is concerned, there is no question as to the fact that the original race was African.

2. What is the Mystery of Melanin?

If, then, the first man on earth was dark as opposed to light, then one of the substantive content questions African Psychology must concern itself with is the role of the skin color-producing substance called *melanin.*

Although the word "melanin" comes from a Greek word, *"melanos"* meaning "Black," in a biological science it is used to designate a pigment whose natural color in human ranges from pale yellow over reddish brown to almost black.

Melanin is synthesized and dispersed by specialized cells, which are called melanocytes. Melanocytes synthesize melanin through a series of bio-chemical reactions beginning with the consumption of the amino acid, phenlalanine. Each subsequent biochemical reaction in the chain is controlled by a specific enzyme. If all the essential enzymes are present the pigment melanin is produced in considerable quantity. When this occurs, an individual has skin, which is dark in color, hair, which is black, and eyes, which are brown. If any of the enzymes are relatively inactive, the pigment production is correspondingly curtailed and the individual manifests a pale skin color, hair that is light or blond, and eyes which are blue. The occurrence defines a state of depigmentation — the genetic inability to produce sufficient amounts of melanin. It is worth noting, however, that all human organisms produce some degree of melanin; variation occurs with regard to the specific level of melanin activity, which takes place within the cytoplasm of the melanocyte.

A major portion of the empirical research conducted in African Psychology involves a systematic examination of the relationship between melanocytes and the nerve cells of the central nervous system. We know, for example, that both are embryologically derived from a single neuroblast in the neural crest of the developing human fetus. This fact leads us to systematically investigate the patterns of neural interdependence that neurons of the brain, neurons of the spinal cord, and melanocytes manifest on human metabolic processes and nervous system functioning. We know that man's central nervous system performs a critical information-processing role, which is essential for optimal neurological and metabolic functioning. Damage to the central nervous system can potentially impair the nervous activity, which is essential to human sensitivity and consciousness.

Our research has discerned a high, positive correlation between specific levels of sensory acuity and states of pigmentation. An examination of neuro-physiological, neuro-chemical, and neuro-humoral data reveals this correlation quite clearly. Relationships have been found to exist between melanin and the cerebellum, between melanin and the red nucleus, and between melanin and the reticular formation. Our research has not yet been able to define the precise nature of these relationships, but we are led to believe (in concurrence with Professor Welsing of Howard University) that melanin *refines* the central nervous system and, in so doing, produces a highly sensitized sensory-motor network.

It is interesting to note in this context that Parkinson's disease, a hereditary disease of the central nervous system, is associated with loss of melanin-pigment by the cells of the *substantia nigra*. It is for this reason that it is a disease, which is largely confined to whites. Lesions to the *substantia nigra* (literally, "black substance") produce the complex motor syndrome *(Paralysis agitans* and *akinsesia)* commonly seen in Parkinson's disease. The *substantia nigra* is located in the mid-brain (mesencephalon) near the cerebellum and forms part of the cerebral peduncles near the red nucleus. Research has suggested the *substantia nigra* has a critical relationship with the reticular formation in the sense that it provides "starter" impulses, which facilitate phasic muscular contractions. The muscular contractions are important for postural adjustment and the rapid and exact movement of specific muscle groups.

Other evidence of the importance of melanin in preventing central nervous system disorders is found in research concerning the hereditary disease known as phenylpyrie oligophrenia or PKU. This disease, again more common among whites than Blacks, is characterized by purposeless movements such as pill-rolling movements of the hand and irregular tic-like motions.

The occurrence of PKU is caused by the absence or ineffective performance of an enzyme called *phenylalanase*. This enzyme, when present in humans, catalyzes the amino acid phenylalanine and forms one of the raw materials out of which melanin is formed. Phenylalanase is necessary to convert phenylalanine into tyrosine; if phenylalanase is absent, the phenylalanine is converted instead to pehnylpyruvic acid, which is excreted in the urine. This mis-conversion process also results in certain mental defects that are associated with PKU disease (hereditary idiocy).

Thus, we are convinced that the absence of melanin is directly associated with the mal-functioning of the central nervous system. However, we are also convinced that the presence of melanin is directly associated with the proper functioning of the central nervous system. It must be admitted, however, that the bio-chemical processes involved in this latter relationship are quite complex and poorly understood. (It is always easier to explain what is "wrong," than what is "right" — since science tends to focus on deviations from normality as opposed to normality itself).

In any case, we can attempt to explain this "normal" functioning by noting that, under normal conditions, the amino acid enzyme tyrosine is formed from the enzymatic action of phenylalanase on phenylalanine. The enzyme tyrosinase then catalyzes tyrosine to produce dopamine. Dopamine is oxidized into norephinephrine and norephineprine is converted into epinephrine. Finally, epinephrine (or adrenaline) is converted into melanin.

Norephineprine and epinephrine are under the control of the autonomic nervous system. The adrenal medulla secretes these in response to conditions of emotion or changes in the discharge of neurons in the automatic nervous system. Part of the autonomic nervous system (the sympathetic) accelerates the activity of all essential vital organs through the secretion of norephineprine.

From these facts, we conclude that there is a positive correlation between the intensity of emotional arousal and the urinary excretion of epinephrine and norephineprine. Implicit in this conclusion is the belief that emotional arousal is a positive trait; this might be strange to most Euro-Americans, inasmuch as emotional arousal tends to have a negative connotation in the Western psychological tradition.

In fact, this difference of attitudes is one of the basic features differentiating African Psychology from Euro-American psychology. We believe, in short, that non-whites are indeed "more emotional" than whites and, not only is this positive in its own right, it is directly related to that phenomenon we call "intelligence." In fact, the "mystery" of melanin, as we see it, relates directly to the fact that while we have a fairly good idea of the bio-chemical properties of melanin and how these are related to nervous system functioning, we do not yet know the specifics of this in relationship to human intelligence. We do, however, have our hunches, and these are articulated in more detail below.

3. What is the Nature of Black Intelligence?

From our research into melanin, we are led to believe that it is the concept of sensitivity, which is of fundamental importance to human intelligence. A related concept, consciousness, is also considered important in our consideration of human intelligence.

Consideration of these two concepts — sensitivity and consciousness — underscores the fact that African Psychology adopts a different philosophical base than contemporary Euro-American Psychology. Our ontological position asserts that there is more to the world than meets our material eyes (which are always limited by the present state of technology). In this sense, we agree with those modern physicists who recognize a non-material or spiritual reality underlying all observed material phenomena. Whether one prefers to call this non-material reality "energy," "spirit," "manna," or whatever, is of little significance; what is important is the recognition that it does exist. We believe that any psychology worthy of its name must incorporate this reality into its philosophical premises, if not content domain. African Psychology, of course, does both and, for this reason, the concepts of sensitivity and consciousness are of paramount importance.

The word consciousness" means "with knowledge" and thus, to the extent that intelligence is related to knowledge, the concepts are fundamentally related. The type of knowledge with which African Psychology is concerned is not, however, that type commonly associated with traditional psychology. It is more closely associated with an Eastern esoteric tradition, which recognizes *self-knowledge* as the ultimate source of all knowledge. Thus, our epistemological position also differs from Western, Euro-American psychology. That is, our position recognizes the supremacy of internal (or self) knowledge, as opposed to external knowledge.

While there are a few Western-trained scholars who agree with us in this regard (notably Michael Polanyi), the dominant thrust of Western Psychology has been the acceptance of an epistemological position, which accepts external sources as the only sources of valid knowledge. This position is incorporated in the very foundations of positivist, empirical psychology.

This, of course, does not mean that African Psychology dismisses empirical research; indeed, our research into the melanin stands in sharp contradiction to such a stance. What it does mean, however, is that external, empirical types of knowledge represent only one source and, insofar as the discipline of psychology is concerned, a relatively insignificant one. It is insignificant in the sense that it does not contribute to the acquisition of self-knowledge and that, we feel, is most important.

In accord with Eastern esoteric traditions, African Psychology recognizes the total field of (self) knowledge as consisting of 360 degrees. Complete knowledge of self expresses all 360 degrees and is frequently referred to as "wisdom." There are, in all societies and at all times, various institutions, which have been established to guide students in their search for self-knowledge. These are not, of course, "schools" in the sense that most Americans recognize them; i.e., they are not publicly supported, nor do they provide training in the various disciplines that are characteristic of established universities. Most of these institutions (variously referred to as lodges, temples, orders, etc.) are designed to "raise the level of consciousness" of their students to 33 degrees or more. The pursuit of such degrees may occupy a person's entire lifetime, but the type of knowledge acquired is considered well worth the effort.

It is important to recognize that "intelligence," as measured by "degrees of consciousness" or self-knowledge, is completely independent of success in public schools or occupational ranking. Thus, it is not surprising to find a highly "intelligent" (as we define it) person having less than a high school diploma and perhaps working at a very low-status occupation. This is not surprising to those familiar with Eastern intellectual traditions, because it is recognized that money, status, and prestige (whose traits are usually associated with "intelligence" in this country) have little to do with intelligence, as conceived outside of the Western world. The correlates one should thus look for in regard to intelligence are not the material ones, but the spiritual ones: happiness, peace of mind, good health, longevity, humor, etc.

There is one aspect of the Euro-American Psychological tradition, which relates to the Eastern and African conception of intelligence. This aspect involves a field of psychological inquiry, which has only recently been granted scientific legitimacy. Generically, this field is known as *parapsychology*. Because of the peculiar position of Black people in America (genetically Eastern and socially Western), it is the area of parapsychology, which we find the most useful in bridging the East-West gap and, at the same time, providing an additional empirical orientation in African Psychological research.

The field of parapsychology is related to the African conception of intelligence in the following sense: As self-knowledge (consciousness) approaches 360 degrees, the individual becomes better equipped to manifest those mental abilities associated with parapsychology. These abilities can be classified in two general categories: "mind over matter" or *psychokinesis* and "mind-reading" or *precognition*. (Clairvoyance, or "seeing into the future," is a derivative of these.) African Psychology, then, if called upon to provide an operational definition of "intelligence" or "consciousness," would cite as representative the manifestation of these psychic abilities. Eastern psychological traditions have, of course, long-recognized these abilities, but only recently have they begun to be accepted in the West. (Interestingly enough, this acceptance has been more at the hands of physicists and other "hard scientists" than it has of psychologists.)

To the extent that consciousness and sensitivity are related to the presence of melanin, and these, in turn, to the development of psychic abilities, African Psychology expects that intelligence (as we define it) is directly related to the presence of melanin. It is this hypothesis, which is currently being investigated in our laboratories, both in America and in other parts of the world. It might be useful for us to mention some of the reasons, which led us to the formulation of this hypothesis relating melanin to psychic abilities. The most significant of these is derived from anthropological research in sub-Saharan Africa, where the largest numbers of high-melanin possessing people are found. This research has documented, for over a century, the Para-normal powers possessed by a large number of Africans. These powers have been frequently referred to as *Voodoo* and/or witchcraft; but, stripped of such (largely pejorative) labeling the observed phenomena represents nothing more than the manifestation of psychokinesis and precognition. Not all Africans possess this ability, of course; one might suspect that they are distributed in a Gausian fashion, as are other human traits, but the evidence certainly seems overwhelming that such abilities are more characteristic of African people than they are of other people on earth. While one might suggest that geographical, cultural, or religious factors account for this, our own position suggests that the dominant factor is genetic and related to the presence of melanin. Thus, one of the major content areas of African Psychology concerns this relationship between melanin and psychic ability, the latter conceived to be the essential material manifestation of human intelligence.

4. *What is the Nature of Black Self and Black Personality?*

Because self-knowledge is considered an important element of consciousness and intelligence, African Psychology defines as an important content area, the nature of the self.

Like many other areas related to African peoples and Black behavior, the research in this area of self-conception is characterized by several important subjective tendencies. First of all, the research about African (Black) people was (and is being), produced largely by non-Black peoples. Secondly, the orientation of most of this research was (and is) to support the pre-conceived notion that African people are deviant from and hence abnormal to white people. The third tendency, related to the second, is the adoption of *a priori* assumptions characteristic of Euro-American philosophy as opposed to African philosophy. The fourth and final tendency is the almost total absence of Africa and Africanity in the theories and research on the so-called Negroes' self-concept.

These tendencies have led us to conclude that if one accepts Euro-American assumptions about African reality then the questions and answers about Black people are going to be — in a predetermined manner — in response to Euro-American reality. Hence, one can see that by the nature of the underlying assumptions characteristic of Euro-American research on the Negro self-concept, the range results (answers) were predetermined and consistent with the questions and assumptions. Thus, if you can accept the Euro-American assumptions and questions, you must also accept the answers (results) characteristic of the Negro self-concept literature. However valuable such an exercise might be, it is not our intent to explain why or how Euro-American researchers have created a pseudo-reality of negative "Negro" self-concept. Our intention is, rather, to suggest some reasons for considering an alternative framework or perspective in understanding African (Black) peoples' conception of themselves.

A. African Self-Concept: The Extended Self

Having implied throughout this article that African Psychology is rooted in the nature of a Black culture, which is fundamentally African (as opposed to European), we contend that a dominant aspect of the black mentality reflects the polyvalent principle of the "Oneness of Being." If one were to epitomize African Psychology, it would be best described as the philosophy of *rhythm* or harmony.

The behavioral modalities, which are therefore characteristic of African lifestyles throughout the "Diaspora", are based on several philosophical assumptions, and a conception of "reality" which when analyzed, reflects a sense of ontological harmony or rhythm. Related to this is an African philosophical orientation, which emphasizes the *notion of interdependence*. This notion conceives of Man and all the other elements of the universe as being part of a unified and integrated whole. The African philosophical tradition, in turn, determines two fundamental operational orders or guiding beliefs. The first belief is that Man is part of the natural rhythm of nature or one with nature. The second is a conception of the universe as a "vitalistic pneumaticism". This latter conception means a belief in the sense of "vital solidarity," or survival of the tribe. Descriptively, it refers to a kind of vital attitude about one's existence or what Westerners term a sense of "common fate." In accordance with these two motions *(one with nature* and *survival of the tribe),* the African thinks of experience as an intense complementary rhythmic connection (or synthesis) between the person and reality.

How this relates to African self-conception is as important as it is difficult to express in the English language. First, we must recognize that the philosophical orientation determines both what is "real" and how one defines or validates its reality. In terms of self-conception, the African philosophical tradition, unlike western philosophical systems, does not place emphasis on the "individual" or "individuality." In fact, one could say that in a sense, it does not allow for "individuals." It recognizes, rather, that only in terms of one's people does the "individual" become conscious of one's own being. It is, in fact, only through others that one learns his duties and responsibilities toward himself and the collective self (tribe). Historically, initiation rites were designed to instill this sense of corporate responsibility and collective destiny. When we examine closely the African philosophical tradition, we recognize that from this an *extended* definition of self evolved. That is to say, the African self-concept is, by philosophical definition, the "We" instead of the "I."

Africans thus believe that whatever happens to the "individual" self (The "I") also happens to the corporate body (The

"We"), and vice-versa. The cardinal point, therefore, in understanding the traditional African conception of self, is the belief that "I am because we are; and because we are, therefore, I am." This belief under-scores the extent to which the African feels himself to be part of all other African peoples. Descriptively, this relationship of *interdependence* can be termed the "extended-self."

This notion of the "we" (as opposed to the "I") may become clearer through an ontological analysis of the self. It is generally accepted in the Euro-American psychological tradition that the establishment of self is accomplished by recognizing in others qualities or characteristics similar to one's self and/or denying qualities and characteristics similar to one's self. The "self," therefore, occurs as the consequence of either of two processes — opposition and/or apposition. The way in which African peoples are *extended* into themselves, however, is not completely explained by this kind of distinction. What one must distinguish between are the "levels of reality:" the material (lower level) and the spiritual (higher level).

The "oneness of being" is predicated on Man being an *integrated* and *indispensable* part of the universe. Being-in-the-world also means to participate in its social time. Hence, to be is to be what you are because of your historical past as well as what you anticipate to be your historical future. In recognizing the historical grounding of one's being, one has also to accept the collective and social sense of one's history. In taking as one's own the collective and social history of one's people, one in turn, realizes that his "self" is not contained only in his physical presence in finite time. The twin notions of *interdependence* and *oneness of being* allows for a conception of self, which transcends, through the historical consciousness of one's people, the finiteness of both Newtonian space and time. Self-awareness is not therefore limited to just the cognitive awareness of one's uniqueness, individuality and historical finiteness (as in the Euro-American tradition). It is the awareness of self as an awareness of one's historical consciousness (collective spirituality) and the sense of "we" being one.

If we, however, portray the properties of self as *only* collectively intersubjective or as only individually unique we distort the totality of the notion. African self refers both to the grounding of the being, which transcends empirical or physical entities, *and* to the discrete entities, which are capable of being located in space, and having recognizable (and measurable) properties. The self is not only a permanently determined physical *entity*. That is, it is not reducible, or merely equivalent, to the biological organism. It is important, however, to make this "property" distinction clear chiefly for analytical purposes.

The most compelling property, of course, is the ontological grounding of the self in the collective and social sense of history. It is in this sense that the self is portrayed as "transcendence into extendation". That is, the conception of self transcends and extends into the collective consciousness of one's people. However, self-conception is also related to the physically recognizable properties of the discrete entities. And this is a critical point for the consideration of Black ("American") self-concept.

The physical situation in which Africans — particularly in the Americas — find themselves involves the domination and imposition of a fundamental European system of "reality" on an African people. This situation naturally causes confusion because it denies the most compelling property of the African conception of self. It is this situation, which has produced the entity referred to as the "Negro" a concept referring to the African person who attempts to (or is forced to) deny the philosophical basis of his Africanity, even though he cannot negate the recognizable properties (physiological facts) of it. To be a "Negro" therefore, is to be in a state *of confusion*. The infliction of the Euro-American philosophical tradition, as it relates to self-conception (i.e., individuality, separateness, etc.) for African peoples causes many to falsely believe that their natural temperament, tendencies, and characteristic spirit were and are "wrong." Such conclusions have been created and sustained by the Euro-American psychological tradition. The results of such beliefs naturally lead to negative conceptions of self and attitudes of self-hatred. This, in turn, has implications for certain other maladies affecting the Black personality a content area of which we turn our attention below.

5. What is the Nature of the Black Personality?

Traditional (i.e., Euro-American) theories of personality functioning all adopt as a norm those behaviors, which are derived from the European lifestyle. The above discussions of intelligence and melanin have already suggested some of the basic normative differences in the Black and white personalities. If these differences exist, and the social milieu systematically rewards those behaviors, which are in accord with the society's norms, it is not surprising that a child will come to respond negatively to his natural tendencies when they are not in accord with the existing social order. A repeated association of one's natural tendencies with painful or negative stimulation leads to a conditioned inhibition of those tendencies in himself and a rejection of similar tendencies in others. This results in a psychologically unhealthy form of conditioning, which most whites (and many white-educated Blacks) confuse with "success."

The most extreme examples are those attempts at physical alteration in which Blacks have tried to alter their appearance by bleaching creams, hair straighteners, etc., to bring their physical appearance into accord with the social norm of physical attractiveness. (Some popular race-intelligence theoreticians have equated such imitative behavior of the holders of power as evidence of the inherent superiority of the white race. Interestingly enough, these same theoreticians do not concern themselves with such "anomalies" as white efforts to produce melanin via sun tanning).

The more subtle yet more insidious form of this conditioned self-rejection is its psychological manifestation, well documented in the voluminous research on Black self-concept. Low self-esteem is almost a *sine qua non* of living in an environment of oppression. A major problem with such research, of course, is that it focuses attention on the *results* of oppression rather than its causes. Attention is focused more on the effects of low self-esteem rather than the origins of low self-esteem.

Perhaps more important than just differences in orientation, African Psychology differs radically from Euro-American psychology in the assumptions concerning the basic nature of man. In this regard, we unashamedly align ourselves with the majority of the world's population in our rejection of Cartesian duality and our acceptance of man as a divine (spiritual) being. Even though Western observers have historically described these assumptions as primitive, heathenistic, superstitious or pagan, the point remains that, without exception, Black behavior is most clearly understood by Black people as extensions of a spiritual core. An assumption of a spiritual core implies the existence of an irreducible element in man, which has a divine origin, an eternal fate and a moral function.

With such differences in basic assumptions about the nature of man, one will necessarily find wide disparities in the organization of societies and the behaviors, which are considered normative for those people. If one follows the history of Black people from West African societies (as a recent referent) through the American slavery experience and neo-slavery experience, one finds as a thread of continuity the religious nature of the Black man.

The European's intrusion into African society was permitted without resistance largely because the African assumed that he lived in a religious world and that strangers were to be accepted as creatures of a similar divine origin and with high moral intent. The faultiness of this assumption is evidenced by the next four hundred years of the Black man's history following this intrusion. However, even this condition (of slavery) was made meaningful as a religious experience for Blacks.

The adaptation of Christianity to the Black religious experience maintained and cultivated the idea of a divine plan at work. The problem continued to be one, which assumed the universality of that divinity which, as viewed retrospectively, too frequently permitted a passive adaptation to an alien way of life. The alien (Euro-American) way of life assumed man to be first and foremost a material being in search of physical gratifications. Normative behavior is thus viewed in terms of the maximal gratification of one's material ambitions (variously referred to as achievement motivation, territorial dominance, political power, etc.). The exploitation of people and resources is considered of little consequence, inasmuch as the core of it all is believed to be dispensable material. One can thus readily perceive the incompatibility of the victim assuming that even his exploitation is of a spiritual quality with the oppressor viewing the spiritual as material.

The emphasis on the spiritual core summarizes the African Psychological perspective on Black personality. All descriptions of the normal functioning Black personality are thus viewed in the context of this core. For example, the recent upsurge in Black homicides, drug usage, mental disorders, and the virtual disintegration of the Black society within the American context can be systematically correlated with the deterioration of the religious function in Black personality. The increased adoption by Blacks of alien assumptions of materialism has resulted in a concomitant adoption of European lifestyles. Such an adopted life style is dysfunctional when it is superficial and contrary to the natural Black lifestyle. This adoption is viewed as superficial because even when the Black man succeeds in emulating the white lifestyle it frequently results in neurosis or other forms of implicit self-rejection. The spiritual tendencies of African people are antithetical to the material tendencies of Europeans and acceptance of the one almost invariably requires rejection of the other.

The Black personality, which has ostensibly adjusted to Western Society, is characterized by what Euro-American psychologists would call a "schizoid" adjustment. This means that he lives in two worlds, which diametrically differ on many key dimensions. He works to foster an image, which will make him acceptable to the material world of the European (e.g., high achievement motivation, emphasis on cognition to the exclusion of affective experience and individualism. And, on the other hand, he will attempt to maintain at least tenuous ties to his opposite Black origins. The growing failure of such schizoid adjustment is seen in the increase of suicide rates among middle class Blacks as well as the growing incidence of depression and general malcontentment.

African Psychology, in short, does not assume that the similar behaviors of the white majority and Black middle-class have the same origins. Because of this, we recognize that a renewal of the spiritual core of the Black man is the most effective therapy for his adjustment disorders. This perhaps begins to explain the very high level of success achieved by the followers of the Honorable Elijah Muhammad in resolving those problems of Black people where traditionally trained psychologists have been utter failures. This has been particularly true of drug addiction and other so-called "incorrigible" conditions.

We can finally (after four hundred years) begin to understand that the solutions to the problems of the Black man are different from the solutions of the problems of the people of European descent. People of African origin cannot be made citizens of the world by acting in accord with the European model of behavior, despite material inducements to do so. The price is too high, and the ultimate rewards too low.

Conclusion

The four content areas discussed above do not, of course, exhaust the list of various subjects with which African Psychology is concerned. The four, which have been discussed, do, however, represent the foundations of our inquiry into the psychological nature of the Black man.

We should perhaps mention, in this context, that we are under few illusions concerning the difficulty of the intellectual work ahead of us. Nor do we have any illusions concerning the extent to which the adversaries of Eastern social and intellectual freedom will go in their attempt to hinder our progress. Indeed, some of us have already been refused academic jobs or fired from them because of our determined efforts to forge a psychology, which validates the experience of Black people. If American history is any kind of accurate reflector of what is held in store for us, we should perhaps consider ourselves fortunate that we are not killed or imprisoned for our work— so bitter is white resistance to independent Black thinking.

Despite expected obstacles (from both whites and Blacks), we are assured of final success. This is because our work does not represent a reaction against anything so much as it is a *response* to certain things. It is a response to the call of incarcerated Black men who seek answers to the why's and wherefores of their miserable condition; it is a response to Black women who fall victim to the politics of population control carried forth in the name of science; it is a response to Black children who are to survive in North America. It is a response to these and many other calls emanating from the mouths of Black people. It is, in short, a response to something which few whites understand—a response to a divine call.

Being thus, it is at once divinely inspired, divinely guided, and (hopefully) divinely expressed.

First published in *The Journal of Black Psychology,* Vol.1, No.2, February 1975 edition. Reprinted in *The Black Pages.* Chicago: Institute of Positive Education (1976). Also reprinted in Smith, W.D., et als (1979) *Reflections on Black Psychology.* Washington, DC: University Press of America, Inc. The authors of "Voodoo or IQ . . ." are the founding members of the **Society for the Study of African Sciences.

Chapter II

THE AFROCENTRIC PARADIGM

OVERVIEW

One aspect of the early presentations that were done in African Psychology required a rather extensive explanation and justification for choosing an alternative paradigm. The important scientific work of deconstruction required a clarification of the limitations of the existing approaches to understanding African American behavior. As the "Voodoo or IQ" paper laid out the broad justification and perspective for African Psychology, many of the early papers that I did continued to address this issue of differentiating between the Eurocentric and Afrocentric approaches to scientific inquiry.

There were numerous conference presentations and several papers that were published during the late 1970's and early 1980's that were very similar in their focus on defining the parameters of the Afrocentric paradigm. The paper "Paradigms of African-American Research" that is printed in this collection was actually the revision of a paper published in 1974 entitled "Black Community Research Needs: Methods, Models and Modalities." The paper originally appeared in a volume edited by Dr. Lawrence Gary (1974) entitled: *Social Research and the Black Community.* This book was actually generated by a conference sponsored by Dr. Gary that was intended to look at some innovative paradigms for conducting research in the African American community.

Other variations of this paper were published as: "Africentric Social Sciences for Human Liberation" in the *Journal of Black Studies* in 1984. In a 1985 volume edited by Harriette and John McAdoo entitled *Black Children,* another variation of this same paper was published under the title: "Our Destiny: Authors of a Scientific Revolution." This paper grew out of a presentation that I did in 1984 at the "Empirical Conference in Black Psychology," an annual gathering convened in part by Harriette and John McAdoo and a variety of important researchers in Black

Psychology. Though these researchers were engaged in the traditional social science research methods for understanding African American people, they incorporated in their analysis and discussions the deconstruction notions that we were developing in these early days of African Psychology. It was the sympathetic ear of our colleagues in settings such as these that gave broad exposure to the same radical ideas that were being developed with the Afrocentric paradigm.

All of these papers were defining and addressing the characteristics of the African Psychology paradigm. These papers, by and large, had two basic components: a *deconstructive* component that critiqued the dimensions of the Western Psychology paradigm for social science and social science research. The other component was a *reconstructive* approach that began to identify the dimensions of the Afrocentric paradigm. This component of definition gave greater detail to the work that we had begun in the premiere introductory article presented in the first chapter of this volume.

The two articles in this chapter summarize the major deconstruction and reconstruction ideas that the early papers dealt with. Both of these papers were published in the 3rd Edition of Reginald Jones' (1992) important collection, *Black Psychology.* The first of these papers provides my most comprehensive discussion of a rationale for a Black Psychology that utilizes a philosophy of science that expands the parameters of our investigations consistent with the worldview of African people.

The second paper offers an early summary of the evolving thinking in the field of Black Psychology and the meaning of each of those perspectives. That thinking has certainly continued to evolve in the nearly twenty years since this paper was initially written, but the dialectic in thought between the Eurocentric and Afrocentric perspectives continues in contemporary efforts to view African behavior within an appropriate context as opposed to alien European hegemony.

In compiling these papers for this volume, I tried to preserve them in their initial form even though I found that my own thinking had evolved since these papers were initially written. I thought it was important to present the papers in the form of their original preparation since the language and the ideas are responding to a certain social and philosophical context.

Though, I have no major disagreement with the fundamental ideas that exist in these papers, I am not sure that I would hold to some of the phrasing and the stridency that characterizes some of my own rhetoric. The language and the approach are all very important to the evolution that is on going in the scholarship and in my personal analysis of these concepts. The revisions from the original that I made in these articles were few and more structural. I did not feel it appropriate to critique myself with the benefit of hindsight. My subsequent writings offered that critique as my ideas have evolved while remaining loyal to the original tenets that I sought to address.

Paradigms Of African American Research (1989)

There has been a growing awareness over the last twenty years that science is not sacrosanct. The recognition that science is a method and not *the* method of observation has increasingly been suggested in the writings of philosophers of science, scientists and scholars in a wide variety of disciplines. Scientific paradigms themselves are unstable and are subject to frequent transitions. Paradigms, as discussed by Thomas Kuhn (1970), are a set of implicit assumptions held by members of a particular scientific community, be they physicists, mathematicians, psychologists or others. The paradigm is the shared conception of what is possible, the boundaries of acceptable inquiry, and the limiting cases. Within science a paradigm allows certain stability in models, methods, and modalities of knowledge, but at the price of certain insensitivity to new input. African American scholars, particularly those in the social sciences have been most vocal and critical of the scientific paradigms, which exist in Euro-American social science (Akbar, 1981; Baldwin, 1981; Clark, 1972; Dixon, 1976; Ladner, 1973; Nobles, 1978 and Richards, 1981.) According to these scholars, traditional scientific paradigms have served the function of perpetuating oppression and erroneously depicting the reality of the victims of oppression.

The assumption guiding the traditional paradigms often couched in esoteric and obscure scientific jargon has essentially been: normative reality is that reality characterizing the observations, behaviors or aspirations of middle class, Caucasian males of European descent. Concepts, models, methods and modalities, which reaffirm the normality, superiority and legitimacy of this group, are the models, methods and modalities with axiomatic legitimacy within the Western scientific arena.

Webster defines research as "investigation or experimentation aimed at the discovery and interpretation of facts, revision of accepted theories or laws in the light of new facts, or practical application of such new or revised theories or laws." Unfortunately, "research" is not like the "searches" which characterized the Ancient African scholars who devoted their scientific endeavors to the pursuit of "Truth." Research does, however, involve a careful, systematic, patient study and investigation undertaken to establish facts or principles. African American scientists must devote themselves to gain knowledge of the facts of ourselves, of our condition and establishing principles for the restitution of ourselves and the amelioration of our condition. Research is an instrument and as with any instrument, its benefit or its danger rests upon its usage. There is neither implicit benefit nor danger in the instrument of research, but the research must be guided by a set of principles, which insure the ultimate utility of that research. The principle, which must guide African American research, must be an objective of self-knowledge and collective liberation. Research is actually a product of certain presumed paradigms or particular models, methods and modalities. The paradigms dictate the parameters of certain models, the validity of certain methods and the appropriateness of certain modalities for investigation. The paradigm dictates what to look for, how to look as well as how to use what is found. The models constitute the definition of what to look for. In sociology, the model is the underlying theory of society; in educational and psychological research, it is the underlying theory of man or mind.

The model determines the answers of your research in that it predetermines what will be seen when the investigation begins. The questions predetermine the answers (Clark, et als, 1976). The method determines how to look. The method, predetermined by the model dictates how the questions are going to be answered. The method is selected as an instrument of the pre-established model. Contrary to the usually more objective view of research methodology the emphasis here is that the model precedes the search determined by the qualities pursued and it is selected to identify those qualities to the exclusion of other sets of qualities. Scientific methodology is only one such instrument of pursuit. The modality determines the expression or implementation of what the method has identified. Structured by a model, guided by a method, the modality becomes the particular form or matter of expression to be determined by the research investigation. Given this progression both the questions and answers of the research agenda are actually predetermined by the paradigm.

This discussion will first of all look at some examples of research based on the traditional paradigms for investigations of the African American community. It will demonstrate how the models, methods and modalities of this traditional research have been counteractive to the needs of African Americans and how they have perpetuated the racist and destructive motives of the exploiters of those communities. The second part of the discussion will suggest an alternative paradigm and some models, methods and modalities that are consistent with the survival, growth and perpetuation of African American communities.

The Traditional Paradigm and Its Models

Kuhn (1970) asserts: "for a time paradigms provide model problems and solutions to the community of (scientific) practitioners." The paradigm that has operated throughout much of the Euro-American history of social science has been the affirmation of the normality of the male, Caucasian of European descent and his relative superiority to other peoples.

This paradigm delimits the array of questions that may be raised in investigating the human being in their varied forms and sundry environments. Whether the investigation is anthropological, sociological or psychological, the normative model is the male Caucasian of European descent. Even the U.S. Census statistics have been broken down into the categories of "whites" and "non-whites," that implies a racial identity only relative to the "norm." White is assumed to be "normal" and anything else is a deviation from that norm, and therefore designated as non-white.

The model dictated by this paradigm is one that has been identified as a "Eurocentric model" (Baldwin, 1976, 1980). The more one approximates this model in appearance, values and behavior, the more "normative" or "normal" a person is considered to be. The problem created for African American communities by such a model is the implicit assumption of deviance on the part of anyone who varies from this model. As early as 1840, medical researcher, Dr. Samuel Morton (Stanton, 1960) concluded from his craniometric research that the brain of various races of man became successively smaller as one descended from the Caucasian to the Ethiopian. Dr. Morton continued: "The brain differential accounted for those primeval attributes of mind, which, for wise purposes have given our (white) race a decided and unquestionable superiority over all nations of the earth."

A brief look at the models of prominent figures of Euro-American psychology reveals the prominence of the paradigm of white supremacy. G. Stanley Hall, founder of the *American Journal of Psychology* and first president of the American Psychological Association states in his classic 1904 textbook entitled *Adolescence* that:

> Certain primitive races are in a state of immature development and must be treated gently and understandingly by more developed peoples. Africans, Indians and Chinese are members of adolescent races in a stage of incomplete development.

Carl Jung (1935, 1968) in a similar implication of "primitiveness" stated "he (the Negro) has probably a whole historical layer less (in the collective unconscious) than you (Caucasians). The different strata of the mind correspond to the history of the races."

A perusal of the traditional social science literature reveals consistent assumption of white supremacy. Almost without exception, the research that has been conducted on black bodies, minds and groups within the model of traditional western science shows blacks to be categorically inferior to whites. The mere fact that blacks are only studied in comparison with whites reveals that the underlying model is whiteness. McGee and Clark (1973) appropriately observe that:

35

> Where there is equality between things, there are no differences and therefore no psychological research. The way a person frames a question determines the limits within which his answer can possibly fall.

White supremacy is not the only characteristic of the traditional Western model. The model is also primarily individualistic. It assumes that the person is best understood as separate from others and characteristics suggestive of interdependence are viewed as deviant. In the psychological literature, dependence has been identified as endemic in a broad array of mental abnormalities from depression to schizophrenia. As a result, the general motif of the culture is one of individualism and a defiant independence. The idea of internal fate control pervades the literature as a preferred personality characteristic. Concepts of internal fate control and independence as desirable personality traits are essentially camouflaged descriptions of the "rugged individualistic immigrant from Europe who conquered and settled these shores of North America." It is a desirable quality to view nature as an enemy and to subdue it at all cost. The idea of subjecting environmental obstacles to the control of the powerful is implicit in such conceptualizations of human personality and motivation. It is only incidental if those obstacles happen to be other people such as Native Americans, African or Aboriginal Hispanics. They are all dispensable if they stand in the way of European fate control.

Predictably, the literature shows African Americans to be consistently in the pathological or abnormal direction along these individualistic dimensions. Blacks show higher tendencies of interdependence, dependence and internal fate control. The mutual reliance and cooperation (that has a natural ecological parallel in all dimensions of nature) is viewed as pathological dependence when African Americans are (invariably) compared with Euro-Americans. The consistently strong faith in a Supreme Being and belief in a systematic and orderly universe by African people throughout the Diaspora is viewed as "low internal fate control" by the psychologists, "superstitious behavior" by anthropologists, pagan practices or pantheistic by theologians and a variety of other pejorative descriptions by other social scientists. In point of fact, these data merely confirm another characteristic of the Eurocentric model that maintains that the Western worldview is the normative worldview. It also structures the observation so that those characteristics where there is evidence of difference are the ones that are investigated.

Another assumption of the Eurocentric model of human beings is that men of the mentally healthy and effectively functioning people are competitive. Human beings are axiomatically assumed to be in conflict and human accomplishment is realized through the triumph over conflict. David McClelland (1965) writes in the *Harvard Business Review,* "The need for achievement is an essential ingredient for entrepreneurial success." Of course, he concludes, "South Americans, East Indians, poor people from other countries and Black Americans lack this (achievement) drive." The assumption of course is that the drive for power, control and authority that characterize high, need achievers is desirable. McClelland and other psychologists who have lauded the benefits of high need achievement have failed to consider the marked parallels in the correlation between the manifestation of this drive and the less desirable characteristics of the authoritarian personality. They are both characterized by a rigidity of thought process, a tendency to manipulate people as objects and an excessive sense of ones own moral rightness as reflected in the high achievement orientation as well as the characteristics of the racist. This characteristic of the model adds to white supremacy some socially desirable characteristics of European American masculinity.

Another assumption of the traditional Western model or conceptualization of the normal human being that guides research activity is the idea that what is real or knowable is material, quantifiable and directly observable. As observed by McGhee and Clark (1973), Clark, et als (1976), and many others, Western *"man"* has all but lost "his" sense of spiritual and non-material reality. In the light of this epistemology it becomes clear why Western thinkers, consistently equate material affluence and technological opulence with strong social and cultural development. Chief Fela Sowande (1971) observes:

> But, of course when an individual has grown so insensitive to the non-material world that he can no longer look at things of the flesh through the eyes, but sees instead the things of the spirit through the eyes of the flesh, then he has indeed become a witting or an unwitting victim for the forces of destruction.

This emphasis on the material, the observable and the quantifiable is the hallmark of scientific method and it reveals the critical role played by models in determining "what to look for." Our suggestion is that the characteristics of white supremacy, individualism, competitiveness, authoritarianism, sexism and materialism characterize the traditional Western models for research.

Therefore, any research that operates from this paradigmatic position utilizing models of Western science, would observe the African American community from this particular point of reference. "Non-whiteness," communalism, cooperation, femininity would all be in some way viewed as deviant or at best, non-normative.

Methods of Traditional Research

As we have discussed above, methodology follows from the model and determines *how* to look. Based upon the assumptions of the model, it dictates how the researcher should proceed in affirming his model within the guidelines of his paradigm. The model determines the methodology or how to do the research. In the words of Dr. D. Phillip McGee (1974):

> Because the empirical foundations of Western science find their generic antecedents in the philosophical assumptions of the oppressor, we can easily understand why their primary premise becomes: 'that which is like me is good while that which is different from me is bad, or white is good, black is bad.'

The traditional researcher, then, on the basis of the aforementioned model can safely establish his behavior, his group, and his culture as a norm and seek to assess predictable deviations from that norm. An example of the consequence of such methodology is the frequent deficit model of research. The poor and Black are identified as "culturally deprived," "socially handicapped" and "disadvantaged." These states of being are ascribed to them on the basis of their deviation from affluent and White groups along several observable, material dimensions, in other words, according to Thomas and Sillen (1972): "the behavior, language and thought of the poor represent deficits that are not present in the middle class." One would similarly expect that good research methodology would require comparisons with "appropriate normative" groups and those normative groups to which Blacks are compared are invariably similar to the white supremacy model.

Another characteristic of the traditional methodology is its approach to sampling. Those African Americans identified for sampling are those who typify the expectation of deviance from the model. Disproportionate numbers of studies on African Americans look at prison inmates, delinquents, academic non-achievers, poor, welfare recipients, single parents, etc. The focus on this population becomes a methodological self-fulfilling prophecy of the characteristics already implied in the model. As the white, male college sophomore has been the model used for volumes of psychological research, the marginalized, poverty stricken, educationally deprived, socially destitute African-American male or female has been the comparable population among "non-whites" that has served as the typical case example to study the behaviors of "non-white" subjects. If such studies followed the claimed standards of Western scientific research, then because of the inadequacy of the controls, whites and non-whites should never be compared along the objective dimensions that have been generated from the human equivalent of the white rat in social science research and that is the white, male, college sophomore. Certainly one would at least expect that evaluation measures would be re-normed on groups of "non-whites" who are otherwise comparable.

Much research has focused on clinical case histories as a model of black personality. Notorious among these are the studies of Grier and Cobbs (1968), Kardiner and Ovesey (1955) and others. These writers operate within the tradition of the model by assuming personality deficiency by over generalizing the crippling impact of oppression. The methodology focuses on a sampling approach, which assumes African Americans to be disfigured victims of oppression, or in some way deviant when the behavior observed is actually realistic and normally adaptive within the social context. Another aspect of the methodology has to do with the guidelines for observation. Phenomena that are observed and those selected to ignore are determined by the methodology of the research paradigm. For example, objectivity is assumed to be the greatest virtue of the scientific methodology (which is the method of choice in traditional Western research. Several writers have questioned the limitations of objectivity (Akbar, 1981; Carruthers, 1972 and Clark, et al., 1976).

This writer (Akbar, 1981) has argued elsewhere that one fact often denied is that the use of an "objective" approach *is* a value. When an observer chooses to suspend from his observations certain dimensions of data, then a value judgment *is* made. This is, in fact, a very important value because implicit in this decision is the choice to ignore certain sources of information which could critically alter ones observations and conclusions. Particularly, the social scientists create an unreal and unnatural situation by assuming that the observer is not a participant in his observations and that the observer or his surrogate (in the form of observational instruments) does not generate a reaction to the characteristics of her/himself.

As noted above, the surrogate of the observer is the instrument used to collect observational data. The usual instrument in traditional research is testing. No particular test has been any more destructive in its conclusions about African Americans than the IQ test. The IQ test is utilized as a very common research and assessment instrument. It assumes that conditions surrounding the test behavior are constant and differences in scores reflect "real" differences in the subjects and their abilities. Consequently, it is not unusual to find statements such as the following by Dr. Carl Brigham (1932):

> ...the army tests proved the superiority of the Nordic type over the Alpine, Mediterranean and Negro groups as racial admixture increases, American intelligence would decline at an accelerating rate owing to the presence here of the Negro.

Comparative performance on an instrument constructed on the basis of certain restricted learning experiences is used to affirm the basic difference between groups who primarily differ in precisely those experiences under consideration. The test given rather readily assumes, however, that differences in scores on such a fabricated instrument reflect differences in factors, which have undefined origins and nature. It is not unusual that we err along the lines described by Guilford (1967):

> In comparing two social groups on the basis of scores from a particular test, it would be important to know that test measures the same ability or abilities in both groups. If it does not, the use of the scores would be like comparing the weight of one group with the metabolic rate of the other.

For example, an African American taking an intelligence measure constructed and administered by whites or white institutions could be a measure of courage by those subjects or their compliance with the impositions of white supremacist institutions, rather than a measure of intelligence. Perhaps, the lower the IQ score may mean the greater autonomy of this African American subject and the degree of their resistance to the imposition of white values. Such a question could never be appropriately answered because the methodology does not allow the possibility of such observations. What is true of the IQ test is equally or more true of most tests used in traditional research. They all reflect the perspective of the model being utilized. The structure, the content and the behaviors that are sampled are all reflections of the model described above. The tests of personality, motivation and other characteristics are all directive in determining what will be observed. The compelling conclusion is that the methods perpetuate the model in that the types of instruments, the identification of subjects and the samples of behavior to be observed are all predetermined by the paradigm shaping the researchers' observations.

Modalities of Traditional Research

The method confirms the model; then the model is perpetuated in the modalities of implementing the research findings. The modalities are the ways in which the research findings are implemented. Based upon a firm adherence to the methodology described above the researcher systematically chooses the behaviors, the subjects and the instruments that assume a particular model of community and of the human being. The results of the investigation are then interpreted in the light of the preestablished model from which the observer began. The cycle is almost complete, except for the perpetuation of the model by research-based programmatic interventions. With the legitimization of "science," the policy-makers are equipped with the kinds of conclusions that continue to establish the conditions that maintain their idealized human model. Of course, in the instance of traditional American social science research, these policies perpetuate the white supremacy paradigm.

An example of such conclusions, bolstered by research is one by William Shockley (1966) based upon his studies and those of other researchers who have predictably concluded the intellectual inferiority of African-Americans:

> Can it be that our humanitarian welfare programs have already selectively emphasized high and irresponsible rates of reproduction to produce a socially relatively inadaptable human strain?

Once his studies have demonstrated the "inadaptability" of that human strain (i.e., African Americans) he is only a step away from suggesting controlled growth of that "inferior strain." The policy was implemented by accelerated efforts to develop birth control policies and family planning for this "human strain." The justification for such provision is never connected with the potentially genocidal implication, instead the argument is made that such policies improve ones economic well being because "the poverty of Black communities is perpetuated by their tendency to have such large families." Of course, no mention is made of the fact that the infant mortality rate is three times higher among those same families. The important fact is that the modality of policy implementation is consistent with the preliminary model that assumes the inferiority of non-White persons from the outset and concludes through selected research methods that strategies or modalities must be chosen that will enhance the effectiveness of the "superior" group and to reduce or even eliminate the inferior group.

Conclusions such as the one above by Shockley and the one below by Arthur Jensen have had disastrous effects in terms of public policy for African Americans. Jensen (1968) observed that:

> Attempts to provide compensatory education for disadvantaged children have failed because they are based on the assumption that blacks could attain the same level and quality of intelligence as whites.

43

The government, during conservative political times, is willing to eliminate or greatly reduce support for effective education of all its citizens. Such a policy decision is a direct outgrowth of research-based" conclusions such as these by Shockley and Jensen. One might, of course, question whether Blacks *should* "attain the same level and quality of intelligence as whites." Since intelligence is a non-specific factor determining a person's effective adaptation to *his or her* environment and realizing the critical distinction between white and black environments in the American context, then it could be potentially self-destructive for a black person to have the same level and quality of intelligence as whites.

Unfortunately, the modalities chosen for the implementation of traditional research findings are ones that encourage Black or other non-White groups to become more in accord with the original paradigm of masculine Caucasian, middle class American behaviors. As Glazer and Moynihan (1963) conclude: "The Negro is only an American and nothing else. He has no values and culture to guard and protect." But, such a conclusion is utterly dehumanizing as is suggested by Andrew Billingsley (1968), when he observes:

> To say that a people have no culture is to say
> that they have no common history which has
> shaped and taught them. And to deny the history
> of a people is to deny their humanity.

Denial of the African American's humanity simply confirms the original thesis that being human means that one is necessarily a male, Caucasian of European descent.

The Paradigm and Model of African American Research

The paradigm that must emerge to structure our models must

be one, which facilitates the best of development for all human beings. It must be a "natural" or generally human paradigm (Akbar, 1980) rather than the narrow ethnocentric paradigm that describes a particular group of humans.

The new paradigm should offer a balance between the materialistic preoccupation of the Western or traditional Eurocentric paradigm and the extremely spiritual and esoteric perspective of the Oriental paradigm. This paradigm that emerges from an African worldview does not presume that the only normative form of the human being is African or the member of any racial or cultural group. The paradigm suggests that the ideal or model human being should be those people who represent consistent and harmonious relationships with nature. It adopts the basic ontological position of the Africentric worldview of "I am because we are" (Mbiti, 1970; Nobles, 1980). It also views spirituality as being endemic to the human make-up; therefore behavioral observations are at best partial observations of the whole human being.

The model, which emerges from this paradigm, has several characteristics. It assumes that all human beings should be (1) free to grow and realize their highest potential as spiritual (as distinct from necessarily religious) beings; (2) free from oppressive and humanly demeaning environments; (3) free to live cooperatively with any human beings that are respectful of their humanity; (4) free to develop knowledge of oneself and/or ones historically and culturally determined identity; (5) free to defend oneself against the dehumanizing influences of anti-human forces and (6) free to achieve human dignity without artificial barriers that negate your access to the fields for human growth. This model is intended to structure the nature of research conducted on African Americans, other so-called "non-White" people as well as even White people who choose to participate in human culture of mutual respect and spiritual consciousness.

The model intentionally and appropriately biases our observations of African Americans and their communities. As the Western social science models described above are designed to perpetuate the oppression of Blacks and affirm the superiority of

Whites, the bias of this model is to facilitate the liberation and enhanced development of people who have been oppressed under models and methods of science that have simply disguised insidious and humanly destructive environments. At the same time it does not assume a contrasting inferior/superior relationship to other human beings in order to affirm its parameters. The Western model of research identifies the characteristics of the researcher's scientific skills should have been acquired and legitimized by way of educational training such as a PhD or some similar initiation bestowed by the doorkeepers of the traditional models of research. In developing an alternative model, we suggest another form of credentialing that is consistent with Chief Fela Sowande's (1971) criteria for meaningful research. The criteria that he identifies for such research are:

> Relationship index (which is) the extent to which the researcher identifies with the culture within which the subject of research is found and the individual conducting the research, by which his personal 'Worldview,' his concept of 'Nature,' etc., indicate what possibilities there might be that research results may be unwittingly filtered through unsuspected or unacknowledged prejudices.

Methods of African American Research

Two issues must be addressed in a discussion of methods of African American research. One issue should be how the aims of the foregoing model will be investigated and pursued. The other issue is the types of research and instruments, which should be used in these investigations. In the light of the first issue, Dr. Dubois McGee (1973) makes a relevant observation:

Racial ascription is the common denominator that is systematically woven through the international fabric of human life on this planet. Thus, understanding the depth, height and width of our experiences as a collectively common one, makes our study of black self imperative to our survival and advancement as well as critical to a more comprehensive understanding of the nature of universal man.

This quote addresses two components of the methodological question. The first component that is delineated is that the subjects for investigation will be Black people. Unlike the traditional research models, which almost invariably focus on Black/White comparisons, the African American research model views, Blacks as normative for Blacks. The diverse occurrence of Black people in a wide variety of social, economic, political and even cultural environments produces a broad base for identifying meaningful variables of similarity among Black people.

The second component identified in Dr. McGee's quote is the need for "study of the Black self." This self-study will generate theory from an appreciation of the culture and history of Black people and will supply new concepts and instruments for observation. Both the content and instruments for Black research should emerge from the fertile cultural ground of the African and African American (African West Indian or other appropriate groups') experiences. For example, rather than asking "How should blacks be involved in Euro American constructed mental health centers?" we should ask, "What kinds of mental health structures do Blacks have and use?" Rather than test children's knowledge of alien environmental artifacts to determine intelligence, they could be tested on their knowledge of indigenous cultural artifacts. Rather than study ways of teaching Black mothers, middle class non-black techniques of child-rearing, researchers might look at "successful" Black children and determine by what techniques were they raised and acquired the impressive adaptive skills that have permitted them to succeed in often overwhelmingly oppressive environments. Somehow, mothers and fathers raise very adaptive Black children who manage to live bi-culturally in happiness and emotional stability. Those Black parents never read a Dr. Spock or any other European American expert on child-rearing. Why not enhance these impressive skills and identify their essence so that they can be shared with non-African Americans (and other African Americans) who have superior European American resources and experiences but manage to raise incredibly neurotic and self-destructive children. Why learn techniques that fail for the very people they are articulated to assist when the evolution of your own child-rearing techniques has given you the real goals of human aspiration: peace, love, joy and harmonious relationships

The African American model in its holistic approach encourages methodologies that look at people in a non-fragmented way. McGee and Clark (1973) observe:

> The Western inability to synthesize body (material) and mind (spiritual) has led some respected scientists to make the absurd comment that black people in America are "good" in athletics but poor in thinking. Such scientists fail to recognize that to have a good body means that one has a good mind and vice versa; one cannot exist without the other. If the body is poor, the mind is also, and vice versa.

The second issue of methodology is the "how" or types of research procedures that appropriately address the model. There are four (4) general types of research which are most relevant to an African American paradigm: (1) theoretical, (2) critique of falsification (deconstruction) research, (3) ethnographic and (4) heuristic (construction or reconstruction) research.

Theoretical research is for the purpose of generating questions. Theory development grows from self-reflective observation and the introspective analysis of ones (collective) experiences. No data beyond ones subjective and affective appraisal of the observer's experience are necessary. This is not unlike the procedure for the ground-breaking and paradigm-setting work of Sigmund Freud, Carl Jung, William James, B.F. Skinner and the vast array of luminaries in all fields of social science research who never produced a control group while laying the cornerstone for Western thought. Once a logically coherent and systematic theory is in place, then one elaboration may be to raise questions that may require empirical answers. The empirical question is neither necessary nor sufficient as evidence for the validity of theory. Considering the conspicuous absence of introspection and self-study within the context of the appropriate worldview for African people, then it would seem that empirical questions would be premature in the absence of a theoretical base from which to generate such questions.

Curtis Banks (1980) has identified "deconstructive" or falsification research as another type of research. Such research is concerned with an analysis of the construct validity of traditional research. The falsification researcher is concerned with demonstrating the fallacy of the inferences and the methodological distortions of that traditional research. This is a process of beginning to undo the kinds of destructive inferences about African Americans such as we have described above that emanated from traditional research. Falsification research involves both theoretical dismantling as well as empirical rebuttal.

Ethnographic research is probably the only authentic form of empirical research that is appropriate for this point in our scientific method development. This approach permits the researcher, having passed the "Relationship Index," (Sowande, 1971) to observe black people where they are and to try fulfilling the criteria of a worker within the African paradigm who can begin to identify those characteristics of Black people that are most fruitful in the light of our research model. Rather than cataloging deficiencies of Black people, the ethnographic researcher can identify those strengths and self-affirmative patterns that have facilitated our growth.

Finally, *heuristic research* offers the bridge to our discussion of modalities. This research follows from the ethnographic research in that it begins to articulate culturally adaptive styles and begins to demonstrate the benefits, which come from adapting that style. The objective of this research is to fortify those structures that have been demonstrated to be beneficial to the survival and advancement of Black people. If tests are to be used, what kinds of tests would be most appropriate in identifying those qualities that have emerged as valuable and effective for survival from the ethnographic research?

Modalities of African American Research

The enactment or implementation of the research findings from the research methodologies is an inseparable part of our observations. Policy and institutional application may or may not follow directly from Western research and its methods. If vital institutions, that maintain our model of human excellence, are already in existence, then concerns about implementation are not as urgent. In the case of African Americans with few, if any, vital institutions, the modalities of implementation are urgent. This becomes the process of liberation and institution building for a historically oppressed people. The interpretation and implementation of our research must not fail as Carter G. Woodson (1931) described the higher education of the African American which:

> . . . .has been largely meaningless imitation. When the Negro finishes his course in one of our schools he knows what others have done, but he has not been inspired to do much for himself.

The programs that emerge from our research should have immediate relevance in correcting our oppressed condition and advancing us in the light of the model of enhanced human growth described in the research model that we described above.

One modality, which should be considered, is that our research should be problem-oriented. Heuristic research must affirm benefit and not function as research for research's sake, as is the case for some traditional research. The objective should always be to apply directly research findings to some problem or goal, which would enhance the development of our communities. Even in the case of the destructive or falsification research, which we discussed above, the ultimate objective should be to define an alternative and constructive direction.

An example of the problem-orientation modality can be seen in research on hypertension. Most of our communities are plagued by deaths related to hypertension. We should combine the efforts of the physicians, social scientists and affected groups to understand the interrelationship of nutrition, stress, racism, and social organization on hypertension. The specific goal of the research should be a reduction of the death rate from hypertension. As is implied in this example, we must focus on interdisciplinary approaches to research. Narrow, traditional disciplinary lines must not restrict our efforts.

Another modality of our research is an outgrowth of the holistic model of human beings that requires us to transcend the conventional parameters of research. We must be willing to recognize the metaphysical dimension of human experience. It is important to begin to investigate systematically arenas of nature and human experience, which have been traditionally viewed as "unresearchable." Certainly, the spiritual dimension is a critical component of the Black experience and research, which ignores this dimension, ignores the assets of an important aspect of the total human experience. Psychic research must be included in our investigations because psychic phenomena are an important aspect of the African experience throughout the Diaspora. We must understand how faith, prayer and meditation work since such forces have guided so much of our history. It is critical to understand if consciousness is a continuous state and what consequences ensue from altered states. These are questions that have been eliminated from consideration in the Western scientific model but must be encompassed in the broader model that we are proposing. One cannot adequately study the experiences of most people of color on the planet without considering spirituality, communality, psychic phenomena and consciousness since such experiences are the essence of "non-White" peoples experiences.

The final modality of our research must be directed towards the development of institutions. Institutions are the forces that maintain and perpetuate the paradigm or model of humanity that people select or determine for themselves. If the model that we have articulated is necessary for the liberation and advancement of African people, then it is critical to establish institutions that will accomplish that objective. As we identify the adaptive strategies and characteristics for our advancement from our research methods, then those strategies must serve as the guidelines for structuring our institutions. Educational institutions must offer content that advances self-knowledge as well as offering instruction through the demonstrated modalities that build on our strengths. Economic institutions must be built that address our critical survival needs while being consistent with our model of humanity and community. Our religious institutions must be critiqued and developed along lines that foster our spirituality and enhance our collective development. All of these modalities provide the ultimate objective of augmenting and institutionalizing the African American paradigm rooted in nature and respect for humankind.

Conclusion

Traditional research in black communities has been based upon a model that fosters the advancement of White people at the expense of "non-White". This research has emanated from a set of paradigmatic assumptions that assume that normative reality is defined by those characteristics of male Caucasians of European descent. The human being is assumed to be at their best when *he* is *white, materially* accomplished, achieved through *competitive, independent* assertiveness and evolved from European roots with American fruits. *She* who is *black, poor, coop-*

erative, spiritual and evolved from a cultural experience in the Southern Hemisphere is by definition inferior, abnormal, unintelligent, uncivilized and superstitious according to this model. The methods of traditional social science research have been selected in order to underscore and legitimize precisely those qualities that the model has identified as normative. The "how" of the research simply reaffirms what the model or paradigm has defined, as should be the "what" of the research. The modalities of traditional research become the policy implementation that confirms, sustains, and perpetuates the original model.

An African American paradigm is proposed which is essentially humanistic and holistic. It establishes a model of the human being, that stipulates how freedom for complete human development and self-knowledge can be achieved. The methodology fosters this development and four (4) types of research are proposed that would advance this model for African Americans. Finally, the modalities of problem-resolution, metaphysical qualities and the institution building are suggested as the essential path for implementing the research. The urgency of human liberation and development is advanced as the major determinant of effective implementation of our research and the model of the African American paradigm.

In conclusion, we must carefully evaluate the approach to human observation that has emerged from traditional Euro-American social science research. We must understand that methodology is not free of bias and in fact, methodology is a form of systematic bias. The application of that method must be consistent with our paradigm or the outcome will only confirm the paradigm that gave rise to the original alien methodology. This means that the persisting effort to investigate the African American experience from the Euro-American framework will only perpetuate the notion of deficient blacks. If the research in our communities is to foster the growth and development of those communities, then we must be clear about the goals of that research. If our research is to be in the African universal tradition of the great scientists of ancient times, then we must expand our vision to greater horizons for study.

References

Karon, B. (1958*).* *The Negro personality*: Λ rigorous investigation of the effects of culture. New York: Springer.

Kuhn, T. (1970). The structure of scientific revolutions. *International Encyclopedia of Unified Science*, 2(2). Chicago: University of Chicago Press.

Moynihan, D. (1965). Employment income and the ordeal of the Negro family. *Daedulus*, 94, 745-770

Nobles, W.W. (1980). African philosophy: Foundations for black psychology. In R. Jones (Ed.), *Black psychology*, (2nd ed.). New York: Harper and Row.

Richards, D. (1980). European mythology: The ideology of progress. In M. Asante, & A. Vandi (Eds.), *Contemporary black thought*. Beverly Hills: Sage Publishers.

Shockley, W. (1972). Possible transfer of metallurgical and astronomical approaches to the problem of environment versus ethnic heredity. Quoted by Thomas, A., & Sillen, S. in *Racism and psychiatry*. Secaucus, NJ: Citadel

Stanton, W. (1960). *The leopard's spots: Scientific attitudes toward race in America*, 18 15-1819. Chicago: University of Chicago Press.

Thomas, A., & Sillen, 5. (1972). *Racism and psychiatry*. New York: Brunner/ Mazel.

Woodson, C.G. (1933/1990). *The Miseducation of the Negro*. Trenton, NJ: Africa World Press, Inc..

*Earlier forms of this paper were originally published as:
Weems, L.B. (1974). "Black Community research needs: Methods, Models and Modalities," in L. Gary (Ed.), *Social Research and the Black Community*. Washington, DC: Howard University Institute for Urban Affairs and Research.

Akbar, N. (1984). "Africentric Social Science for Human Liberation," *Journal of Black Studies*, (14(4), June, pp. 395-414. Also in R. Jones(Ed.) (1992) *Black Psychology* (3rd ed.), Berkeley: Cobb & Henry Publications.

Evolution of Human Psychology For African- Americans (1990)

There has been a rapid evolution in the thinking about the psychology of African Americans since 1970. That evolution has progressed from a self-negating perspective that viewed the model human being as necessarily nonblack to a self-affirmative perspective that sees the African as a model of universal man. In a relatively brief time, scholars have dissected the youthful psychology that has grown-up in Europe and America over the last 100 years and has sought to salvage human psychology from the precipice of mechanized, human destruction. This discussion is a brief review of the evolution of that thinking about the psychology of African Americans.

Several scholars have presented extensive comparisons regarding the philosophical basis of conceptualizing the world from European vs. African perspectives (Akbar, 1976; Clark, 1972; Clark (X), et al. 1975 and Dixon, 1976). The differences in these philosophical perspectives have been cited as the basis of the differences in European and African behavior as well as differences in the methods of observation of those behaviors (Baldwin, 1976; Jackson, 1976, 1979 and Nobles, 1974, 1976). Jackson (1979) in a provocative study reviewed the origin and development of "Black Psychology" and some of the key issues regarding the development of that field of inquiry.

This discussion draws upon the valuable discussion of Jackson and perhaps extends his observations a step further into analyzing the conceptual development that has occurred in the thinking of, particularly, African-American psychologists over the last 20 years. We shall characterize the three major developments in the conceptualization of African-American psychologists as "Euro-American," "Black," and "African" perspectives.

These three orientations have certain characteristics that de-

fine their methodology, and by implication structure the definitions and ontology that emerge from these perspectives.

Orientations (Norms)

These three stages of conceptual growth have first evolved
in terms of their orientation. An orientation determines one's reference point for assessing normality. Throughout most of the
history of observations of African-American behavior in the West,
that reference point has clearly been Euro-centric. Baldwin (1976)
observes that the standards of observation that have led to persistent conclusions of the "social pathology" of black behavior
has resulted from the Euro-centric assumptions in the use of
measures of black behavior. Baldwin (1976) continues:

> The traditional social pathology view of black
> behaviors is therefore based on a European con-
> ception or definition of reality, or more precisely,
> a European distortion of the reality of black people.
> Its rise to prominence in the psychological litera-
> ture, naturally then, merely reflects the vested so-
> cial power of Euro-American psychology (and
> white people generally in European American
> culture) to legitimate European definitions of re-
> ality rather than the necessary objective credibil-
> ity appeal of its presumed validity (p. 8).

From this Eurocentric reference point, normality is established
on a model of the middle class, Caucasian, male of European
descent. The more one approximates this model in appearance,
values and behavior, the more "normal" a person is considered
to be. The major problem with such normative assumptions for
non-European people is the inevitable conclusion of deviance on
the part of anyone, unlike this model. In fact, the more distinct or
distant you are from this model the more pathological you are
considered to be. The obvious advantage for Europeans is that
such norms confirm their reality as *the* reality and flaunts state-

ments of their supremacy as scientifically based "fact."

Even a casual observation of the history of psychology will well-demonstrate that the volumes of psychological literature from the last 100 years have been based on observations primarily on Europeans, exclusively Caucasian, predominantly male and overwhelmingly middle class. Thomas and Sillen (1972) have well demonstrated this fact in their extensive review of *Racism and Psychiatry*. The formulations of such notable thinkers who have shaped the thought of Euro-American psychology such as Sigmund Freud (1953), G. Stanley Hall (1904), Carl Jung (1953), William McDougall (1908) and B. F. Skinner (1971) have all directly or indirectly asserted the superiority of European races over non-European races. Despite the diversity of the so-called "Schools" of Western psychology, they seem to merge unequivocally in their assumption of the Euro-centric point of view and the superiority of people of European descent. It is not surprising that the conclusions reached from the application of their concepts and methods have concluded the invariable inferiority of non-Caucasian peoples.

The use of this Eurocentric reference point by non-European (Caucasian) observers has resulted in many non-Caucasian observers having become advocates of their own inferiority. It is for this reason that many so-called "black psychologists" have been identified with the same racist tradition that has characterized the majority of Western psychology and its research findings. Such findings have obsessively dealt with the alleged self-rejection, inferior intellect, defective families and contorted motivations of African Americans. These conclusions are not unlike the typical conclusions of the European American psychologist. As I have observed elsewhere (Weems, 1973):

> The logical fallacy in this inappropriate attribution of normative statements about non-white people is the assumption that to be intelligent (or for that matter, psychologically healthy in general) is to act like a European rather than as an agent of your own culture.

The orientation of "Black Psychology" is "ghetto-centric." Jackson (1979) has accurately portrayed the early development of Black Psychology as "reactive." He further observes:

> (Black Psychology) can be readily traced to the 1920's when Afro-American psychologists first published research studies to dispel the notion of Afro-American inferiority and sought to increase the psychological services rendered to the Afro-American community. These heuristic works and pioneering efforts were, for the most part a reaction to the existence of institutional racism and individual acts of discrimination, and, therefore, merely constituted a racist perspective (p. 271).

This reactive aspect of "Black Psychology" was necessary and served a vital purpose in the evolution of thought about the psychology of African Americans. It was probably one of the initial insights of the African American scholars that one of the primary shortcomings of traditional psychology was its fallacious normative definitions. It was clearly perceived by writers such as Kenneth Clark (1965)—who has condemned the Black Psychology movement since its inception—that the insistence upon viewing African American behavior in the light of European American norms was clearly conceptually faulty.

The response was to decry the Caucasian, middle class norm and to assert the necessity of analyzing African American behavior in the context of its own norms. These norms were assumed to be the behaviors of southern-born, working class, African American ghettos-dwellers. Such a norm, though introducing bias against large numbers of African Americans was certainly more valid than the traditional norms, which had been applied.

Joseph White (1972) in his landmark piece "Toward a Black Psychology" asserted the need for this new norm. He states:

58

> ... it is vitally important that we develop, out of the authentic experience of black people in this country, an accurate workable theory of Black Psychology It is very difficult, if not impossible to understand the life styles of black people using traditional theories developed by white psychologists to explain white people. Moreover, when these traditional theories are applied to the lives of black folks many incorrect, weakness-dominated, and inferiority-oriented conclusions come about (p. 43).

White continues in identifying the real adaptive strengths of African American youngsters when they are evaluated within the confine of their own cultural norms:

> These black youngsters know how to deal effectively with bill collectors, building superintendents, corner grocery stores, hippies, pimps, whores and sickness and death. They know how to jive school counselors, principals, teachers, welfare workers, juvenile authorities, and in doing so, display a lot of psychological cleverness and originality. They recognize very early that they exist in an environment, which is sometimes both complicated and hostile (p. 44).

The irony of this black norm assertion is that it invariably validates itself in comparison with whites. White's assertion that such a perspective actually makes "them superior to their white age-mates" is the consistent conclusion from the black norm. Ultimately, the norm remains the same as it is in the Eurocentric approach since African American behavior is still being compared with the rejected norm. The statement of what it meant to be "black" was never considered an adequate statement unless that condition was in some way compared with whites. The consequence is an inevitable entrapment in the same circle.

The other limitation of the "black norm" as adopted in the Black Psychology movement is the conclusion that the adaptation to the conditions of America by African Americans constitutes a reasonable normative statement about African American behavior. The problem with such an assumption is the acceptance of many adaptive but ultimately self-destructive behaviors as legitimate. For example, the pimp becomes glorified as a cultural hero because of his material attainment. For very much the same reason, the drug pusher can become a hero because he, in White's words, "is the black culture hero who messes with the system and gets away with it." As a consequence, such destructive adaptations emerge as new cultural norms for the African American community.

Utilization of the ghetto-centric norms rendered "Black Psychology" irrelevant to a large middle class of African Americans who were, ironically, the authors of Black Psychology. A classic example of this irony was the robust condemnation of the Moynihan conclusions about the African American family. Based on the Euro-centric norm and models of Freudian psychology, Moynihan concluded that the "Black Family" is essentially pathogenic or responsible for the origin of many psychological and social problems of African Americans. The outcry was intense and extreme from black and "liberal" white psychologists, sociologists, and other social scientists. Typical of this outcry was the statement by psychologist Joseph White (1972):

> When the black family is viewed from a middle-class frame of reference, which assumes that the psychologically healthy family contains two parents, one male and one female, who remain with the child until he or she becomes a young adult, the fact that the same black male is not consistently visible to the white observer of the black family leads to a conclusion that the black family unit has a matriarchal structure... A closer look at the black family might show that the matriarchal or one parent view fails to take into consideration

the extended nature of the black family (pp. 44-45).

Though the description of an extended family is true from a point of view, it inadvertently establishes a new and equally biased norm based upon the ghetto-centric perspective. The large numbers of intact African American families are then suspect in regard to the "black norm." Though the extended family concept is valid as a structure of African American families, it is important to realize that the nuclear family can also have validity for African Americans. The assumption that one must choose one or the other due to majority participation raised serious questions about the validity of the norm being applied. As we shall see below, the application of a more universal norm could legitimize either pattern.

The weakness of the Euro-centric and ghetto-centric perspectives is their reliance on a statistical norm as the model of human order. Implicit in both perspectives is an assumption that a majority in a particular context can effectively determine what is natural for human beings. In fact, throughout European American psychology, there is a serious fallacy that confuses normative (or normal) with natural. Elsewhere, we have seriously criticized this tendency that we call "democratic sanity," (Akbar, 1979).

The orientation of African Psychology is nature-centric. It takes as its norm, the nature of the human being and the functioning of nature in general. It is important to note at this juncture that we use the term "African" advisedly. In fact, we might more appropriately describe this approach as "natural psychology" (Akbar, 1976). This reservation is crucial because of the numerous distorted images that can be observed in post-colonial, modern Africa. A misapplication of the concepts of African Psychology has come from the effort to document or disprove this African Psychology model by conducting field surveys or studies of contemporary urban African behavior. The assumption of the African Psychology theoreticians has been since its inception that the philosophical foundations of African Psychology (Nobles, 1972) represent a pure model of the African person in particular and universal man in general. "African Psychology" has gained growing popular usage over the last several years, so we use it here, but with the aforementioned reservations.

The writer is aware that the use of vague language like "human nature" is a harping back to the "pre-scientific" assertions of 19th century European philosophy. Precisely because of the false security in such pseudo-objective notions as "behavior" and "statistical norms," we reassert the validity of concepts such as "human nature." The use of a nature-centric perspective maintains that there are absolute standards and principles guiding human behaviors.

For example, one of the principles of African Psychology is "survival of the Tribe" or the principle of collective survival. Under the influence of this principle, one can observe a wide variety of behaviors geared towards that end. Many behaviors can fit this standard of human nature. The critical point is that the norm is not a statistical majority, but a life concept of collective survival. From this point of view, we can more fully appreciate Nobles' (1978) description of the African American family structure as "elastic." Such a family can be as effectively nuclear as extended, depending upon what kinds of circumstances were necessary for survival of the family (tribe). The same point is true of functions within the family. According to Nobles (1978):

> Functionally, or the performance of its (family) functions, would be fluid or elastic. That is, the performance of a particular function does or can "expand" into many other functions.

The whole notion of fixed and inflexible role definitions does not become a criterion of effective family functioning. As a consequence, an argument for the presence or absence of a physical father is a moot question regarding family effectiveness. Instead, the issue becomes adequacy of function rather than the presence of a particular role occupant. The concept of a matriarchy or a patriarchy is a meaningless analysis. Equally useless, is the argument of a nuclear as opposed to an extended family, for the same reasons.

There are other absolute norms about the nature of man that are drawn from both historical, philosophical, religious and eso-teric descriptions of man and his nature. Assumptions about the perfectibility of man, his capacities for self-mastery, conscious-ness and conscience as well as man's inseparability from man, are viewed as preeminent influences in human nature from the African Psychological perspective.

Axiology (Values)

Issues of values are seldom discussed in scientific enterprises. This is in part due to a pervasive denial of the role of values in guiding so-called "scientific" activity. In fact, it is the erroneous claim that values are absent in the "objectivity" of science that rather systematically excludes values as an issue in the discus-sion of science. Dr. Jacob Carruthers (1972) observes rather as-tutely:

> ...the science or (experimental) methodology is neutral or objective, it is the science of control through intervention and/or the unnatural alter-ation (if possible) of all objects (p. 3). So, what is assumed to be value-free is itself a value. The choice of values or the values guiding ones pur-suit constitutes one of the critical distinctions be-tween approaches to the study of man.

The essential axiological (or axiomatic, if you will) position taken by the European American psychological perspective is the value of objectivity. It starts as Carruthers (1972) continues by assuming:

> A theory about harnessing certain forces and subduing certain oppositions to the deserved change. Western science assumes that any desir-

63

able modification of nature is dictated....thus not only is it right to modify nature to supply needs, but it is also right to conform nature to all other tastes, in keeping with the doctrine of enlightened self-interest. (pp. 3-4).

In other words, the value of objectivity adopts a point of view of the essential relationship in nature to be man-over-object. Man is viewed as the instrument of control and all other things (and occasionally people of lesser power) are objects subject to that control. The individual self is viewed as the center of reality and all else is object. So if self is male, then all that is female is object; if self is Caucasian, then all that is non-Caucasian is object and is therefore subject to male, Caucasian, etc., control or unnatural alteration. Social science is replete with examples of this tendency to objectify by ordinal or nominal classification. Again, Dr. Carruthers (1972) observes:

...modern methodology is based upon ordinal classifications. The various phenomena are ranked according to imagined or imposed objective values such as magnitude or complexity or natural arrangements derived from so-called systematic comparisons (p.4).

Classifications which are frequently encountered in social science literature of the European American variety frequently reduce people to categories like "the aged," "the schizophrenic subjects," "the culturally deprived," etc. Such categories, which are initially nominal, are invariably treated in some qualitative fashion resulting in an ordinal classification based on Superordinate-subordinate arrangement. The necessity to refer to people involved in psychological studies as "subjects" is clearly instructive about the goal of such studies which is to subject. This is the value of the "valueless" European American experimental methodology.

A final value implication of the European American methodology is the assumption that the observer is not a participant in what he observes. This arbitrary suspension of universal interconnection is an astounding feat of logical fallacy. By altering the classification or depersonalizing the personalities into an (E)xperimenter and a (S)ubject, there is an assumption that the E is free to peek without detection or intrusion. Such an assumption perpetuates the platonic notion that man and nature are two different realms of being. This assumption frees man to run amok in his role as master over nature. In fact, Carruthers (1972) goes on to point out:

> The assumptions are based on the so-called self-evident notion that nature is uneven in supplying the needs of man; thus, the maximization of individual survival can be achieved by modification of natural supply (p. 3).

The axiological position of Black Psychology is racialism. This value assumes race to be the critical human issue in the study of African American behavior. As the European American operates effectively from his position of man-to-object, the Black Psychologist views the critical relationship of black-to-white as the paradigmatic relationship. The condition of white oppression of blacks is accepted as a given and the essential value of Black Psychology is mastery over oppression and the oppressor. In fact, psychiatrist Frances Welsing (1974) defines "Black Psychiatry" as "counter racism."

The works of eminent black scholars such as Clark (1965), Fanon (1967), Grier and Cobbs (1968) and non-black scholars such as Kardiner and Ovesey (1951), Karon (1958) and many others have well-illustrated this position. The assumption that black personality is a cumulative by-product of sustained oppression is one of the major positions of these writers. Furthermore, it is assumed that the only meaningful approach to the study of black persons is from the perspective of oppression and in terms of the black experience with whites in America. In fact, the idea is that African Americans would be just like European

Americans or perhaps, more appropriately would be European Americans if it were not for oppression. There is also an assumption of commonality among those who have experienced oppression. It is not unusual for some African American social scientists to adopt a Marxist position that uncritically equates the racial oppression of people of African descent with other economically and/or socially oppressed peoples.

The extension of this value perspective asserts that essentially whatever is black is of positive value and what is white is of negative value. This is in direct contrast to the Caucasian domination and exploitative use of "objective" methodology, which has objectively concluded everything "white" to be positive and everything "black" negative. The reactive quality of Black Psychology is reflected in this mirror image of European American psychology. The "Black Psychologist" involves himself with the process of delineating those "black" positive characteristics and those white negative ones. In other words, it follows the tradition of Dr. Welsing's "counter-racist Psychiatry."

The essential value of the African psychological system is the centrality of the human being. In the African Cosmology, man is the center (Nobles, 1980). "The animals, plants, and natural phenomena constitute the environment in which man lives" (Nobles, 1980). Nobles (1980) continues: "everything was functionally connected; to destroy one category completely would cause the destruction of the whole of existence, including the Creator." Man and his world are clearly interdependent and the objective approach that completely excludes subjectivity is logically fallacious.

The African approach identifies the relevance of psycho-historical traumata such as slavery and the cultural barbarism of certain people but these considerations are not reactive. Though the experiences of oppression are critical in terms of assessing the contemporary African experience, this cosmology evolved long before the coming of the European and it would be self-effacing to reduce its perspective to "racialism" or experiences with the European. The Axiology of African Psychology identifies a Divine Creator as the originator and sustainer of man. Nature is in harmony with herself and the desirable state is a harmonious relationship with nature. Consequently, mastery over environment is not the essential value of African Psychology. Neither is mastery over oppression viewed as a preeminent concern because without oppression man would find himself in a teleological vacuum. However, the preeminent value is self-mastery, which presupposes the active elimination of oppressive yokes in order to realize this value. Man is conceived as a microcosm of the universe; therefore, in mastering self one has mastered the essential processes of nature.

Those things that facilitate effective human development are valued. Human values are paramount and objects are evaluated as they impact upon the human situation. Objects are never evaluated as having greater prominence than people.

Conceptions of Self

The three approaches also differ in terms of how they define self. The definition of self or "person" in psychology is critical because such a definition determines both the approach to description, assessment and ultimately reconstruction, if such should become necessary. In other words, ones conception of consciousness is at the foundation of ones approach to method in the study of the human mind.

European American Psychology takes as its arena of study the individual ego, behavior and consciousness. The commonality in the European American approach to personality is its emphasis on individuality. From Adler's "creative self" through Maslow's "actualized self" and Mead's "looking glass self," the conception is consistent that self is an individual phenomenon. All of these approaches give the highest credibility to the individual and his unique experiences. So from Skinnerian to Freudian psychology, we can observe that there is a common emphasis on individual differences as being the best description of human experience.

Black Psychology describes the arena of study as being the

collective experience of oppression. What must be studied to understand the human experience is the shared experience of oppression or the shared phenomenon of being an oppressor. The degree to which one is conscious of shared oppression is assumed to be a measure of "black awareness" or "black personality." Therefore, we get models of black personality such as the Cross (1971) model that describes development of black personality as growing from Negro (or unawareness of oppressive realities) to black (hyperawareness of oppression and the oppressor) to transcendence (where blackness is integrated).

Semaj (1980) introduces an excellent critique of the limitations of this analysis, which would take this discussion somewhat afield to fully review. However, the essential issue is that personality for African Americans is conceptualized as the emergence of consciousness of oppression. This approach that begins to see personality as a collective phenomenon is a critical contribution of "Black Psychology." It makes a radical departure from the European American preoccupation with the individual and his isolated experience. There is a "quantum leap" in this conceptualization though the intention was to merely address the shared reality of oppression.

African psychology conceptualizes self as an unqualified collective phenomenon while respecting the uniqueness of the individual self as a component of the collectivity. Nobles' (1980) description of the African ethos as a "collective consciousness" typifies this notion, The African conception of personality is captured in the formula given by Mbiti (1970): "I am because we are; and because we are therefore I am," Whatever happened to the individual impacted on the corporate body, the tribe and whatever happened to the tribe reverberated into the individual. This conception identified the appropriate arena of study as being the collective consciousness or again, what Nobles (1980) refers to as the "experiential communality" or the sharing of particular experience by a group of people. Nobles (1980) argues that the experiential communality is important in determining society's fundamental principles—its beliefs about the nature of man and what kind of society human beings should create for themselves. In other words, description, assessment and even reconstruction are assumed to be collective rather than an individual phenomenon. This is critical not only in terms of how people define their psychology, but also in terms of the kind of society, one would expect many Africans well adjusted to their "experiential communality" to be quite deviant in such an alien society (see, Akbar, 1979).

Time Orientations

Another distinction in the approaches is in terms of how time is conceptualized. Time conceptions are critical in that they determine which events are most significant. Most importantly time becomes that which maintains the cadence of people's lives. It determines their rate and intensity of activity as well as their priorities about life. Their motivations and orientations are determined through the cadence established by their time orientation. Time is such a powerfully subjective factor that people seldom consider that their time orientation is actually idiosyncratic. They rather automatically assume that everyone else is out of order if they are not moving consistent with their rhythm. This is particularly true when there is a strong investment in objective measures of time.

Certainly, the most extreme of these objective time-measuring cultures is the European American culture. Their approach or orientation to time is predominantly futuristic. Their rhythm as a consequence is exceedingly urgent and pressured since it is essentially impossible to ever catch-up with the future.

This futuristic orientation is played-out in their study of human psychology. The objectives of their study are focused on the goal of prediction and control. The concepts, instruments and methods of European American psychology are ones that are geared towards future outcomes as opposed to enhancement of the present or elaboration of the past. For example, there is often greater credibility given to predictive assessment devices than is given to the actual here-and-now performance of people or the history of their prior performance. Child-rearing practices, learning methods and even psychotherapy are future-oriented.

Non-Europeans have often been described as deficient because they have an inadequate future-orientation. This is another example of the attribution or projection that emanates from the ethnocentrism. As we commented above, ethnocentric time is probably the most notorious of the projections that come from ethnocentrism. Time is as idiosyncratic as is the heartbeat responding directly to ones own life (cultural) experience and reality.

Time in the European American system is a concrete materialistic commodity: it is bought and sold, as is any other product. In many systems of psychotherapy, for instance, the time is viewed as a critical dimension of the psychotherapy. The "clock time" is strictly adhered to regardless of the emotional state of the client. Scheduled meeting times are viewed as sacred and clients are routinely charged for their appointment times whether they keep them or not. Though elaborate theoretical justifications are given for such actions, this is still a graphic illustration of the concrete conception of time in the European American's orientation.

The mathematical reality of the clock has the same tyrannical hold on European American's conception of reality, as does quantification throughout their science. The symbolic numbers that are associated with the rhythm of time are literally assumed to be the abstraction of time. With the projection towards the future working with this concretizing of time, human conduct actually becomes a servant to time and behavior is judged by its adequacy in responding to time.

The Black Psychology time focus is on the recent past of the African American experience and the present conditions of oppression and its multifarious manifestations. The future is not considered as relevant. There is actually no consideration of prediction since racism is considered a constant and the experiences and behaviors of African Americans are determined by racism. The African American rhythm is assumed actually to be determined by its reaction to racist oppression.

The time orientation is primarily past and present in this system of thought. The assumption is that to understand current behaviors, one need only understand the history of racism and to be conscious of contemporary expressions of oppression. Time is actually reckoned by the pain of oppression. This condition and when it has been manifest is the focus of the rhythm of time. So one is a victim of time because time itself actually becomes a part of the oppressive process in an oppressive environment. In the African system, time is viewed as cyclical rather than linear. Consequently, "now" is the past and the future since those dimensions are immersed in the present. The past was focused upon as the source of instruction because "the direction of one's life system was from the present dimension backward to the past dimension" (Nobles, 1980). Nobles goes on to describe the African conception of time thus:

> For the people, time itself was simply a composition of past events. Very little concern was given to time in and of itself. It existed, but the African time concept was (is) very elastic...Time was reckoned by phenomena...

In order to make sense, or be real, to the West African, time had to be experienced; and the way in which one experienced time was partly through one's own individual life and partly through the life of the tribe, which went back many generations before one's birth. We see in this description a very distinct orientation to time from the European American perspective, which we described above.

There is first of all, a basic acceptance of the notion that time is a subjective phenomenon, so the likelihood that one feels compelled to impose his time perspective on others is reduced in the African system. This might in part account for the absence of colonizing and proselytizing activities historically on the part of Africans. Many of the differences in motivations and behaviors among people of African descent and people of European descent can be seen to be attributable to their differences in conceptualizing the rhythm of life, which we call time. Jackson (1979) makes a compelling argument for the African American's treatment of time as growing out of this African conception of time.

It is important to observe however that though the future orientation does not predominate in the African system, there is a consideration of the future. History informs us that Ancient African people established the first clocks and calendars. The ability to plan and develop for crops, migrations, etc., was well entrenched in the African lifestyle. Certainly, much of the metaphysical life of African people was relegated by a future orientation, but the future was understood to be contained in the present. The future is conceptualized as a repetition of the infinite cycles of being which all meet in the powerful experience of the present. The future is actually viewed, as a reenactment of the past and progress is the application of the best lessons of the past and the avoidance of repeating disastrous errors from the past.

Human Goals

The next area of difference in the approaches to human psychology is in terms of the conceptualized goal or purpose of the human being. The conceptualization of goals determines the basis for effectiveness of the human being. Therefore, mental health and mental disorder are determined by effectiveness in achieving the goals of the self or personality. So, the theoretical import of hypothesized goals is critical in terms of evaluating the adequacy, effectiveness, i.e., sanity of the person. Variation in perception of goals can lead to serious discrepancies in the assessment of mental health as well as the prioritizing of energies for groups of people.

The European American approach sees the person as essentially directed towards pleasurable gratification based on material achievements. The Behaviorists assume that, all behavior hinges on rewards and punishments. Freud assumes the primal need of immediate gratification of either sexual or aggressive drives and Maslow assumes a hierarchy of needs for gratification at various levels. Again, the diversity of the schools merge in the shared assumption that the critical goal of human personality is the desire for gratification.

The emphasis of Black Psychology is that the essential goal of human behavior is survival. The emphasis on survival skills characterized the majority of the literature in this area: Grier and Cobbs (1968), White (1978) and other similar writers have emphasized the survival skills of African Americans as being the primary goal and accomplishment of personality. The constant confrontation with racism and oppression is viewed as the consistent reality and strategies to out-maneuver threats to survival by African Americans is the goal of personality. Staples (1974) for example, builds his theory of the black family on a survival-adaptation basis. His assumption is that confrontation with slavery and subsequent oppression shaped the African American family through its struggles to survive. The essential goal of the Black Psychology orientation was formulated as in this example as: 'how do we overcome the oppression of European Americans?"

Though survival, no doubt represents a basic goal of human existence, as it is a goal of all life forms, the limitation of the Black Psychology orientation is that it views the goal of survival only vis-à-vis the oppressive European American. It does not address the goal of personality in the absence of oppression. The goal of African American existence again takes its form in reaction to the conditions of oppression.

African Psychology offers the goal of self-affirmation and self-perpetuation as the objective of human personality. It advocates that the affirmation of ones unique history and the perpetuation of ones collective self and cultural reality is the goal of human personality. The human being is focused on the full manifestation and perpetuation of who we are as a collective phenomenon. This clearly is not oppositional to the Black Psychology perspective of "survival against oppression." African Psychology sees oppression as an incidental but disturbing obstacle to human self-affirmation that is not unlike many similar issues.

Epistemology

Epistemology defines "how we know, what we know." What is the legitimate form of acquiring knowledge and how do we identify that knowledge has been acquired? The latter part of this question has, of course, become a major objective of the psychologist and educator. The way that the psychologist defines what is authentic knowledge and how it is acquired becomes paramount in his determination of who has adequate knowledge facility. The degree to which measurement of intelligence has permeated the concern of psychology throughout its history is an indication of how critical this question is. The fact that alleged discrepancies in intellectual faculties has served as the justification for the discriminatory treatment of African Americans also indicates why this issue of epistemology is so important for conceptualizing human functioning.

In European American psychology, knowledge of the outer environment particularly as it is experienced by the European American person is considered as the basis of legitimate knowledge. The concept of IQ is rooted in the idea that the greater is ones store of information about the typical middle class, Caucasian American environment, attitudes, values and techniques, the greater is ones IQ=Intelligence=Knowledge. The issue of self-mastery, the applicability or even the validity (Truth) of the acquired knowledge is not an issue. The European American epistemology identifies knowledge as essentially recall or recognition of essential objects, processes, or experiences within the typical European American experience. The key element of this epistemology is that what is to be known is external to the person and ones knowledge pool is assessed by what is known of his external world.

The reactive quality of Black Psychology is again reflected in its epistemology. The assumption of Black Psychology is that intelligence for African Americans is the knowledge that he has of the working class, traditional African American environment. This is well demonstrated in Robert Williams' (Wright and

Isenstein, 1975) approach of culture-specific testing, which he bases on a principle of cultural match or mismatch:

> Learning one activity either facilitates or hampers the learning of another, contingent upon the similarity or dissimilarity between the learner's cultural background and the material to be learned (p.9).

On this basis, Williams established the Black Intelligence Test of Cultural Homogeneity (BITCH). He devised the test by drawing from a glossary compiled of African American slang, "his personal experiences and that of his friends who had lived in the African American community" (Wright and Isenstein, 1975). Dr. Williams' approach is not unlike that of Drs. Wechsler, Terman and others (in this regard) who have developed European American instruments for measuring "intelligence." The difference, of course, is the cultural experience being called upon as exemplary of knowledge. The limitation in both approaches is its epistemological conclusion that what is knowable is external and the inevitable bias that comes from variations in experience of the external. Williams did not advocate the innate intellectual inferiority of European Americans due to their consistently lower performance on the BITCH, as do his Caucasian counterparts.

African Psychology assumes a universal knowledge rooted in the awareness of the make-up of the human being. The most direct experience of the self is through emotion or affect. Vernon Dixon(1976) observes:

> Homeland and overseas African persons know reality predominantly through the interaction of affect and symbolic imagery, i.e., the synthesis of these two factors produce knowledge. In the "pure" Africanized worldview of the unity of man and the phenomenal world, there is no empty perceptual space between the self and phenomena. Affect refers to the feeling self, the emotive self

engaged in experiencing phenomena holistically
(p. 70).

Dixon (1976) makes another important distinction in this regard, relating to African epistemology. He says:

> Affect, however, is not intuition, for the latter term means direct or immediate knowledge (instinctive knowledge) without recourse to inference from or reasoning about evidence. Affect does interact with evidence, evidence in the form of symbolic imagery (p. 70).

This knowledge via "self" or holistic knowledge is critical in terms of understanding African Psychology. The relationship to reality inferred by African Psychology is one that relegates as doubtful any of the measures of knowledge that identify only external reality. A possible measure of intelligence in psychology would be observed in "effective living and development." Effective living would not be demonstrated on a typical European American IQ measure. Instead, one would need more dynamic evaluation of a person's experience of himself as well as an evaluation of the socio-cultural environment surrounding the person. In other words knowledge would be reflected in the degree to which a person is capable of maneuvering an environment offering obstacles to his development.

So, intelligence would entail (1) knowledge of the collective reality of self, (2) knowledge of environmental obstacles to effective (collective) self-development, (3) actions initiated to remove or master such obstacles and ultimately (4) knowledge of the Divine and universal laws which guide human development into ultimate knowledge of the Creator. These components of knowledge are most directly "known" through the "affect-symbolic imagery" as described by Dixon above. Dixon (1976) notes: "symbolic imagery is the use of phenomena (words, gestures, tones, rhythms, objects, etc.) to convey meaning." Consequently, an adequate inference of intelligence would require effectively tapping the full-range of a people's symbol imagery as well as ascertaining, which are the most effective forms of such imagery that are used. One could not evaluate a person's "knowledge" without knowing how effectively that person conducts his full being.

Therefore, the possibility of a man being adjudged a genius on the basis of his external knowledge yet proving to be morally inept would be impossible in African Psychology. Genius, by definition, would identify not only what you knew, but the kinds of judgments and prudent uses made of what you know. The four (4) dimensions must be understood as interdependent in terms of assessment of knowledge.

Another example would be that knowledge can only be adjudged or assessed as adequate if it is used in the service of the collective self. Cognition is not presumed to exist independent of self-liberating action. Unlike the European American and Black Psychology approaches that assess both knowledge (cognition) and achievement independent of self-affirming activity, the holistic reality of African Psychology could not hypothesize such an inconsistency. The most "intelligent" among those assessed through African Psychology would in the extreme show the greatest self-knowledge and higher knowledge of the Creator and his mission for man as understood through universal wisdom. In the light of such an approach, it is not surprising that the leaders perceived as most intelligent by the majority of African Americans (who view their experience from their perspective) would be people such as Nat Turner, Harriet Tubman, Martin Luther King, Malcolm (X) Shabazz, Elijah Muhammad, Marcus Garvey, and others. All of these models invariably came equipped with Universal wisdom as well as secular knowledge of the external world. The kind of response to such leadership (knowledge) as well as the expression of such knowledge is done via the affect-symbolic imagery defined above. The ideas are communicated and received, not by words alone, but from the full range of affective and symbolic imagery.

The intelligent being from the perspective of African Psychology is a moral being. Morality represents the imperative of ordered life functioning for the purpose of effective human development. Knowledge of such principles and, of course, the implementation of them is as much a measure of intelligence as is the shrewd and facile manipulation of principles of material creation. The holistic conception of human life requires attention to and progressive understanding of laws that regulate the outer life "and" the inner life. The degree to which the person understands and utilizes these laws for the purpose of collective self-liberation is the supreme measure of intelligence and well-adjusted functioning. In the light of such an approach to intelligence, the assessment of intelligence is not a quantitative phenomenon. It is seen in the quality of life that a person maintains.

There is an assumption that the quality of ones life is determined by the knowledge of the inner self and not subject to influences from the outside. Such an approach makes moot the issue of racial superiority/inferiority and nature/nurture controversies as they relate to intelligence. The assessment of superiority and inferiority is done on the basis of the quality of life chosen and the utilization of human growth potential. Again, the assertion is that material accoutrements constitute only a limited portion of life quality, and such achievements must be evaluated in the light of humane and just usage of such resources. Ultimately, the intelligent person finds peace and helps to bring it to others. This image of the effectively functioning person is viewed from the perspective of the nature of the harmonious universe and is therefore within the natural potential of all human beings.

Another aspect of epistemology that directly proceeds from the above discussion is the assumption made about the essence of things. Particularly, in attempting to understand the human being, ones definition of the human essence is crucial. The definition of essence merely represents the conception of the lowest possible form to which the human being can be reduced. European American psychology views this essence as material. It is this materialism that has devolved psychology from the study of the psyche (or soul) to its current status as the study of behavior. The European American preoccupation with mind=brain formulations, hypothesizing that the totality of human life can be understood from brain functioning and physiology represents the epitome of the European American concept of essence as material. The pervasive conviction that what can be observed by the senses represents the essence of human life defines this epistemology. The direct inference epistemologically is: what can be observed and is material is real and therefore knowable. What is unobservable and not material represents the unknowable or unreal. Therefore, the equation of external or outer technology with human superiority and even reality becomes understandable in the light of their epistemology. It is not surprising how people with less opulent outer appearance are adjudged inferior, uncivilized, undeveloped, unintelligent or savage, even when such people may far-surpass European Americans in justice, charitableness, compassion, contentment and peacefulness.

Black Psychology followed a similar course because of its emphasis on the physical exploitation of oppression. The tendency to view the essence of human life as the outcome of struggle and oppression results in a materialistic conception of the human being. The view that blackness is sacrosanct is the obverse of the view that whiteness is supreme. Frances Welsing's "counter-racist psychiatry" epitomizes such an approach. As the European American has justified his exploitation of non-Caucasians on the basis of his superior material (i.e., white skin color), Welsing (1979) argues that the basis of such exploitation is due to their inferior material (i.e., color inadequacy) and their fear of the superior material (i.e., significant skin pigment) of black, brown, red and yellow peoples. The goal of "counter-racism" according to Dr. Welsing (1974) is to "efficiently and effectively checkmate the behavioral system of racism (white supremacy)." The essence of this conceptualization of the human being is to view the person as essentially material.As we have suggested throughout this discussion, there is considerable justification for the spokespersons of "Black Psychology" to focus on the exploitation of African people by Europeans as a central issue in conceptualizing the psychology of African Americans. As Baldwin (1986) concludes in his analysis:

"(Black) Psychology is therefore proactive as
well as reactive, and it is most certainly political.
Notwithstanding its reactive aspects, however, its
thrust is clearly toward proactivity, that is self-
definition and self-determination". The urgency
of the historical oppression of African people by
Europeans demands urgent and unprecedented
attention. However, it is ultimately debilitating to
ones conceptual development if a battle strategy
becomes ones "Weltanschauung."

Fanon (1968) insightfully notes:
But, if nationalism is not made explicit, if it is
not enriched and deepened by a very rapid transformation into a consciousness of social and political needs, in other words into humanism, it
leads up a blind alley (p. 204).

There are some who would argue that such a position is
accommodationist and advocates transcendence beyond the persisting realities of racism and oppression. Such is clearly, not the
position of this discussion. What is described, as an evolution is
that which has become increasingly more expansive in addressing the total needs of human beings, particularly the historically
exploited and excluded from conceptualizations of humanity. It
also recognizes the real limitations of field weaponry when the
struggle has moved into the halls of scholarship addressing the
control of minds rather than bodies. African Psychology affirms
itself and in so doing counteracts whatever is destructively alien.

African Psychology maintains that the essence of the human
being is spiritual. This means that human beings reduced to our
lowest terms are invisible and of a universal substance. This writer
(Akbar, 1976) has discussed elsewhere that the African conception of personality is fundamentally built on the notion of a force
that defines the person's continuity with all things within the
world. This implies that the person is ultimately reducible to the

universe itself, which gives the human being universal potential. This assumption of the ultimate spiritual nature of the human being hypothesizes the potential harmony of people with each other and the remainder of the universe. There is no assumption of essential conflict in an interdependent cosmos. Material by its very nature is fragmented and in conflict. The material world operates on principles of polarity and conflict and if ones system of thought remains at this level, conflict becomes inevitable. The Freudian conclusion of the essence of the human being as being in a perpetual state of conflict between the life force (*libido*) and the death force (*thanatos*) is not surprising. The Skinnerian notion of the essence of man's development centering around the conflict of avoidance of punishment and the acquisition of rewards is also consistent with this view. We can see the same dialectic functioning in the Black Psychology epistemology that posits the on-going conflict between black/white as being inevitable.

African psychology sees the human being as ultimately reducible to a universal substance that affirms our oneness with the essence of the universe. Man's worth is adjudged potentially as compatible as are the relationships between all of the mutually facilitating components of nature itself. The human being is considered as potentially harmonious and vast as the universe itself. With such a definition of the essence of the human being, we can better understand the conceptions of intelligence that were discussed above.

As a final aspect of "epistemology," the issue of "how" we know becomes a point of significant departure among the various approaches to human psychology that we have identified in this discussion. The conceptualizations of intelligence and essence identify what is knowable within an epistemological framework. How what is knowable becomes known is highly significant in conceptualizing the workings of human psychology.

European American psychology identifies this process as rational thought or cognition. Cognition or thinking is considered to be a rather mechanical process that follows certain systematic rules of logic. Logic, objectivity and rationality automatically preclude affect in terms of Western thought. Thinking is considered to be effective only when it is free of subjectivity (i.e. emotion or affect). The only things that are validly known are known by this process. As we discussed above, objectivity is a prime value in European American axiology, because it is presumed to be the only appropriate and reliable way to obtain knowledge. Feeling is identified as a contaminant to "good and pure" thought.

Syed Khatib (a/k/a Cedric Clark, 1972) observes that:

> Our philosophical heritage—that is, what is taught in our public schools—is firmly grounded in European conceptions of reality. The dualistic conception of Descartes, as defined by the British Empiricist thinkers, particularly Hume, Locke, and Mill, still stands as the scientific foundation of contemporary psychology. The only "truth" that matters according to these thinkers, is that which is given to us by our sensory experience with things. The mind may exist, but it is totally independent of matter, and what "matters" (i.e. is important) is the reality of the matter. Matter is sense; the mind is non-sense, or would result in nonsense if one philosophized on it too long (p. 12).

This observation well-characterizes the modality of European American epistemology. From such an orientation we can see how psychology has reduced human intelligence to a score on an IQ test, human misery to a score over 70 on the MMPI (The Minnesota Multiphasic Personality Inventory.) We can also see why a psychotherapist who "feels" with a suffering client is described as experiencing "counter-transference" rather than sharing with another human being. Khatib (Clark, 1972) quotes the historian of psychology E.G. Boring, as claiming that the science of psychology "first lost its soul then its consciousness." He goes on to observe that, "at least one contemporary writer has since added that psychology threatens to go out of its mind completely." Even human identity is characterized through rational experience: *"cogito ergo sum* (I think therefore I am)" which comes from the French Philosopher, Rene Descartes captures this cognitive orientation of European American psychology. It is a brief step to conclude that one who is not adequately cognitive (i.e., with a low IQ score) is an inferior human being.

Black Psychology takes a completely opposite point of view. The assumption in Black Psychology is that the best way to know what we know is through affect or feeling. Joseph White describes the culture of African Americans as a feeling-oriented culture. White (1972) says: "In a feeling-oriented culture, apparent and when examined closely, superficial, logical contradictions do not have the same meaning as they might have in the Anglo culture." White (1972) continues:

> Closely related to the easy style of handling contradictions, it can also be stated that black people have a greater tolerance for conflict, stress, ambiguity, and ambivalence. White psychologists fail to take this into consideration when they assume that because we have a lower class background, black people are therefore more impulsive, emotionally immature and have less tolerance for stress. (pp.46-47).

Such an approach to characterizing "black culture" is appropriate in the light of the negative characterizations of African American affectivity that have grown out of the Anglo approach to psychology. The black psychologist reacted in self-defense in declaring black culture as a "feeling" culture and therefore appropriate in many of its responses viewed as pathological by European American Psychology.

Again, because of the focus of Black Psychology on oppression as the critical human experience, there is a focusing on the hatred or negative feeling of the racist and the suffering and pain (feelings) experienced by the victims of oppression. One is tempted to conclude from the analysis of Black Psychology that the predominant human feeling modality is pain or suffering. African Psychology assumes a rhythmic balance between affect and cognition. As we quoted Dixon (1976) above: "Affect does interact with evidence, evidence in the form of symbolic imagery." This process of synthesis is essential to the African Psychological perspective because it gives a balanced perspective on feeling and cognition.

There is recognition that knowledge is acquired from sensory experience as well as the subjective experience of affect. African Psychology assumes that the perimeters of knowledge are rational, affectional and moral boundaries. Rationality represents the order of exoteric or outer principles of reality and morality represents the order of principles of esoteric or inner reality. Feeling is the mediating process between these dimensions. Such an approach provides a guide and a context for the often-ungrounded nature of rational knowledge. The classic example is the kind of human suffering that has emerged from the exclusively rational approach to nuclear weapons in contrast to the potentially great human contribution that could come from a morally guided use of the knowledge of nuclear energy.

As we observed previously in this discussion, balance is considered critical in African Psychology. Moral or affective dimensions unchecked by rational or cognitive dimensions result in an human imbalance that ultimately lays the conceptual foundationfor human destruction.

Summary

Black Psychology emerged from the volumes of negative statements about African Americans that have characterized the vast majority of the European American psychological literature. Black Psychology was a reaction. It remains the political or militant arm of the study of African Americans within the European American context. Black Psychology is self-affirmative, particularly in its denial of the self-denigrating conceptualizations of European American psychology.

African Psychology attempts to look at some of the basic philosophical assumptions about the nature of man and the universe as it emerges out of classical African Philosophy and worldview. It attempts to identify the characteristics of the human being in the light of Divine revelation as well as modern science.

This discussion has looked at the basic philosophical assumptions of the three basic approaches to the study of human (primarily African American) behavior as stages in the evolution of our thought about the psychology of African Americans. The conclusion that we draw shows a growth in our conceptualization, which gives us an ever-expanding horizon for study. European American concepts are appropriate for a time and a context, i.e. the time and context which views the African American as a deviant from the Anglo world for those observers who maintain the insignificance of race and cultural plurality may still find such an approach appropriate and valuable.

Black Psychology represents an effort to come to grips with the overwhelming ethnocentrism of European American psychology with a counter-ethnocentrism. The approach is emphatically reactive and predicates its existence on the postulates of European American Psychology. African Psychology may more properly be characterized as natural psychology, in that it attempts to identify the natural laws of the universal human experience. It does not deny the necessity of the often "-militant" stance of Black Psychology, nor does it deny the considerable distance of Europeans from this model of natural human form. It asserts, however, that the principles of African Psychology represent the Creator's model whereby a people most in accord with the original and natural laws of human nature are likely to find compatibility with these principles. In order to do so, the human being must be liberated from the contaminants of materialism, individualism, dualism and hedonism that obscure universal vision and proper human evolution.

References

Akbar, N. (1980). Mental disorder among African Americans. *Black Caucus Journal, 2,1,* 1-7.

Akbar, N. (1976). *Natural Psychology and Human Transformation.* Chicago: World Community of Islam in the West.

Akbar, N. (1976). Rhythmic patterns in African personality. In L. King (Ed.), *African Philosophy: Assumptions and Paradigms for Research on Black Persons.*

Baldwin, J. (1976). Black psychology and black personality. *Black Books Bulletin, 4,3,* 6-11, 65.

Baldwin, J. (1986). African (Black) psychology: Issues and synthesis. *Journal of Black Studies, 16, 3,* 235-249.

Carruthers, J. (1972). *Science and Oppression.* Chicago: Center for Inner City Studies. Northeastem Illinois University.

Clark, K. (1965). *Dark Ghetto.* New York: Harper & Row.

Clark, C. (1972). Black studies or the study of black people? In R. Jones (Ed.), *Black Psychology.* New York: Harper & Row.

Clark, C. X. (1976). *Voodoo or IQ: An introduction to African psychology.* Chicago: Institute of Positive Education Black Pages .

Cross, W.E. (1971). Negro to black conversion experience: Toward a psychology of black liberation. *Black World, 20, 9,* 13-27.

Dixon, V. (1976). Worldviews and research methodology. In L. King (Ed.), *African Philosophy: Assumptions and Paradigms for Research on Black Persons.* Los Angeles, CA: Fanon R & D Center.

Fanon, F. (1968). *The Wretched of the Earth.* New York: Grove Press.

Freud, S. (1953-74). *The Standard Edition of theComplete Psychological works.* J. Strachey (Ed.). London: Hogarth Press.

Grier, W., & Cobbs, P. (1968). *Black Rrage.* New York: Basic Books.

Hall, G. (1904). *Adolescence.* New York: Appleton.

Jackson, G.G. (1976). Cultural seedbeds of the black backlash in mental health. *Journal of Afro-American Issues, 4,1,* 70-91.

Jackson, G.G. (1979). The origin and development of black psychology: Implications for black studies and human behavior. *Studia Africana, 1, 3,* 270-293.

Jung, C.G. (1953-78). *Collected works.* H. Read, M. Fordham, & G. Adler (Eds.) Princeton: Princeton University Press.

Kardiner, A., & Ovesey, L. (1962). *The Mark of Oppression.* Cleveland: World Publishing Company.

Karenga, M. (1982). *Introduction to Black Studies.* Inglewood, CA: Kawaida Publications.

Mbiti, J. (1970). *African Religions and Philosophy.* Garden City, NY: Anchor Books.

McDougall, XV. (1908). *Social Psychology.* New York: Luce.

Mosby, D. (1972). Toward a new specialty of black psychology. In R. Jones (Ed.), *Black Psychology.* New York: Harper & Row.

Nobles, W. (19741. Africanity: Its role in black families. *The Black Scholar. 5, 9,* 10-17.

Nobles, *XV.* (1976). African science: The consciousness of self. In L. King, V. Dixon, & XV.

Nobles (Eds.), *African Philosophy: Assumptions and Paradigms for Research on Black Persons.* Los Angeles, CA: Fanon Research & Development Center.

Nobles, W. (1978). The black family and its children: The survival of humaness. *Black Books Bulletin, 6, 2,* 6-14.

Nobles, W. (1980). African philosophy: Foundations for black psychology. In R. Jones (Ed.), *Black Psychology.* New York: Harper & Row.

Semaj, L. (1980). *Models for an Africentric Psychology.* Presented at the Community Clinical Psychology Conference, Southern Regional Education Board, Atlanta.

Skinner, B. F. (1971). *Beyond Freedom and Dignity*. New York: Knopf.

Staples, R. (1974). The black family in evolutionary perspective. *Black Scholar, 5, 9,* 2-9.

Thomas, A., & Sillen, 5. (1972). *Racism and Psychiatry*. New York: Bruner/Mazel Publishers.

(Weems) X, L. (1973). "Guidelines for African humanism ". Presented at the meeting of the International Association for Cross-Cultural Psychology. Ibadan, Nigeria.

Welsing, F. (1974). *Definitions in counter-racist psychiatry*. Unpublished manuscript. Washington, D. C.

Welsing, F. (1974). *The Cress Color Confrontation Theory*. (Private printing). Washington, DC.

**This article was originally published in Jones, R. (Ed.)(1991) *Black Psychology* (3rd ed). Berkeley: Cobb & Henry Publications.

Chapter III

CONCEPTS OF AFRICAN PERSONALITY

Overview

The personality structure and functioning of African people (or people in general from the African perspective) is the area of my major interest in formulating and reconstructing African Psychology, as was foreshadowed in the "Voodoo or IQ" paper. The nature, structure and functioning of the human personality is an essential aspect of a people's view of their world and themselves. This view of a people's fundamental human identity carries major implications for their moral, social, intellectual and motivational life. This concept of what makes a person a person determines the parameters of normality and abnormality. It is this definition that serves as the core of the human identity in any given culture or human setting. Whether detailed and explicit as it is formulated in European American psychology or abstract as it is in the myths and symbols of traditional people, the definition of the human character is the ethos for human functioning and interaction. The right to articulate this formula of the human make-up is fundamental to the effective functioning and freedom of any people. The imposition of an alien definition of this human character on a people is tantamount to the theft of their humanity. In other words, only a defeated and captured people succumb to their conquerors' definition of their humanity. On the other hand, the ultimate manifestation of freedom and the dismissal of the shackles of conquest is to restore ones culturally appropriate and self-generated definition of their identity.

Guided by this perspective I viewed the issue of personality order and disorder to be a critical component in the reconstruction of African reality. Not only was this redefinition an empowering process, it was a crucial part of negotiating a political environment that used definitions of us as inferior human beings as the basis for the exploitation and oppression of African people in America and throughout the Diaspora. It was in the simplest sense, an act of defiance to affirm our peoplehood and an act of emancipation to rediscover how our people understood their humanity before it was desecrated on the altar of white supremacy and

African captivity. It became an act of ultimate liberation to re-claim the right and ability for African people to rename and re-define ourselves.

These papers were all originally, written and presented in the late 1970's and early 1980's. Certainly, the other pioneer who entered this particular arena early in the 1970's was Kobi Kambon (Joseph Baldwin) who also devoted considerable energy to this issue of re-defining African personality. His work is laid out in rather considerable detail in his book, *The African Personality in America: An African-Centered Framework*, published in 1992 encompassing nearly twenty years of his work in this area.

My four papers in this section delineate my major ideas about personality from an Afrocentric perspective. The major distinc-tion that I lay out in these papers is the idea that personality has a cosmogenesis as opposed to the European view of personality as having a biogenesis. This means that the African conception of the person is of a spiritual creature with an animal façade rather than being an advanced form of animal.

The other concept is the centrality of the interconnectedness of people with each other as opposed to the insular notion of the individual that characterizes the Eurocentric approach to under-standing personality. Finally, there is the assumption that the laws of personality are ultimately continuous with the laws of nature, and normal functioning has certain universal and metaphysical principles that it follows. These fundamental assumptions have remained unchallenged among the numerous younger scholars who have taken up the mantle of defining African personality. Wade Nobles' work applying the Afrocentric concepts to the understanding of the African family and this work of applying the concepts to understanding personality were the earliest ef-forts to move beyond the definition of the paradigm to the initial efforts to apply the concepts. Learning to use the paradigm was the task of the second decade of this work of reconstruction. These papers in their original form represent my efforts to come to grips with these concepts as guidelines for understanding the human personality and to reformulate the African system of conceptual-izing the human being.

African Roots of Black Personality
(1979)

There has been considerable confusion and misrepresentation regarding Black personality. Theoreticians have insisted upon describing the Black person's personality with the terms and assumptions which have grown form the Western Caucasian man's study of his personality. The use of such concepts and assumptions has resulted in repeatedly negative or pathological conclusions regarding Black behavior. It is necessary to draw from an alternative structure and set of concepts in order to assess fairly the behavior of the Black person.

The real or complete definition of an event is based on its origin because the origin establishes the identity of that event. The origin equals the essence, which in turn defines the destiny of that phenomenon. Unfortunately, it is necessary to repeatedly reflect on the European-American's theories in order to understand our own thinking. So much of African-American thinking is determined by the influence of European-American thinking. In order to effectively describe our point of view, it is necessary to contrast the European American conceptualizations because we often fail to remember why it's necessary to develop an alternative conceptualization and without the comparison many students of African-American behavior are left standing with an alien theoretical cap on their heads. Many scholars don't even realize that there is an alternative point of view. It is therefore necessary to make the proper connections in order to address our problems and begin to grow as people.

The Western Conceptions of the Origins

Western psychology deals with this important question of "origins" from three basic viewpoints. There is the Freudian conception that pervades much of Western thought. This viewpoint suggests that the root or core of the origin of the human

93

being is something that is sexual and aggressive. According to this view, when you reduce the person to their lowest element, you essentially have an animal whose primary orientations are pleasure seeking and violence. The evolutionary implication of the human being as originating from animal origins characterizes the identity and the destiny of the human being. The conclusion that human beings are essentially these animal creatures confines our possibilities to the ultimate destiny to survive by defending ourselves from predators, reproduce and then die.

A second viewpoint is that of the behaviorists. Their essentially mechanistic approach sees the human being as a machine, modifiable consistent with some environmentally imposed program. The only thing one needs to concern oneself with is understanding the schedule and system of environmental input into the individual. They conclude that whatever constitutes the inner fiber is unimportant. The human being is essentially a well-constructed programmable machine who has no destiny other than what is programmed into the machine. Therefore, there are no real limitations as to what possibilities can be programmed into the person. The "behavior modifier" is morally at liberty to manipulate the human being in whatever way they are shrewd enough to implement. The scientist may plug electrodes into his subjects' brains and stick them into a computer to make them do what he wants them to do and there are no moral compunctions against it. The assumption is that the person is whatever kind of environmental experiences he happens to have. In a way very similar to the Freudian assumptions, the human being is a biologically evolved machine, whose origin is in its biology and the environmental modifications that have occurred as a result of the individual's separate experience. Once again, the assumptions about origins determine destiny, expectations and treatment of human beings.

The third viewpoint that we find in the Western approach to understanding personality is the Humanistic approach. This approach makes a determined effort to speak to the uniqueness of the human being. Though it seeks to view the human being as more than an animal or a machine, it finds itself limited in terms of what it can assume about the human make-up and still maintain their scientific credibility. The outcome of this ambivalent approach to the human make up is a kind of "artificial humanism"(Muhammad, 1976). In terms of the issue of origins, this "Humanistic approach" is as limited as are the other two approaches because it assumes that the person's essence is their basic animal survival needs. These students of human personality are much more optimistic about the human's ultimate possibilities and they attribute a destiny of growth and transcendence that is not even considered in the Freudian and Behaviorist approaches. The problem is that this "actualized" human being is restricted by the animal nature that rests in the core of their being. Mastery of the material world and a certain level of economic achievement must occur as a basic requisite for the transformation as an actualized "human." As a result, the best examples of truly transformed and actualized people were those who had achieved a certain level of economic affluence that afforded them the luxury of study, esoteric pursuits and philanthropic indulgence, which are the ingredients for ultimate actualization.

Based on your understanding of the origins of an event or of the human being, you can begin to understand what kind of expectations you might have about where it can ultimately go. We find that a people's assumption about their origin or core defines not only their psychology but also their economics, politics and even their religion. It is revealing that the Western scholar, in speculation on his genesis, chooses theories that characterize the human's growth and evolution in terms of their being a more efficient killer than other animals (Morris, 1967). The human essences characterized by these types of animalistic images restrict ultimate growth because of the assumptions about the origin of the human nature. The Darwinian assumption that man is a glorified ape tells us much about the low-level moral expectations that typify Western societies. Conceivably, the European American is acting out a destiny described by their scholars in the conception of their origin as human beings.

The African Conception of Human Origins

The African or Asiatic assumption of the human being and their origin is quite different. When we say African or Asiatic we are not talking about the contemporary African and Asian mentality. We make a firm distinction between what is traditional African/Asian thought and what has happened to Africa and Asia in response to the destructive influence of the Western mentality. It is important to keep this in mind because, with the recent yearning for Black Nationalism, we have indiscriminately imitated some continental Africans. Unfortunately, many of these continental Africans have retained only vestiges of their indigenous culture and have been as self-alienated by colonialism and foreign invasions as have Africans captured and brought to America. When we say African, we are talking about a deep inner sense of self that reaches back before the intrusion of the Caucasian mind into the African life style and the African mentality.

In traditional African thought, the core of the human being is a Divine core. When we are reduced to our lowest human common denominator, when you go to the very root of what the person is, you are going to find a Divine substance. You are going to find a substance that has a spiritual origin. This substance is from the universal all-encompassing mind. The idea of such a substance has an impelling moral implication. The belief is that somehow this inner self has come from a Divine source (call it "God" if you wish). Because of its universal origin, it is something that unites man with everything else in the Universe. In other words, there is a strand that flows through the personality of the person and unites that individual with all things in the Creation. From the African point of view, we are dealing with an assumption that the human being is more than the product of a material environment. Though physically tied to all things in the material world, our essential origin is Divine.

Based on this assumption, we begin to get into other kinds of things that define what the human being is all about and what should be expected of us. Different groups of African and Asian people refer to this inner core by different names (Weems, 1975). The Honorable Elijah Muhammad (1965), the late spiritual leader of the Nation of Islam, had a concept that he called the "Original Man" or "Asiatic Black Man." When he identified the "Original Man," he was describing something that emanated from the Divine order of things. The human being is interconnected with everything that constitutes the physical and so-called spiritual world. This concept of the "Original Man" is an effective metaphor for helping us to understand what we are calling in this context our "African essence." It is the African essence that defines where we came from and where we are going.

Let us consider briefly some characteristics of that "Original Man." The human personality operates according to certain principles that determine what motivates people. The force that motivates the personality draws from various energy systems. From the point of view of Western Science, the primary motive or energy behind human activity or behavior is the quest for something that offers the body pleasure. (For example the alleviation of hunger, return to a steady balanced state from disharmony such as too high or too low body temperature, etc.) According to Western Theorists, this feeling of pleasure is a natural experience when certain basic survival needs are satisfied. The Western student of human behavior has concluded that the basic thing that determines the drive of the human being is the desire for gratification of certain types of physical needs associated primarily with the process of survival.

When we look at the human being from the African conception, the assumption is that the personality emerges from that Divine substance that created it and operates on the basic principle of rhythm or connectedness. Rhythm is flow; flow is interconnection and it succeeds in unifying those things that ostensibly appear to be separate or disconnected. Rhythm is the drive to be reunited with that from which we were dispersed or separated in our "individual" creation. Rhythm draws the separated or disunited things back together. The basic or essential energy that drives the human being is the energy towards reunification or reconnection with nature and the Divine source of our origin.

AL-IKHLAS
UNITY (HQ)

97

Rhythm orients a culture of people to focus on ways to affirm their interconnection or similarity rather than being preoccupied with their difference and separateness. African Scholars have observed that most of the cultural activities in the African traditional life style are group activities (Ani, 1994; Clark et al., 1976; Kambon ,1992; Nobles, 1972 and others).

These group activities reaffirm the essential oneness of the people that has been disrupted by the material and physical distinctions between them. The physical differentiations are consumed in the rhythms that reunite the people. On a material plane, this reunification can be seen in music and dance, therefore, the prominence of musical and dance expressions in the African life style. One may observe a similar phenomenon in the traditional Black church. One is likely to enter the church environment consumed by the influence of the material world that enforces a perception of one's individuality and separateness. It isn't long, however, before the rhythms of the music and the gathering of people begin to absorb the preeminence of separateness as one rises to a spiritual perception of interconnectedness and unity. Often, in episodes described as being "in the spirit," the hat will be thrown in one direction, the pocketbook goes another, and many of the other indications of individuality disappear in the communal enjoyment of being reconnected with each other in the vibrations of a spiritual communion.

The usual evaluation of what constitutes an effective and meaningful gathering in Black communities is the degree to which the ties of togetherness have been reactivated. In contrast with the European American context a highly evaluated gathering is one that gives the greatest support to one's validation as a separate and distinct individual. Such a perspective focuses on separateness. The key to understanding the motor or drive of the inner spiritual core of the Original Man is to see it as operating on a principle of self-transcendence. The basic motivation of the African/Asiatic self is a striving for something that reaches beyond the confines of the separate individual and reconnecting with the extended self. Relationships are vital (literally, "life") from the African view of personality (Nobles, 1974).

In earlier discussions, we (Clark, et al., 1975; Nobles,1974; X Weems, 1975) have used this model as a way of describing the African personality throughout the Diaspora. As a conceptual scheme, this African view of the human personality with a spiritual core is a convenient model for understanding everything from the expression of the African extended family to understanding the significance of dance and music that is a prominent universal among people of African origin (Akbar, 1975.) There is considerable appeal in this African model. It captures the unique and distinct character of the Black person. It shows that, despite any affectation we may have assumed or the superficial qualities we may have adopted, at core we are the "Original Asiatic Black Man," as described by Honorable Elijah Muhammad.

Despite our conscious self-concept, there is a shared African consciousness that is at the root of our being. As students of the African mind, we can only speculate about how these patterns are transmitted. Genetic transmission; a metaphysical transmission or an information transfer through socialization could pass them along. We know that these "indigenous" African patterns are persistent. The patterns seem to be maintained among African people regardless of where we are found in the Diaspora, which suggests a very refined process of transmission that has been able to endure even the most horrendous efforts to impede any form of cultural transmission. This rhythm certainly seems to be a fundamental part of the root of African personality. It has such a powerful influence over the disposition of the African person that there is a consciousness of interconnectedness among African people throughout the world. It is this innate consciousness that the European slaveholder fought so hard to destroy. It could be distorted but not destroyed, as the present so-called "Third World" consciousness suggests.

The Creation of the Negro (*Necro*)

Unfortunately, this basic African consciousness has become distorted by something that is known as a "Negro." This Negro predominates in North America, but he is found wherever the

Caucasian has significantly affected the thinking of Black people. The "Negro" constitutes the distortion of African consciousness and is the root of most of the basic problems for Black people. The fact that we have contaminated our core self with this superficial "scab" known as "Negro" is the source of many of the psychological problems of Black people.

"Negro" is a very interesting word because first of all it comes form a Greek origin meaning something that is dead. Negro comes from the same origin as *"necro"* and *"nekro."* In Greek there is no difference between these words. Some wise and devious white scholar knew what he was saying when he decided to call black people Negro (or necro). If the originator of this concept had been using the Latin or Spanish origin, as is often suggested, he would have called himself *blanco*, which means white. He did not call himself *blanco*; he called himself "white" and he called black people Negro, likely meaning *necro*. There is a semantic message hidden in this word and it seems that it might lie in its Greek origin intending to describe the Black person as a "dead substance." The manifestation of the distorted African self found in the characteristics of the "Negro" is something that stands as a barrier to the real expression and real essence of the African person. The *"necro"* refers to a mentally, socially and culturally dead person.

One of the ways that human beings are able to maintain a conception of themselves and maintain their mental life is through the maintenance of certain self-affirming institutions. People, therefore, have spiritual celebrations, rituals, memorials, museums, books, monuments and all kinds of things to reaffirm their group definition. They constantly reaffirm and celebrate what this inner core is all about. Europeans and all mentally alive people do it.

People of Western Culture repeatedly reaffirm the inner core of themselves as distinct individuals motivated by this sexual and aggressive drive that we discussed above. Their major holidays and monuments either commemorate a war or celebrate a day of significance by either symbolic or actual celebration of these carnal animal drives. The noblest of all their holidays –

Christmas – is notorious for its drunkenness, high death rate, and adulterous office parties. Even Thanksgiving is commonly depicted showing a Pilgrim with a musket in hand. America and Europe celebrate their violent tendencies and the heroism of effective killers in their history. The independence of America is commemorated by celebrating the American Revolution. Fireworks, dramatize "the rockets' red flare and the bombs bursting in air."

Such institutions reaffirm the basic mentality of the Caucasian. This stands in contrast to the preponderance of religious monuments and holidays found throughout the Asiatic and African world. We assume that such a warlike disposition is the basic nature of all people. It is important to understand that the Black American and other Blacks around the world have been subjected to the Caucasian institutions and their mentality. This subjugation accounts for most of the similarities between Western and African/Asiatic cultures in this respect. Indigenous people around the world find their highest celebrations to be of qualities of beauty and power in nature and in the celebration of spiritually accomplished human beings.

The slavery experience destroyed the Black Americans' institutions; therefore, we lost those mechanisms for reaffirming this inner core of who and what we are. The disposition has remained, however. In any of those cultural forms that were adjudged innocuous and left intact, we can see evidence of that inner self-seeking expression. The prominence of traditional religious patterns despite the imposed images and concepts of European Christianity reflects the African person's preoccupation and desire for the Divine.

The social life reflected in the song and dance of black culture show a yearning for togetherness instead of individuality, which is the prevailing ethos of the Western mentality. Surprisingly these African patterns have been maintained by the inert "Negro" (*necro*) who could only imitate and react but had lost the power to initiate. The activities of the real inner life were always limited because of the absence of cultural activities to stimulate the inner life of the African person. The real self-remained encapsulated in the "Negro" disposition that could only imitate the European American patterns that fed it. The real African self was made to seem as unnatural to Black people, as did our black skin; even when his latent disposition surfaced, the inert Negro attempted to counteract it.

The slavery experience was destructive to the historical identity of African people. The repeated separation of mothers and children and the loss of language, culture, and natural religion worked to depose the real African self. Another process that occurred in quieting the influence of the African self is similar to the hypnosis or trance induction that comes from hyper-stimulation. This means that if you put people under enough physiological stress, at the same time removing from them vehicles by which they can transcend those physical stresses, then those people are left psychologically vulnerable and exposed.

The slavery trauma was obviously such a hyperstimulating event. If you were suddenly exposed to excessively loud music and flashing lights, the hyperstimulation would soon dull your sensitivities until you entered a trance-like state. Excessive pain has been shown to result in coma or shock. Physiological psychologists have been able to show that hyperstimulation leads to hypnosis or a trancelike state. Such a trance-like state makes a person thoroughly suggestible to whatever kind of input happens to be present. The result is that the person is only able to react. The Negro has been able only to react. The Negro adopts the issues and behaviors fed to him by the world of his captors. Hypnotized by the trauma of slavery and the horrors of his neo-slavery experience, he is only able to react rather than being able to act in terms of his self-survival mechanism.

It is awareness of the inner self that makes people operate in their own self-interest. It is awareness and consciousness of this inner and extended self that transcends the individual ego. It is this inner being that reaches back to the very African essence of us that energizes and motivates the African person with self-preservative and self-maintaining activities. This "Negro" fabrication has made African people self-destructive. It has, in fact, made us contradict the realities of who we are. Black people have become much more interested in the survival of those enemy forces acting against us than we are in the survival of ourselves. Too often, we find ourselves much more oriented towards the physical and philosophical maintenance of an alien people than we are committed to the affirmation and expression of our true self. Because the authentic "Original Man" has been hypnotized by hyperstimulation, the Negro manifestation becomes thoroughly manipulable, conditionable, and responds directly to whatever input happens to come in from without.

Resurrecting the African Self: Burying the *"necro"*

In order to solve some of the problems and reestablish the sovereign personality of the Black person, it is critical to penetrate through that "Negro" barrier into the Original Man. This is done by resurrecting the real inner self. Many Black activists have traditionally made the mistake of trying to eliminate the Negro façade by altering it's outer appearance. They have dressed the "Negro" up in African clothing, given him a new haircut and taught him a couple of African dances and assumed that this would begin to alter the death process of the Negro. Even in African Cultural Nationalist settings, too much attention has been directed to the external manifestations of the "Negro". The adherents to this newly restored African orientation are exposed to certain external stimulation in an effort to resurrect their Africaness. These well-meaning Nationalists have been attempting to destroy the "Negro" from its strongest front – the external.

Unfortunately, many of the children and the adults initiated into these external alterations quickly resume their "Negro": practices as soon as they find themselves in another non-African external environment.. All of the cues in the external dominant society are telling black people not to be themselves and rewarding any behaviors that are inconsistent with their own advancement and self-interest. Any manifestation of an independent self definition coming from a view of oneself in a broader global and universal context is severely condemned as irrational, fanatical or radical. In order to resurrect the real African inner self, the

Negro has to be uprooted – not from the outside, but from the inside. The first step to the inside requires that we know the identity of that inner core that Africans have invariably characterized as spiritual.

Activists and others have tried, unsuccessfully, nearly every material definition imaginable in order to help African people resurrect themselves. Black people have tried everything from "afros" to dashikis and back to processed hair – the whole gamut of the material. We have tried almost all of the external revisions possible to get us back to being ourselves. None of these external or cosmetic solutions have worked. In order to reconstruct our true selves we must identify that inner substance that makes us who we are. Once we have restored our true selves we will be characterized by our commitment to maximize our individual and collective survival.

Conclusion

A basic assumption of this discussion is that none of these methods will ever work until we recognize the essence of who we are as a spiritual people. We must conceptually appreciate that the outer material begins with an inner thought. We must trust the direction of our intuition. We must seek successful, wise leadership from among ourselves. We must restore the valid cultural rituals that bring us together for constructive purposes. We must make a clear distinction between being spirited and spiritual. "Spirited" is the emotional response to music, parties and religious arousal-tactics. This is thoroughly emotional and usually unproductive. True spiritual growth is guided by the knowledge, which cultivates the growth of the mind. Being spirited has kept us in our long-standing condition of mental slavery. Being spiritual will release us for transcendental growth and self-mastery. "The Original Man" is really a mentality and it must be restored by knowledge rooted in an authentic reconstruction of who the African person is.

Such knowledge becomes the foundation for establishing the new cultural forms that maintain the true inner self. This knowledge must be universal as reflected in the Divine order of the natural world. It must be knowledge that draws upon appropriate interpretation and application of the ancient religious wisdom of Black civilizations. It is only with such knowledge that the dead mental life of the Black person can be resurrected. With such a resurrection, the black man's personality may once again become a functioning entity and engage in the kind of constructive processes that facilitates all human beings to achieve the vision of their greatness.

References

Akbar, N. (1976). "Rhythmic patterns in African Personality," in King, L.M., Dixon, V.J. and Nobles, W.W. (Eds.) *African Psychology: Assumptions and Paradigms for Research on Black Persons.* Los Angeles, CA: Fanon Research and Development Center.

Ani, M. (1979). *Let the Circle be Unbroken: African Spirituality in the Diaspora.* Trenton, NJ: African World Press.

Baldwin, J. (1976). Black Psychology and Black Personality: Some Issues for Consideration. Chicago: *Black Books Bulletin,* 4(3), 6-11, 65.

Clark, C. S. (1975). et al. Voodoo Or IQ: An Introduction to African Psychology. *The Journal of Black Psychology,* 1(2), 6-29.

Morris, D. (1967). *The Naked Ape.* New York: McGraw-Hill.

Muhammad, E. (1965). *Message to the Black Man.* Chicago: Muhammad's Temple of Islam #2.

Muhammad, W.D. (1975). "Artificial Humanism." Chicago: *Muhammad Speaks,* 14.

Nobles, W. (1974) Africanity: Its Role in Black Families. *Black Scholar,* 5 (9), 10-17.

Weems, L.X. Rhythm of Black Personality. Proceedings of the 1974 Convention of the Association of Black Psychologists, Nashville, Tennessee, 1975. Reprinted in *Southern Exposure,* 1975, Vol III. Atlanta, GA: Institute for Southern Studies.

**This article was originally published in Smith, W.D., Burlew, K., Mosley, W. & Whitney W. (1979). *Reflections on Black Psychology.* Washington, DC: University Press of America.

Cultural Expressions of African Personality (1980)

There have been two major trends in the interpretation of the many apparent differences between the African-American and the Caucasian child in North America. These interpretations have come from the Social Scientists and Educators primarily, whose entire history as a "science" has been the repeated demonstration of supposed differences between the "races." The first of these trends has been to assume that the difference observed in the African-American child meant deviance from the Euro-American norm and should therefore, be evaluated as either inferior or pathological (Jensen, 1969; Thomas and Sillen (1972). The other trend has been to assume that the differences were deviant but adaptive forms of behavior for living in environments of oppression and poverty (Kardiner & Ovesey, 1962).

Both of these interpretations assume that the norm is the typical expected behavior of the middle class Caucasian child. All other behaviors were considered to be unquestionably abnormal. Insufficient consideration has been given to the possibility that despite a shared cultural geography, African-Americans and Euro-Americans may conceivably have different cultural personalities. The " melting pot" concept assumes a kind of homogeneity despite the compelling evidence of considerable cultural diversity in North America. The dangers of economic, political and social reprisals by the dominant culture have led to a growing denial of evident racial differences. Since so many charlatans have paraded in the name of science the idea that difference automatically meant African-American inferiority, African-Americans have become seriously fearful of any suggestion of possible variation from the Euro-American norms. As a result, much obvious dissimilarity between the two groups has remained unexplored. Such negligence rests solely on the shoulders of the African-American scholar because only he would have been equipped to surface these issues from the very essence of the African life experience in North America. The African-American scholar has instead dissipated his energies attempting to counteract the cry of "black inferiority" coming from the vocal and ever present Caucasian scholars.

The severest casualties of the American educational and social system remain disproportionately and overwhelmingly African-American. Despite all kinds of innovative methods to bend the African-American child into the appropriate Euro-American middle class mode, the parade of failures is still led by the child who is poor and black. Head Start programs have been one such attempt to bend the early "twig" in the "acceptable" direction. Many other programs, dating from the mid 60's, have sought to "redeem" the African-American child. The inevitable outcome has been continued failure for the African-American child that has been even more devastating than the failures in the destructive system of enforced segregation. The decrease in academic success, the increase in dropouts, the decreasing age of drug addicts and the general social casualties among African-American youth attest to the overwhelming failure of the educational system and the social sciences to appropriately address the needs of the African-American child.

Increasing numbers of African-American social scientists are now approaching the issues of African/European differences as blatant realities that must be confronted. Psychologists such as Syed Khatib (a/k/a Cedric X. Clark, 1976), D. Philip McGee (1976), Wade Nobles (1976,1978), Gerald Jackson (1976), psychiatrist Frances C. Welsing (1970) and some others are seeking to formulate theoretical notions and programmatic interventions that take cognizance of these differences without necessarily seeking to modify the child out of them. These African-American scholars all agree that the so-called "science of human behavior" has been little more than the outgrowth of Caucasian social scientists seeking their own images in the mirror of human experience. Though much of the work from these scholars is still in its infancy, the implication of their research is that most of the normative statements about human behavior are little more than ethnocentric projections rather than generalizable statements about the human make-up.

In this discussion we will attempt to identify some of the rather dramatic examples of behavioral patterns of the African lifestyle. Though mostly anecdotal in format, our discussion is intended to be suggestive of trends for further investigation in the light of more attention being given to such behavioral forms and their psychic or environmental source.

African American Language

Language variations are very critical in understanding the personality functioning of groups of people because words are critical in the formation of the thinking of a person. Psycholinguistics is an entire specialty that addresses this reality. There has been considerable documentation of linguistic differences in the African-American culture. These differences have been alternately described as dialect, subcultural idioms, or as simply unstructured distortions of standard English. The African scholar views the language variation as an attempt by the African speaker to milk from an alien tongue the verbal expressiveness that is reflective of the widely different mental experience of the African in America. (Smitherman, 1977; Williams, 1975).

The African mental experience is highly affective or is one marked by considerable feeling, not only in response to the chronic tension which characterizes the oppressed environments, but as a continuity of the high feeling tone of the African experience among African descendants throughout the world. Frantz Fanon (1967) and others have suggested similar variations among the African speakers of French in Africa and the West Indies.

The language is at best a symbolic expression of one's mental contents. The language evolved is based upon certain shared experiences and agreed upon symbols for the expression of those experiences. The English language and European languages in general have evolved to reflect the modal Caucasian experience. Characteristics such as the limited number of interjections in the English language fail to reflect the subtleties of emotions of a highly affective and sensitive people. Rather bland words such as "wow," "gee," "golly," etc. are woefully inadequate for the highly charged life of being African in America. Consequently, one finds a wide use of profanity and coined interjections among African-Americans in an attempt to reflect the more highly charged mental experience.

The limited and contextual meaning of the language is given additional flexibility by the considerable amount and highly meaningful body language adopted by the African speaker (Majors, 1989.) It is important to note that the body language is not of the Freudian symbolic form that has gained considerable popularity among the psychodynamic psychologists. Such sexual interpretations of body language are far-fetched in appreciating the vast range of communication in Black body language. One source of considerable misinterpretation of African-American behavior is the tendency to view that behavior from the same reference point as similar behavior might be viewed in European-Americans.

The African body language is a modality for maintaining rhythm in expression as well as dramatizing that which the language fails to communicate. In fact one might view the body language of the African speaker as a highly exquisite form of pantomime. One observation frequently is that there is a scarcity of communication between parents and children within the African home. This observation has been used to explain the alleged language deficits of the African-American child when in fact such an observation is a misperception of a highly intricate and intimate imbedded communication pattern.

The mother who "cuts" her eyes at a "poked-out" child is communication that occurs between that mother and child, which transcends verbal communication. Despite the absence of words, there is considerable communication going on between the two parties. Most African-Americans recall vividly, instances of a parent throwing a casual glance (as seen by an outside observer) at them from the opposite side of a huge room and having that glance lead to immediate modifications in their behavior. The instructions are not spelled out in explicit terms as they may be in the typical Euro-American family setting, but the message is clear and emphatic. The numerous connotations of shrugs and head scratchings are quite pregnant with meaning far in excess of the simplistic interpretations ascribed to those patterns by un-initiated observers. The flexibility of frowns, grins, and eye-movements would be too voluminous to catalogue. The child described as "non-verbal" in the classroom has frequently baffled unaware observers by his considerable popularity, leadership and apparent communicativeness outside the classroom.

This apparent paradox would resolve itself for the observer familiar with the diversity of communication patterns among African-Americans. Many of the realistic dangers of the alien American environment has led to the African speaker develop-ing many deceptive grammatical maneuvers of considerable subtlety and ingenuity. One such maneuver is the adjectival meaning reversal. One very common contemporary maneuver of this nature is the use of the word "bad." A "bad ride" is an exceptionally good automobile. Some "bad stuff" is a product of exceptional positive quality. "Bad," however, in unpredictable instances can maintain its conventional meaning that requires an astute attunement to the subtle changes in intonation and per-haps accompanying body language in order to recognize the switch.

Another such maneuver that camouflages meanings from unwanted audiences is the multi-connotation expression. One of the most pejorative expressions which can come from the lips of a non-African is the word "nigger." Within the African cul-tural linguistic community the word has massive flexibility. It can be a term of warmly intimate endearment such as: "Yeah, Baby, you sure are my nigger." Or it can be a term of poisonous attack such as: "You, d— nigger!" The differences in intona-tion, the time, the place, and the speaker will determine the mean-ing of the word. Again, the meaning shifts are indicated by tone changes, eye movement, raising of eye-brows and often even more subtle indicators which are very likely to by-pass the unfamiliar observer.

It is because of such subtle patterns that African-Americans are often misunderstood when communicating to an unfamiliar person. The child is likely to respond to the frustration by either rebellion or retreating from interactions with the non-comprehending listener. It is obvious that many of the inappropriate labelings of African-American children as deviant is a consequence of such misunderstandings.

Similarly, many of the behavioral problems encountered by the Caucasian teacher may be a consequence of such breakdowns in communication. The opposite case is less true because of the considerable and widespread influence of "Standard English" the African-American child is more likely to be more familiar in recognizing the language of the Euro-American speaker.

Oral Patterns

A direct derivative of the ideas presented in the discussion on language is the importance of the spoken word in the African life experience. Different life experiences place less or greater emphasis on various sense modalities. For example, the European-American people demonstrate a highly developed visual orientation as is evidenced by the bibliomania that characterizes the Western Cultures. This does not suggest any negation of literacy or the written forms of communication. The present correlation of a written tradition with technological progress and modernism has legitimized such a preoccupation with written material. Unfortunately, it has by implication served to disparage alternative modes of communication such as the richness and interpersonally intense oral tradition that still characterizes much of the traditional world.

Certainly, an oral system of communication is woefully inefficient in a culture such as this, but it is still the predominant mode for transmission of information throughout most of the world. The importance of oral or spoken communication to the

African-American lifestyle is an example of one of the many continuities with the African tradition maintained in the African-American experience. A casual observance of any community's African-American radio station, church, even community leaders will demonstrate how well developed is this skill of verbal language.

Oral communication remains the predominant means of information transmission within the African-American community. Considerably more than in the broader Caucasian culture, the spoken word is relied upon much more than the written word. This emphasis on spoken communication results in a highly developed auditory or listening facility on the part of the African-American child. This child develops an acute sensitivity to subtleties in expression and intonation often unobserved by the Euro-American speaker. Consequently, the child often responds to feelings communicated in the verbal expression that may even escape the conscious notice of the speaker. There is a particular sensitivity to hostile tones that the child perceives and responds to despite efforts to veil them on the part of the speaker.

It is for this reason that often African-American children respond to unexpressed prejudice and hostility on the part of non-African personnel when the personnel may perceive themselves as carefully camouflaging or being unaware of their feelings.

Very often, being read the written word can enchant the same child who shows little or no emotion or interest in the written word. The European child will usually seek to orient himself through visual modes because this has been the conditioning of his culture. His African counterpart with less efficient visual-motor coordination demonstrates superior difference in dancing abilities and other gross motor behaviors. Particularly with dance are we able to observe the marked difference between Europeans and Africans and the relative aural-motor "deficiency" in Caucasians and the considerable advancement of Africans in this area. However, an African-American child with such highly developed coordination is likely to be assessed as "cognitively challenged" if he is unable to demonstrate a similar facility with visual-motor coordination.

Dancing is actually the translation of certain auditory rhythms into motor activity. Reading is the translation of certain visual rhythms into a motor behavior. Though the prior training for the latter activity is greater than for the former, there is no available evidence that necessarily suggests that the former activity is any less complicated or suggestive of inferior cognitive capacity. Unfortunately, the IQ tests do not have a scale for the measure of aural-motor activity though there are several scales that measure visual-motor activity.

With this kind of analysis, we can begin to get a better comprehension of the disproportionate African-American failure rate in European structured modes and media of education. These media overwhelmingly emphasize the visual modalities for instructional purposes and for assessment. In fact the educational and psychological literature is practically void of any data on aural-motor coordination and its relationship to learning. Only in cases of its absence, such as educational programs for the deaf, does one find any suggested relationships. In the meantime this highly developed facility on the part of the African-American child must be dissipated in recreational dance when in fact it may hold the key to some of the educational deficiencies confronting children of African descent.

People Orientation

One very important element of the oral tradition that distinguishes it from the visual tradition is the centrality of a speaker in the former case and his dispensability in the latter. This crucial difference indicates another significant characteristic of the African-American child's cultural experience. This characteristic is the considerable "people orientation" of the African culture. Experiences are significant to the degree that they relate to people in some very direct way. The charisma of many African-American heroes such as Dr. Martin Luther King, Jr., Malcolm X, and Barbara Jordan was linked to their considerable verbal eloquence. The facility of such leaders in the oral tradition serves to ignite the motivational fuse of African-Americans as they are given instruction in a familiar and forceful medium. The dual medium of the spoken word and the living person serve to motivate, inform and inspire African people. It is interesting to note that much of the response to the orator is only incidental to the verbal content of the message. The rhythms, the cadence of the storyteller is as important as what he is saying. For effective communication, one would hope that there exists a correlation between the rhythm and content or the message and the medium.

The lesson in this for one who is interested in reaching the African –American child is an appreciation of the "griot" or "storyteller" in the African tradition. We can incite interest in the child by using the medium with which he is most familiar and most easily attracted. This can serve as a transitional method to move the child to exploring other areas of learning. For example, a story read with the lore of the storyteller can offer an exciting inducement for learning to read.

There are other examples of this important characteristic of people orientation throughout the African-American life experience. Because of its prominence it has been viewed as a maladaptive dependency in the personality of many African-Americans. There is a marked group orientation among African-Americans that stands in sharp contrast to the wider cultural norm of individualism and independence. Writers such as Kardiner and Ovesey (1962), Grier and Cobb (1968) and many other traditional thinkers have related this orientation described by them as "dependency" as being an important factor in many mental disorders affecting African-American people. The sensitive observer would accurately observe that any African-American person who did not show such a high people orientation was, in fact, abnormal in the light of his own cultural experience. In an increasingly insulated and "inner-directed" society, the African-American encounters considerable conflict in adjusting to such alien behavior patterns outside of his cultural environment.

The young child is immediately faced with this conflict when she is encouraged to be more of an individual (as school emphasizes) rather than an integral component of her group. When social cooperation is valued over competition as it is in the educational environment, the socially oriented person is destined to suffer effectiveness in the alien environment.

Interaction vs. Reaction

Another pattern of considerable prominence found in the African-American life experience is the interactional pattern of "call-and-response." This pattern has its most dramatic example in fundamentalist churches in which one finds the preacher's speech transformed into a litany of sentences and responses from the listeners. The spontaneous reactions and supportive statements of encouragement involve the speaker and listeners in a dynamic interactional dialogue. This stands n contrast to the traditional Euro-American speaker/audience setting in which the speaker or expert dispenses wisdom and the audience listens attentively and reacts only at appropriately defined moments.

This pattern, though most colorful in the speaker setting, is a pervasive occurrence within African culture. This on-going system of interaction and social reinforcement maintains relationships between people in almost all settings. Even a brief observation will reveal a considerable difference in the classrooms of many African-American teachers (if they are true to their cultural forms) will have much more of an interactional relationship with their students. This is an alternative to the more passive requirement of the traditional classroom where the child is expected to quietly, and passively absorb and react only in some systematic and pre-defined form.

The passivity requirement of the traditional classroom probably accounts for one of the most common complaints of behavioral problems among African-American children. This complaint is one of hyperactivity and general classroom disorder. The hyperactivity has been attributed to everything from broken homes to brain damage. More often than not, such hyperactivity is an adaptation to boredom. The boredom is in direct response to the excessively low activity level of the classroom that so sharply contrasts with the home environment with which they are familiar.

The use of instructional methods that would maximize student response and involvement are likely to be much more effective in reaching African-American children. The teacher benefits form the direct and immediate feedback and the student gains a sense of connectedness with what is being presented. Singing activities often stimulate such resounding interest because they involve the kind of group participation that reaffirms the sense of oneness, which is such a critical cultural motif among African people (Nobles, 1978).

African Thought

Another distinctive characteristic of the African-American child is the form of thinking and problem solving that they have acquired from the conditioning of their cultural and life experiences. This characteristic is a strong reliance on internal cues and reactions as a means of problem solving. This is in contrast to the enforced reliance on external cues that is required for most problem solutions in a classroom setting. This form of problem solving receives very little respect in Western culture because it is viewed as too subjective. Objectivity is considered as the hallmark of scientific enterprise. Though objective observation is critical in the acquisition of certain kinds of knowledge, it is not the exclusive means of acquiring knowledge.

This form of thinking has been called the function of "intuition" by Carl Jung (Jacob, 1963). He is one of the few European theorists who has described this characteristic in some detail. As observed by Dr. Jung, this particular thought function does not have any considerable prominence in the West though it is a highly developed function among African and Asian peoples. We might add that it has persisted as an essential dimension of African-American thought. There is a cultural respect for internal cues and "hunches" as a means of acquiring information. Despite the scientific unreliability of this form of information getting, it offers some advantages that reliance on the external simply cannot produce because of its limitations in time and space.

Because of this affective component to cognition for the African-American child, he is particularly vulnerable to his emotional reactions interfering with his learning. His sense of being disliked by a teacher can devastate his intellectual performance. On the other hand, his sense of being liked and respected by the teacher can wrought wondrous improvements in his intellectual performance. This probably accounts for the frequent observation of rather extreme fluctuation in performance between classes for the same student. His subjective reaction to the teacher can have a rather severe effect upon his performance.

This reliance on intuition is very adaptive in an environment where learning and problem solving usually occur in relationship to people. Such inner processes are very informative about inner processes of other people and provides information beyond the particular information that is verbally communicated. However, in a setting where the focus and the orientation is on objects, then there are predictable difficulties when such objects have no inner reality nor is there a medium between the object and oneself that has such an inner reality.

Many African-American children reveal previously unexpressed psychomotor and reasoning skills when object manipulation is placed in an interpersonal context. When the object manipulation is done as a means of interacting with another person, the task that previously received little effective attention from the child suddenly takes on new significance for him. It seems that African-American children are not as disposed to manipulation of objects for manipulation sake as Euro-American children. Even very young children show a decided preference for human rather than object interactions.

Reliance on intuition makes African-American children particularly adept in social relations because such a facility relies heavily on empathy. In fact, many African-American children are so adept at getting people to do what they wants them to do that they have frequently been described as "psychopathic manipulators." In fact, this is only applied empathy and it utilizes the primary social skill that we learn as human beings and that is: how to get people to act, as you want them to act.

So long as the setting is an interpersonal setting, as we observed above, the child is comfortable and efficient. When the learning situation is devoid of human involvement, then frequently, the African-American child experiences difficulty.

Spontaneity

Another characteristic of the African-American child is his capacity to be spontaneous. His facility for easy, rapid adaptation to different situations is one of the most remarkable strengths of the African child. The capacity to respond quickly and appropriately to environmental changes facilitates the African-American child's basic comfort in most settings, where there are positive interpersonal relations.

The African-American environment is a constantly changing and multi-faceted one. From the moment the child is born, within an African home, they are exposed to a world in continuous movement. Many faces constantly passing through; radios and record players often going in conjunction with TV sets; many activities simultaneously in progress requires a facility of ready adaptation. It is important to see the contrast with the middle class nursery where one learns to adjust to little more than mobiles over his crib and an occasional face bringing nourishment. The nursery environment of the middle class child is more often child relating to objects, rather than child relating to people in the African environment.

In these communities the child learns early the importance of constant change and rapid adaptation to that change. Such a facility is a genuine strength in learning to deal with a realistic environment that requires constant adjustment and readjustment. Even such a considerable strength and asset such as this becomes deficiency in an environment that emphasizes constancy of environment and behavior. In the typical classroom setting, this real cognitive asset becomes a paradoxical disability in an environment that is based on rigidity and only stereotyped responses are supported.

Therefore, there is a considerable discrepancy between the

constantly changing environment of the home and the relatively stagnant quality of the classroom. Again, we can see some justification for the behavior difficulties produced by such a radically deviant environment as the typical classroom.

The African-American child's spontaneity is as present in her rapid adaptation to new environments as it is in other aspects of her behavior. These children are equally spontaneous with their feelings, generally responding directly and honestly. The African-American child's spontaneity with well-coordinated motor activity has been well documented (Wilson, 1978). In most instances such apt responsiveness would be viewed as healthy and indicative of a high level of personal adjustment. In environments that are by-and-large unnatural (from the perspective of the native environment of the child) these same behaviors are likely to be viewed as ineffective and in many instances even as disruptive.

Conclusion

There are several assumptions and inevitable generalizations that are made in a discussion of this nature. One assumption is of a fairly homogeneous African-American community. We are aware of class variables and the compelling arguments that suggest that racial differences are ultimately class differences. The characteristics that have been identified herein are fairly consistently present at all class levels of African-Americans. Certainly, the more alienated people become from their indigenous culture the less prevalent are these cultural expressions. However, it is a safe assumption that African-American children are much more likely to act consistent with the characteristics of their indigenous culture than they will act as agents of the more alien Euro-American culture. Many of the deviant behaviors identified in African American children are simply deviations from the European-American normative behaviors and expectations.

The other issue that has been emphasized in this discussion is the degree to which the classroom based on Euro-American assumptions about child behavior are an alien environment for the African-American child. From just the vantage point of the few behavioral examples identified in this discussion, the remarkable fact is that the African-American child adjusts to the classroom at all! A predictable reaction is a minority of African-American children who show some degree of real difficulty in adjusting to the often grossly alien environment of the typical Euro-American classroom setting.

We can only speculate about how much untapped potential has fallen prey to the classroom setting that was unresponsive to these unique characteristics and needs. At a time when the push towards a kind of cultural pluralism is taking over our educational setting we are hopeful that African-American scholars will address these unique and potentially powerful contributions to the so-called educational "melting pot."

References

Clark, C. X., McGee, D.P, Nobles, W. & Akbar, N. (1976). "Voodoo or IQ: An Introduction to African Psychology," *Black Pages* (Chicago: Institute of Positive Education).

Fanon, F. (1967). *Black Skin, White Masks.* New York: Grove Press.

Grier, W., and Cobbs, P. (1968). *Black Rage.* New York: Basic Books.

Jackson, G. (1976). "Cultural Seedbeds of the Black Backlash in Mental Health," *J. Afro-American Issues*, Vol. 4, No.1, pp70-91.

Jacob, J. (1963). *Psychology of C.G. Jung.* (New Haven: Yale University Press.

Jensen, A (1969)."How Much Can We Boost IQ and Scholastic Achievement?" *Harvard Educational Review*, 39 (Winter), pp. 1-123.

Kardiner, A. and Ovesey, L. (1962) *The Mark of Oppression.* Cleveland: World Publishing Co.

Majors, R. (1989). Cool pose: The proud signature of Black

Survival. In M. Messner, & M. Kimmel (Eds.), *Men's Lives: Readings in the Sociology of Men and Masculinity.* New York: Macmillan.

Mayers, S. (1975). "Intuitive Synthesis in Ebonics: Implications for a Developing African Science." In L. King, et al. (Eds.) *African Philosophy: Assumptions and Paradigms for Research on Black Persons.* Los Angeles, CA: Fanon Center Publication, C.R. Drew Postgraduate Medical School, pp 190-214.

McGee, D.P. (1975) "Melanin: The Physiological Basis for Psychological Oneness," *African Philosophy: Assumptions and Paradigms for Research on Black Persons*, L. King et al (Eds.) Los Angeles, CA: Fanon Center Publication, C. R. Drew Postgraduate Medical School, pp. 215-222.

Nobles, W. W. (1974). "Africanity: Its Role in Black Families," Black *Scholar*, Vol. 5, No. 9 (June 1974), pp.10-17.

Nobles, W. W. (1978). "The Black Family and its Children: The Survival of Humanness," Black *Books Bulletin,* Vol. 6, No. 2, pp. 7-16.

Smitherman, G. (1977). *Talkin' and Testifyin': The Language of Black America.* Boston: Houghton Mifflin.

Thomas, A. and Sillen, S. (1972). *Racism and Psychiatry.* New York: Bruner/Mazd Pub.

Welsing, F. C. (1970)."The Cress Color Confrontation Theory," Washington, DC: Howard University.

Williams, R.L. (Ed.)(1975). *Ebonics: The True Language of Black Folks.* St. Louis: Williams & Associates.

Wilson, A. (1978). *Psychological Development of the Black Child.* New York: United Brothers Communications Systems.

*This paper originally entitled "Cultural Expressions of the African American Child" was published in *Educational Resources Information Center (ERIC) Reports.* (Report #ED179633) Arlington: ERIC Document Reproduction Service April. Also reprinted in *Black Child Journal,* 1981, 2(2), pp. 6-15.

Rhythmic Patterns in African Personality (1974)

[Tahid = oness]

African people throughout the world have a worldview that is conceived as a universal oneness. There is an interconnection of all things that compose the Universe. Pierre Erny (1973) has observed that "The African cosmos is like a spider web: its least element cannot be touched without making the whole vibrate. Everything is connected, interdependent." This interconnectedness is conceived as a kind of vitalism or life force which pervades all of nature: rocks, trees, lower animals, the heavens, the earth, the rivers, and particularly man, who is a vessel for this oneness which permeates and infuses all that is.

An African conception of personality must then begin with such an elemental notion of the person. One cannot begin to speak of man without first speaking of this force, which defines his continuity with all things within the world. The Dogon people of Mali refer to this force as *Nyama,* which flows in man's veins with his blood and connects all the man's actions and all his circumstances with the functioning of things in general. The Bambara (Mali and Ivory Coast) call it the *dya, which* serves to unify all things in nature. The Akan of Ghana refer to it as a man's *Okra*— his life force; it is a small bit of the supreme force that lives in every person's body (it is by definition what gives one life and returns to the supreme force when one dies). In the United States, this notion of a universal force is most closely rendered by the American Blacks' notion of "soul." Despite the small variations in the conceptualization of this force, such a notion serves as the basic substratum for beginning to understand the African man.

> Disorder...which for an individual results especially from the breaking of the rules of life, prefigures the universal disorder which spreads by

stages from the individual to his close kinsmen, his family, his clan, his people. But the disorder may be arrested and removed at any stage by appropriate rituals.(Forde,1970)

Even in the United States where the African people are most alienated from their true nature, one finds vestiges of this same pattern. It is considered a real contribution on the part of family members, friends, and religious leaders to come and "sit up" with the sick person. The participation in the cure by visitation and communion is still an important social value among Africans in the United States. One needs to make only a brief visit to a local hospital and watch the swarms of Black family members and friends who come to surround the ailing victim. This is in contrast with the emphasis on isolating, limiting visitors, and restricting visiting hours found in Western settings for treatment of the ill.

Education is another area where an understanding of rhythm and communion might correct many of the errors of educating Black youth, which grows out of the imposition of alien concepts of personality onto the Black student. With a notion of participation, one sees the inappropriateness of a teaching machine or a rigid lecture format as the method of choice in teaching Black people. One is appreciative of the retreat of the Black student from the classroom which forces dreaded isolation. The most common complaint about the Black student is the disorder caused by the excessive socializing that goes on in the classroom. From a perspective of rhythm, one is made aware of the unnaturalness of the classroom setting that fosters isolation rather than the eminent value of socializing.

It is interesting to observe how the phenomenon of participation permeates Black group settings. The common pattern of call-and-response found in all settings from the fields to the church, from political rallies to religious observance; the rhythm of shared participation becomes the tie that binds the diversification of function. The leader in his authority makes a call; the listener shares in the call by responding and supporting the call of the initiator. The rollicking "Amens," "Right ons," That's right," which characterize the ongoing support of the audience soon obscure the distinction between the speaker and listeners. The key idea of this part of the discussion is that it is meaningless to conceptualize an "individual" personality among African people. When such insular notions are used as the basis for intervening into the life processes of Black people, one condemns himself to failure from the outset because such notions are alien to the nature of African people.

Kinship Patterns

The concept of unity or rhythm also explains African kinship patterns. The tribe obtains its group definition based upon its unitary genesis. A man without lineage is a man without citizenship, without identity, and without allies. Nearly all tribes have a mythological system that defines their derivation from one stock. This becomes a critical notion for social organization and social control, as well as reinforcing the notions of rhythmic socializing described above. The often-described extended family among African people is relevant to this notion of oneness. Among the Dogon, for any individual, all uterine kin represent femininity and all paternal kin masculinity. "A man calls all women who are uterine kin, whatever their age, mother *(na)*, he calls all adult men of his patrilineal kin father *(baj)*. Such kinship patterns serve to reinforce the notion of interdependence that is derived from the notion of a single unifying life force, which flows through all people and all things.

Again, there are derivatives of this notion found in Black Americans' family and social patterns. The extensive number of "distant" relatives who are incorporated into the nuclear family often baffles cultural aliens; the inclusion of cousins removed by a factor of fourth or fifth into the immediate family fold is not unusual, particularly in rural settings of the United States. Robert Staples describes para-kinship ties, where males and females who are "unrelated" to one another "go for" or have "play" brothers and sisters who have the same loyalties and responsibilities as "blood" relations. Such relationships even further extend the far-reaching kinship patterns. Particularly among Black Americans, the pattern of referring to each other as "brother" or "sister" serves to foster that notion of kinship among all people. Such kinship ties and titles serve to reinforce the flow among all members of the group.

With this perspective, the Black family is not subject to the considerable criticism it has received from scholars who have chosen to view the Black family as an aberration of the model European family which, like its cosmology, is much more closed and insular. White social workers, psychologists, and educators have found themselves utterly confused when they have attempted to list, define, or describe Black families utilizing the guidelines that have grown from their own experiences. Such extended kinship patterns are as practical as they are spiritually and philosophically significant. Such patterns of kinship serve to establish an implicit social control and morality, which make external coercion unnecessary in observing laws of human relationships.

It is particularly interesting to note that as these indigenous kinship patterns begin to erode, there has been a parallel increase in disharmonious relationships among Black groups. The extensive documentation of Black-on-Black crime, especially in the cities, is the clearest example of the consequences of the erosion of natural patterns of relating. Particularly in the cities, contact with alien people and imitations of their patterns as well as considerable stress of urban living has served to erode these natural kinship patterns.

Disharmony has resulted from the disruption of flow and interconnectedness in these alien environments. The housing patterns the absence of adequate opportunity to form real kinship ties, the excessive crowdedness of urban living all serve to erode these socially facilitative kinship patterns. One observes as a consequence a kind of perversion of these natural patterns. The brotherhood of one's age group mutates into delinquent gangs that must defend their territory as well as their identity in response to excessive congestion, as well as imitative of a modeled life-style communicated by the alien media.

The loss of spiritual definitions of kinship in lieu of the considerable material emphasis of the environment further serves to erode those relationships. The few instances where such kinship patterns have been re-instituted and utilized as a means of social cooperation and social control have been successful only in those contexts where there has been a reactivation of the concept of a unifying spiritual force. Certainly, the Nation of Islam serves as the most dramatic example of the facility of unity within a context of a shared vitalism. It is precisely because of the activation of this spiritual vitalism that such a spirit of fraternity persists within the Nation while it erodes rapidly in more superficial contexts, such as the attempt to use political nationalism as a sufficient cause for unity.

Male- Female Relationships

The energy behind the unifying vitalism is maintained by the perpetual alternation or vibration of opposites, which reflects a principle of twinness that ideally should direct the proliferation of life. "Nothing in the universe can be generated without the cooperation of complementary principles or 'twins' whose archetype is the feminine-masculine couple."(Erny, 1973) The fundamental law of creation is the principle of twinship. Even at the level of the individual, man is conceived as possessing "two souls of opposite sexes, one of which inhabits his body while the other dwells in the sky or water and links it to him." According to the Dogon (Forde, 1970): "Man and woman are each provided with twin souls, one of each sex."(Erny, 1973). The very cohesion of man with nature, man with himself and man with woman is regulated by the principle of 'twinness and the attraction of opposites. "Diverse elements are bound to each other by meaningful relationships. They make a closely woven fabric formed by threads of warp and woof" (Erny, 1973).

The distinction between male and female is the essence of their union. It is in this area that the most serious toll of the slavery experience was taken. The traditional distinction of the roles between the sexes was obscured by the manipulations of the slave

127

master. The persistence of the basic slavery social order that has kept Black men in a subservient and dependent role while fostering the domination of the woman has prohibited the return to more natural patterns of role definition.

The absence of real masculine prerogatives for the Black man has left his role obscure, which has, in turn, obscured the role of his complement. In addition, an identification with the unisexuality of the alien culture, which surrounds us, has further obscured the distinction between the sexes. The pejorative quality of sexism has made the contrast of femininity even more abhorrent to the Black woman. Consequently, the alternation of opposites, which should be personified in male-female relations, is disordered. The cohesion that is achieved by the attractive force of opposites is disjoined by the confusion of roles.

In traditional society, male and female roles are distinct. The separation and interdependence of the sexes is a basic theme of their social organization and ritual. In some societies there is also a marked segregation of the sexes with men and women taking their meals separately, dancing in separate groups. On festive occasions they do not mingle but enjoy themselves in separate groups. The primary necessity to have independence before interdependence among Black men and women has confounded those relationships in the United States from the outset. Most of the conflicts between the sexes emanate either from the economic and status pressures of living in a passionately materialistic culture or from the inevitable jealousies of the dependent and insecure.

Again, we find among the members of the Nation of Islam a return to the cohesive balance of opposites in the relationships between men and women. Without being relegated to an inferior status (on the contrary, the Muslim woman becomes the recipient of considerable exaltation), the woman is able to accept a complementary relationship with the man. The man must submit to real justice and learn to lead in certain arenas of life without exploitation. With an appreciation of the implicit opposition of forces within their roles, they are free to develop individually and collectively in a mutually supportive direction. It is remarkable that submission and sharing that is a preeminent value among most Black people of the world, has attained such a negative connotation as a result of its association with slavery and its aftermaths.

As a result of the support, which the pairs of opposites give each other, there is an equilibrium that the individual being conserves within him or herself. The individual is able to stabilize the twin souls within themselves through achievement of the external stabilization in the balanced male-female relationship. In traditional societies, sexual mutilations are seen symbolically as producing within the person a definite dis-equilibrium, dispossessing him of one part of himself, and compelling him to seek outside in the human community and specially in marriage that which he lacks.

Religion

It is impossible to speak accurately of Black personality without speaking of Black religion. Sterling Plump observes:

> By Black religion I mean those ways in which
> Black people in Africa and later in America, con-
> ceptualized to explain the universe and man's re-
> lationship to it and to subsequently govern man's
> relationship to man.(Plumpp,1972).

Religion became the rituals for regulating the rhythms of life that flow from the force of oneness that permeates all things in the Black man's world. John Mbiti (1970) says:

> Traditional religions permeate all the depart-
> ments of life there is no formal distinction between
> the sacred and the secular, between the religious
> and non-religious, between the spiritual and the
> material areas of life. Wherever the African is,
> there is his religion.

Certainly, the most consistent characteristic of Black people throughout the world is their fervent belief and practice in some form of religion. Though the practice comes in many forms, it consistently seeks to reaffirm the notion of oneness within and between people as well as with the source of divine force that flows through all human beings. Religion becomes the essential regulator for the rhythms of life that are subject to the distortions of- material relativity. Religion is a primary vehicle for reaffirming through shared experience and contacts the communality that exists between the people. It is the vehicle that unified all of the community into a kinship of oneness.

Even the avowed Black atheist finds himself caught up in a religious drama if he maintains any form of in-depth contact with Black people. "A person cannot detach himself from the religion of his group, for to do so is to be severed from his roots, his foundation, his context of security, his kinships, and the entire group of those who make him aware of his own existence."(Forde, 1970). Certainly, the history of Black people throughout the world and in all areas has always occurred within a religious context. From the building of the pyramids, throughout the rich kingdoms of the Black King Solomon, all along the Nile, throughout the Asian world, and into North America, Black people and their offspring have all been involved in a religious drama.

If consistency, as documented by eons of Black history, is a source of data about binding universal laws, then we should look to invariables in that history for definitions of Black normality. From such a perspective it would seem that the most normal lifestyle for a Black person is a religious life-style. The suggestion here is that the spiritual definition of self, which characterized the African, requires that a conceptualization of the personality of the African utilize a spiritual cosmology. The material definition of self that predominates Western psychology, from behaviorism to Freudianism, is inappropriate and inaccurate as definitions of African people. The application of any of these theoretical systems to the minds of Black people of necessity presents an incomplete and inaccurate view of these humans of universal dimensions. The psychology of the Black personality can be no less than a cosmology that takes account of the oneness of the African mind, the rhythms of the African spirit, and the restoration of order where there is a disruption of rhythm.

Though this may sound unduly abstract and impractically philosophical it, in fact, corresponds with the existing realities of the African's world. A survey of the attitudes of the majority of African people anywhere in the world would reveal those attitudes to reflect a religious conceptualization of their lives and their world. If a function of the psychologist is to help describe normative reality, there is no behavior that is more normative than Black religion. It is in religion or through religion that we find the source of leadership, education, counseling, recreation, birth and death for African people. It would not be far-fetched to assert that Black psychology is Black religion.

"NEGRO" Disharmony

A contaminant has affected the traditionally rhythmic Black personality. This contaminant emanated from contact and involvement with the arrhythmic Western personality. Nowhere is this contamination more evident than in the personality of the "American Negro" This so-called "Negro" is an American creation having been spawned from the loins of an insidious slavery system. This slavery system is notorious as the most humanly degrading method of exploitation and abuse in the history of civilized man. Its notoriety primarily stemmed from its long-term effect on the personalities of its victims. Unlike other people of African descent around the globe, the former American slave was thoroughly emptied of his traditions and prohibited from participation in those societal-sustaining systems of shared cultural participation; a disharmony was inculcated into the slave personality.

All societies develop and maintain their integrity as a people of shared origins with shared needs on the basis of their shared cultural experiences and traditions. In being emptied of these traditions the American Black has been left slightly out of harmony with himself and other people of African descent. The sense of oneness and rhythm, which predominates in the traditional

African worldview, has been almost thoroughly uprooted from the conscious personality of the "Negro." The "Negro" has become arhythmic to the extent that he has denied the unconscious prompting of his genetically endowed mentality. He has succumbed to the sway of the alien mentality, which though consistent with the social, cultural and psychological needs of the slave master was and is destructive to the needs of the Black man.

African personality was traditionally viewed as extending into the life space of all life forms, particularly, that of related creatures. That extended self has since narrowed itself into fleshly isolation under the ideology of individuality characteristic of Western mentality. Kinship patterns which radiated outward to encompass all of the identifiable tribe have crumbled under the pressure of exalting a uterine family unit. Male/female relationships are fraught with disharmony as they frantically chase the elusive alien models of beauty and conjugal balance. Religion, which was the nucleus of traditional Black life, has become a superfluous moral annoyance. In light of this, one can only conclude that the "Negro" has become arhythmic to the extent that he has alienated himself from his traditional personality processes. To be restored to "Black" is to grow back into the traditional rhythmic modes of relating discussed above.

Conclusion

Rhythm is the pulse of the unitary vitalism, which flows through and permeates the African's mind and world. It is manifested in everything from Black movements to Black speech, and, in more or less subtle forms, in all aspects of Black life. It is simultaneously the essence of the oneness of the African wherever he is and the motivation for unification that characterizes the proverbial search of the African spirit. When disorder occurs — be it manifested physically, mentally, or spiritually — the disruption emanates from a disturbance in the rhythm, which is the African's gauge of oneness.

Order is restored when he attains a reestablishment of social equilibrium with his brothers and sisters. The kinship patterns of African people are geared toward maintenance of the same harmonious balance between the person and his nuclear group. The striving to extend that balance leads to indefinite extensions of the nuclear group itself. Male and female relationships acquire for the separate partners the same harmonious equilibrium to the extent that the polar, oppositional forces of maleness and femaleness are complementary in the actualization of the separate roles. Briefly, happiness in such relationships is directly proportional to the degree to which the man is fully man and the woman is unambivalently woman. Intra-personal and interpersonal harmony is mediated by religion, which facilitates the unique qualities of rhythm, and unity, which characterize the motivational striving of the African mind.

The essential point is that we must reach beyond the materialistic and physical definitions of mind that characterize Western psychology, and we must seek to understand the African mind within the context of its distinct characteristics and strivings. The concept of a unifying force or vitalism which pervades all of nature and particularly finds its highest expression in man along with its manifestation through rhythms represents the departure of the African psychologist from the personality theorist coming from the perspective of Western psychology.

References

Erny, Pierre (1973), *Childhood and Cosmos: The Social Psychology of*. the *Black African Child*, New York: New Perspectives.

Forde, Daryll (1970), *African Worlds*, New York: Oxford University Press.

Mbiti, J.S. (1970), *African Religions and Philosophy*, Garden City, New York: Doubleday and Company.

Nobles, W (1974), Africanity and Black Families, Sausalito, Calif., Black Scholar, Vol. 5, No. 9. June.

Plumpp, S. (1972), *Black Rituals*, Chicago: Third World Press.

Staples, Robert (1974), "Strength an Inspiration: Black Families in the United States," to appear in *American Minority Lifestyles*, Robert Hahenstein and Charles Mimdel (eds.) New York: Holt, Rinehart and Winston.

** This paper was originally published as Weems, L.X., "The Rhythm of Black Personality" in King, L.M. (1975) (Ed.) *African Philosophy: Assumption and Paradigms for Research on Black Persons*. Los Angeles: Fanon Research and Development Center at the Charles R. Drew Postgraduate Medical School.

African Metapsychology of Human Personality (1979)

One of the many benefits of an African psychology model is that it affords an effective alternative to prevailing ways of viewing personality functioning. The models of personality that have emerged from the European perspective are either that of a mechanistic system that operates as an automated program of inputs and outputs or that of a meaningless cataloging of the infinitude of possible personality traits. Both approaches rob the human personality of its dignity and fail to provide any real insight into the highly refined functioning of the human being.

Freud's devastatingly popular postulates of a conflict-ridden psyche have rationalized several generations of meaningless human conflict—both internally and externally. Freud viewed the dynamism or movement of human personality as resulting from the bombarding confrontation of incompatible energies and impulses. The Behaviorists saw no movement at all, just a passive adaptation to a precarious and sinister environment.

Personality as Conceptualized in African Psychology

African psychology, however, offers some genuine alternatives to all of these crippling perspectives. African psychology views personality as purposeful in its emergence, harmonious with its ecology, and consistent with the laws of life. The human being is neither a passive agent shaped by the environment totally, nor is the person an exalted isolated god without purpose and goalless freedom. The African sees a continuity and harmony between nature and the human being. Though the person is consistent with nature in the orderliness of their being, humans stand above the lowly nature of instinct driven creatures because of their capacity for will, choice, knowledge, and self-government. To comprehend the laws governing their nature, humans have always looked to the laws governing the environment surrounding them. They have sensed the peacefulness of the heavens, the orderliness of the earth, the predictability of the cycles of growth, and the continuity of life as an insight into the unknown laws and principles guiding their own lives. The ancient African people of the Nile Valley saw these forces of the environment as little "gods" or "angels" that they called "*Neters.*" These *Neters* were the principles or prototypical teachers of nature. They were often personified as immortal beings operating throughout time.

With nature in her pristine purity as a model we should be able to postulate a model of human personality that is both meaningful and universal. Such a model, hopefully, would be free of the ethnocentric assumptions so destructively evident in the Euro-American conception of personality. (Though we prefix our model with "African," it is not an attempt to claim an exclusive corner of the universe in this conceptualization; it merely identifies the environment out of which these universally applicable notions have emerged.) Such a model would offer the very universe itself as a laboratory for testing our assumptions. One would expect to find in such a model some absolutes about the human being. The current conceptions of the human being emerging form the Western world say, in essence, that a normal human being is one who is not abnormal.

Western psychology is a pathology-oriented approach to understanding human functioning. Because of the absence of vital universal assumptions or values regarding the human being, there is no absolute standard of defining the nature of a human being. Normal behavior is simply the ability to conform to the predominating patterns of behavior. Abnormal behavior is the inability to conform to such patterns. However, there are no universals or generalizations that can be made regarding the human being's functioning except that deviation from the behavioral norms make one a "deviant." This is of course circular logic that ultimately means nothing. We believe that the African's model of nature affords us an avenue for being able to infer a universal standard for adequate human functioning. An effectively functioning human being should basically agree in form to the definition of any successful life form. At all levels of life, the one pervading motif that seems to identify the life process is the tendency of life forms to preserve themselves. From the one-cell organism to the very galaxy, the entire life process is geared toward maintenance of itself. Certainly, the human being is no different in this regard; in fact s/he represents the highest evolution of this self-preservative process.

Three Components of Being: Physical, Mental, and Spiritual

Let's look at the human being at his/her three levels of being. These levels of the physical, mental, and spiritual self, so alien to Western psychology, form the unquestioned structure of the human being in African and Asian worldviews. The African views the person as spirit in his/her essence with the physical and mental components as tools for spiritual growth and development. The human personality is a composite of these factors being manifested in the environment. The Akan people of Ghana view the *Okra,* as the guiding spirit of man (Abraham, 1962) that is present before birth and continues after death. The African people of the Nile Valley in their advanced culture and concepts saw the human being as *ka* (body) and *ba* (soul), with a variety of related qualities of a spiritual form (Akbar 1986). Spiritual language and its intangible quality create a form of scientific dissonance for the heavily encumbered Western mind that is unable to comfortably conceptualize outside of the physical and observable. The prominence of spiritual considerations in African American life should inform the observer that any science that precludes the spiritual is alien and irrelevant to understanding people of African descent and how they understand all of life.

THE PHYSICAL COMPONENT

This self-preservative drive that was described above can be viewed at each of the three components of being. The manifestations of the *survival orientation* that we observe at the physical plane can allegorically relate to similar processes at the unobservable but more powerfully motivating levels of mental and spiritual life. Certainly, the most prominent characteristic of the physical organism is its orientation to survive i.e., maintain its existence. The basic equipment, motivationally and instinctively, that the human being is born with is geared towards the preservation of the life of that body. The newly born infant immediately responds to hunger, thirst, and pain. Hunger and thirst are drives of such magnitude that the human neonate instinctively responds in an unlearned panic reaction when these needs are aroused.

Equipped with little more than a powerful set of lungs and the ability for crude vocalization, the infant insistently provokes the environment to respond to its need. The infant's demand for food is the untaught recognition that this input is necessary for survival. The magnitude of the response communicates how critical the input is to the life of that organism. So, before food and water have a name, there is a basic consciousness of their necessity for life. Similarly, it doesn't take any lessons in "becoming a person" to experience genuine pleasure in having that hunger alleviated. The response to pain is very similar. To the extent that pain is a danger signal of physical damage to the organism, we can see the self-preservative disposition operative in the response to pain. Pain automatically provokes the person into avoidance activities. Again, the same fundamental consciousness that precedes "knowing" as we understand it has a compelling impact on doing just what needs to be done to insure the survival of the organism.

Even in ways outside of voluntary control the body is programmed for its own maintenance. The homeostatic process is automatic though connected by alarm signals to the conscious being to assist at times of danger. Increases in body temperature that endanger the organism automatically activate the cooling system of perspiration. Decreases in body temperature automatically activate a shivering reaction that generates body heat. Short supplies of oxygen activate yawning and so on for hundreds of unconscious (autonomic) physical processes that maintain a balanced state within the physical organism. The same process of homeostasis activates the subjective experience of hunger when essential nutrients are deficient in the body.

The body is also equipped with a highly sophisticated defense system. The autonomic nervous system is programmed for immediate and assertive defense behavior. Under conditions of danger the physiological response is so considerable that people are capable of feats of strength far in excess of their ordinary physical abilities. With the release of adrenaline into the blood stream, every system of the body becomes mobilized for defense. So critical is survival for the human body that it has a defense system so elaborate that it can literally mobilize every cell of the body for "fight or flight." This level of coordination and intensity of military activity on the part of the human organism can only be imagined among planners for societal military activity.

Even at the microscopic level, dramatic and strategic processes go on constantly within the body, which insure its survival. Highly sensitive microorganisms called antibodies maintain a ready army against any alien intrusions into the body. The liver, kidneys, intestines, and nearly every other organ in the body are equipped with self-maintaining life systems. The writers from ancient Egypt (Kemit) have left us the wisdom: "As below, so above." This informs us that we can find operating at the "micro" level, the same processes that exist at the "macro" level.

In the same way that the body operates to preserve its individual self, it is also motivated to preserve its generic self. To this end, we find the powerful sex drive. Contrary to Freudian interpretation of this drive, we attribute the power of this drive to the urgency of the self-perpetuating motive in the life process. Rather than the hedonistic pleasure seeking attributed to this drive in the Freudian hypothesis of libido, we see a much more profound implication in this drive. Despite the surface incompatibility of Freudian and Behaviorist assumptions, they both attribute a kind of hedonism to the primary rewarding nature of these life-preserving drives. The power of the sex drive as a motivator of human behavior is a coded message of the human's need to perpetuate self and as a consequence, preserve self in perpetuity. We shall see how this function expresses itself on higher planes in our discussion below.

This self-preservative orientation is prototypical for the "normal" or natural human being at the physical plane. There are certainly higher mental and spiritual survival motives that can override these physical drives, but taken in isolation, it is simple to describe the physically normal (healthy) human being as one whose self-preservative functions are operative. Physicians have no difficulty diagnosing dysfunction or abnormality when they find any of these functions impaired. The premature infant is placed in an incubator because it cannot maintain a safe body temperature. The anorexic person causes concern because his or her natural hungers are dysfunctional. Societies have major constraints and taboos on abandoned sexual indulgence because the process of self-perpetuation requires careful protection and maintenance. Cancer is such a deadly disease because the malignant cell fails to respond to the naturally preservative balance and restraint built into its nature. In some forms of cancer, the cells that should protect the organism from alien intrusions begin to attack the life-giving cells. No physician has any philosophical problems in identifying a condition in which the body is destroying itself as being a disease. The deadliness of AIDS is a result of a breakdown in the defense system of the human body and its ability to appropriately preserve itself against invasion and attack from destructive influences. The recognition of the signs of stability and the universal norms of the human body has greatly advanced medical science. Psychology or the science of the mind can be equally advanced when similar absolutes are recognized in human mental and spiritual functioning. "*As below, so above.*"

From an absolute perspective and assuming the absence of more powerful survival motives from the mental or spiritual sphere, any behavior that is intentionally self-destructive is abnormal (or sick) behavior. Such self-destructive processes (such as cancer described above) are universally recognized as sickness because they defy the body's natural tendency to survive and preserve itself. At an unconsciously instinctual level, the body responds by revulsion to toxic substances that are introduced into it. The respiratory system automatically activates to expel smoke entering the lungs. The throat, the taste sensors, and the stomach initially respond in a repulsive way to expel alcohol when it is introduced into the body. The same is true for all kinds of physically destructive activities. There is some signal that the body gives to indicate the danger of any type of toxic agent. Because of the body's adaptive capacity, it fairly quickly accommodates to the insistent intrusion and begins to activate other systems that seek to neutralize the destructive influences. For example, the body's vitamin C supply is utilized to neutralize the nicotinic acid from smoking, which lowers the body's balanced supply of this important nutrient.

Another dramatic—and disastrous—example of the body's submissive accommodation to unnatural conditions is seen in the variety of psychophysiological stress disorders. Hypertension, an adaptive response to conditions of stress, becomes a condition for coronary attacks and strokes if allowed to persist. In unnatural environments (of a social or psychological type), people respond to sustained stress by a condition of constant mobilization for defense. The very survival process can be subverted into a death process in an environment of unnatural conditions. We can effectively operationalize our concept of natural and unnatural as those conditions that foster or interfere with the life processes. The environment that leads to the kind of sustained stress that subverts the body's survival strategies to destructiveness is an unnatural environment. An environment that permits effective survival-oriented behavior and responses is a natural environment. Environments that systematically disrupt such effective efforts towards survival are unnatural environments. We could pursue this argument, if space permitted, to demonstrate a wide range of behaviors, which according to this criterion of self-preservation would be considered sick or disordered. This may sound to some as an axiological or value argument but it can be demonstrated as valid at the most basic level of values, i.e., the value of the survival of the organism. Such a position is able to call for testimony every life process in the universe as evidence of the sanity (health) of self-preservation and the insanity (sickness) of self-destruction. By its very definition, sickness means that there are processes that threaten the survival of the organism. The normal human being is the one who is cautious and protective of their life in all of its dimensions.

Let us hasten to say that we are not suggesting a Darwinian analysis of human behavior that hypothesizes a kind of cold-blooded "survival of the fittest." Though we speak of survival as an essential value, we also accept the African notion that survival for the human being is much more than the preservation of the body, since we understand that the body is only one level (the lowest level) of manifestation of the person. Though preservation of the body is basic, it is only a means of preserving a higher life that inhabits that body. To the extent that the physical body is the womb and medium for the growth of the higher life within it, then preservation and survival of that body does become of crucial importance, but survival of the body is not the highest of human objectives. Let us now turn to a discussion of those higher dimensions of life.

MENTAL COMPONENT: SURVIVAL OF THE MENTAL LIFE

In the Western psychological conceptualizations, we generally do not think of the intelligence as actually constituting a life or "world." We wish to suggest that the intelligence is a system, world, or life that operates according to the same principles or laws as does the physical system of life. The mental or intellectual life is too often equated with the physical instrument panel called brain. Such an inadequate equation is like attributing the musical genius of jazz great John Coltrane to his lips or his lungs. In any event, we introduce here the assumption that the intelligence or mental sphere is a dimension of life and that we can evaluate its effectiveness by the degree to which it preserves and perpetuates itself.

As the body manifests a natural hunger for food in order to maintain itself physically, the mind has a parallel hunger. This hunger that feeds and perpetuates the mind is the nutrition of enlightening knowledge. Knowledge that brings light, guidance, direction, discrimination, and effectiveness to the human being is the food of the mind. Not unlike the body, the mind is naturally equipped with a hunger for such knowledge.

The mind's hunger is initially manifested in curiosity. The two-month, six- month, year-old child is most demonstrative of this hunger for knowledge. So avid is the youngster's appetite for knowledge that it is actually difficult to get it to go to sleep. The child seems to be literally propelled by the hunger for knowledge. As soon as the physical comforts are attended (and often, even before) the eager young mind is off and exploring. In the early months, any novel stimulus fascinates and engages the young mind. It seems that acquisition of mobility is propelled by the desire for wider exploration.

The initial discovery of the child's own body rapidly gives way to the ability to turn that body over and lift it up The wider vision that these skills give propel the child after several months to begin to drag that body around, then crawl, then pull up, and eventually walk. The fuel for this phenomenal acquisition of locomotion is the hunger for knowledge. The greater is the mobility, the wider the field of exploration, and, ultimately, the more knowledge that the developing person is able to acquire. Much of the infant's early behavior can be shown (rather meaningfully) to be geared toward this hunger for knowledge.

Another important observation made by Freud is the prominence of oral activity during the early months of life, in Freud's preoccupation with hedonism; he saw this behavior as being primarily motivated by sensual pleasure. Freud's conviction that sensual pleasure was the most primary goal that motivated human behavior blinded him to the intangible essence of human life. His victimization by the "physical-mindedness" of his time

143

and culture thoroughly impaired his spiritual vision. The early oral preoccupation of the child could more usefully be interpreted as the prototype of incorporation or internalization of the external reality.

Perhaps, the child in its natural reasoning intuitively makes the generalization between the incorporation of physical food for the physical body and the incorporation of mental food for the mental body. Perhaps, the child rather wisely extrapolates from one process of survival to the next level. In the light of such an inference, it is not surprising that the next most powerful hunger is assumed to be fed through the same channel as that which satisfies the physical hunger. The automatic connection of seeing a new object sends it directly to the mouth if it can be grasped. The mother of a young toddler told me recently that her young son was very upset and frustrated one day because he couldn't swallow the wall. As ludicrous as that sounds to our adult knowledge, the child's hunger for knowledge (internalization of the external) is so intense that such frustration is conceivable for the recent arrival into our vast world of experience.

The oral exploration of the young infant is undoubtedly an indication of this rapidly growing appetite for knowledge. The infant wants to be fed information about its world. It wants to take in the enlightenment that brings consciousness and light to the untapped waters of mind. So, *curiosity is hunger of the mind.* It fuels the development of mobility that affords an ever-expanding menu for the mind. The oral preoccupation is the child's initial effort to internalize the world or take in knowledge, using the metaphor of physical hunger and the mode of its satisfaction. Another component of the hunger of the intelligence is the desire for order. The discovery of patterns usually affords the child moments of delight as they find that one action predictably leads to another. This delight is the mental life's appetite for ordered experiences. Relationships and patterns represent the real meat of knowledge. Such orderliness and knowledge of relationships give the human being a sense of mastery over an environment that becomes more predictable as knowledge increases. The mental life has safety valves, as do the satiation levels of the body. Boredom signals the need to move into new arenas of knowledge or to rest for the purpose of digestion and assimilation. Imbalances in the knowledge diet trigger the need to pursue new vistas of experience. Curiosity and interest continue as appetites that guide the mind to ever-increasing horizons of knowledge.

The normal, living mind seeks knowledge naturally. The very nature of the intelligence is to seek enlightenment in much the same way as the body seeks nourishment for itself. Only a mind robbed of its natural dispositions (a common phenomenon in this society) actively seeks unconsciousness, ignorance, or mental death. In this discussion, we assume that the child is naturally "driven" to seek knowledge. We object to the arguments that suggest that children must be artificially stimulated or externally motivated by some new technological toy or device in order to learn. It is certainly difficult to believe that a young mind that was eager to be enlightened only months previously is suddenly incapable of being stimulated once it enters public school (a most serious problem in the United States). Some serious questions must be raised about what happens to that mind between the time of the early enthusiasm and the alleged apathy in the early grades. It would appear that some powerfully destructive force has altered the natural intellectual curiosity that characterized that human mind only months previously.

Knowledge of one's world and knowledge of oneself is the foundation for the self-mastery to which the human being is naturally disposed. The early examples of physical mastery dramatically illustrated in the child's acquisition of balance and walking skills are only prototypes of the inner self-mastery to which the human being aspires. We are suggesting that there is no discontinuity in human growth. The accomplishments at lower dimensions simply find greater expression at higher planes. Learning to propel one's body is the birth of the desire to propel one's world and life. Knowledge of how the mind, body and spirit work, the full dimensions and potential of the self and of the characteristics of one's environment are the objectives of enlightenment. The intelligence of mental life is naturally attuned to receive that data. Without knowledge of one's human capabilities and with ignorance of one's environment, one is rendered essentially blind in the mental world. More consistent with our analogy from above, without such information the person is mentally starved, intellectually malnourished and/or subject to immediate death.

Similar to the self-perpetuating function of the physical life reflected in reproduction, there is a similar urge in the mental life. This urge to express and perpetuate one's knowledge is seen in the basic desire for communication. As with the early curiosity drive discussed above the child manifests very early the desire to know and to spread what he or she knows.

Children delight in the response they obtain from even their early babbles. They eagerly begin to incorporate language as they recognize its capacity to propagate what they know and later they discover that it can also feed their knowledge. Speech or communication is to the mental life what sex is to the physical life. It is the vehicle of self-perpetuation through expression of one's ideas and knowledge. It is also the basis for contact between mental worlds, the vehicle that brings two minds together as sex brings two bodies together.

We described above the body's natural revulsions to poisons. Similarly, the mind has a natural revulsion to ignorance, unconsciousness. Again, this is illustrated in the young child's revolt against sleep, once they have been excited by wakefulness, and they revolt against being locked away from their opportunities to observe and have their curiosity satisfied. The numerous "why's" that characterize the conversation of the three-year-old tells us of their need to have full understanding of the order around them. Under normal circumstances the mind naturally seeks greater consciousness and awareness of itself. (Given the destructive job that has been done on the human mind, I can only offer this as a hypothesis in the light of only limited evidence in the adults of our contemporary world.)

As the human body can rapidly accommodate to ingested poisons despite the initial revulsion, the human mind is capable of even greater adaptation or adjustment. The broader range of receptivity of the mental life over the physical life permits greater

146

flexibility of the intelligence. Though its dispositions are systematically marked out, as is illustrated by the early mental thrusts of the mind coming to life, it is very susceptible to subversion. The intelligence can be systematically molded in a distorted form by the early impressions that are made on it. Rather than seeking consciousness, it can be perverted to seek unconsciousness. Rather than seeking knowledge, it can seek ignorance. Rather than the intelligence striving for self-mastery, it can seek self-indulgence. The signs of mental death from intellectual starvation are not as obvious as are the signs of physical malnutrition and starvation. In fact, mental death can occur in a body that persists in carrying on its physical life functions for some time after mental death has occurred. However, one does not have a human being under these conditions, only a living corpse.

The demand for unconsciousness through alcohol, drug abuse, and general apathy which has come to be the predominant mental disposition in our society today is evidence of distorted human material rather than the true form of the human being. The mental life's natural urge for enlightenment and nourishment has been fed on such a continuous diet of artificial ingredients that the natural appetites have accommodated themselves into non-recognition. The artificial diet has been one of opiates, fantasy, and falsehood. These conditions are a form of mental death and a puzzling form of self-destructiveness that betrays the living body as actually being mentally dead.

As we have described above, the unnatural environment can subvert survival processes and turn them against the life of the organism. This is, of course, dramatically illustrated in the psycho physiological disorders of ulcers, hypertension, and other deadly diseases. It can be demonstrated that the entire array of mental disorders results from a subversion of the mental world's efforts at survival. For example, the painful and debilitating rationalizations and intellectualizations of the obsessive-compulsive, rather dramatically demonstrate the subversion of intellectual processes. The withdrawal into fantasy—i.e., unreality or ignorance—seen in schizophrenics is the most severe form of subversion of the mental life. What is, in fact, adaptive withdrawal away from consciousness or reality under conditions of stress becomes a persistent style under conditions of an unnaturally traumatic and painful environment.

We can see from these brief examples how such a model of "natural human life" begins to give us a universal standard for assessment of mental as well as physical disorders. Cultural context notwithstanding, these are universally identifiable characteristics that affirm human physical, mental, or spiritual survival. Such characteristics that enhance survival and advance human development are universally considered healthy, sane, normal, or similarly designated. Their normality is not affirmed by the popularity or cultural consensus about the conduct, but the degree to which that behavior enhances both the individual and collective well-being. In contrast, there are identifiable patterns that are destructive to human survival. Such patterns are considered to be sick, crazy, abnormal, and so forth.

THE SPIRITUAL COMPONENT: NATURAL HUNGERS OF SPIRITUAL LIFE

Nearly all writers on the African worldview maintain that the human being is intimately tied with the supreme force in the universe through the spiritual life. This spirit represents the human potential for perfectibility from before birth and through the eternal essence that continues after death. The spirit is the transcendent dimension of the person that is of the same universal substance as the Divine. As strange as this language may sound to scientific Western psychology, it has only been very recently that the world's most advanced scientists ever considered speaking of order without affirming Divine processes and a Supreme Being. We believe that one of the great difficulties with modern psychology specifically and Western science in general is its neglect of these transcendent and Divine processes in the universe.

Western Science's stagnation in the empirical world conceals most of the broader dimensions of nature and of the human being, especially. Certainly, the overwhelming failure of psychology to remedy the severe mental turmoil of the contemporary Western world and its inhabitants is in part due to its failure to recognize the spiritual essence of the human being. By relegating the entire spiritual life of the human being to religion, the scientists, have discarded an essential part of the unifying fiber for conceptualizing human functioning. The cultures of Africa as well as much of the Asian world and other traditional cultures, such as Native American peoples, have maintained this integrating principle and have been able to harness resources that maintain mental well-being without having to surgically or chemically alter the structure of the physical dimension of the human being. Unlike the healing arts in most parts of the world that rely on the self-healing capacity of the human spirit, Western practitioners prefer a physical or chemical alteration in order to bring healing to the person.

African students of the mind have never neglected the reality that the human beings at their most advanced and enduring form are ultimately spirit. Whether it's the *Okra* as described by the Akan of Ghana (Abraham 1962), the *nyama* as described by the Dogon (Forde 1970), or *nommo* as described by the Bantu (Jahn 1961), the pervasive African conception is that humans are essentially spirit. Therefore, survival of the spirit represents the ultimate survival of the human being. This message of spiritual survival has, unfortunately, been left to the religious institutions alone. This is unfortunate because in the Western world, religion has been separated from the daily life experience, and the human being has been fragmented. The African, on the other hand, according to Mbiti (1970) "is caught up in a religious drama from long before birth and until long after death."

The psychologist has attempted to attend to the mental life often to the disregard of the physical life and almost invariably to the complete neglect of the spiritual life. The physician has usually attended the physical life to the exclusion of the mental and spiritual lives. The religious practitioner has too often attended the spiritual life to the utter disregard of the physical and mental. The human being is a unity and can only be distorted by a fragmentary approach to human adjustment. According to Pierre Erny (1973):

> ...the African cosmos is like a spider web: its least element cannot be touched without making the whole vibrate.

Certainly if this is true of the African cosmos, it must be true of the human microcosm. The spiritual life, not unlike the physical and mental, has innate survival processes as well. In fact, the survival orientation of the physical and mental planes or dimensions of being are for the ultimate purpose of spiritual ascendancy. The physical and mental spheres operate as vessels for the sustenance, transmission and growth of the spiritual life. The relationship of the physical and mental self to the spiritual self is not unlike the relationship of organs or senses to the physical body. The hand has no life without the body though the body is capable of sustaining itself without a hand. The eye is a source of knowledge into the mind, and the eye has no function without an active mind, though knowledge still comes with no eyes at all. Similarly, physical life and mental life supply the spiritual life, though the spiritual life is capable of maintenance in the absence of either or both of them.

How can we characterize the hunger of the spirit? It is actually a metaphysical hunger—a hunger for the infinite, transcendence and for perfection. The body hungers for finite ingredients—physical food, sensual experience, physical reproduction, etc. The mind hungers for knowledge, enlightenment, order, and communication. The spiritual life hungers for the universal, for the transcendent—for God! It is the strong desire in all people that has led to the establishment of religion and a conceptualization of God. It is the drive in the human being that pushes us to seek goals higher than material, higher than partisan ideology, higher than our own physical selves. It is the drive in the human being that guides us to conceive of the Eternal and of a Supreme and Divine Power and plan.

The universal presence of these ideals and how they override lower level needs of the human being is evidence of the spiritual life and indicative of the powerful significance of spirit in the human life system. Only societies in which human beings have fallen into the most base debauchery and have become less than human is there the absence of a concept of a Transcendent Being. Those societies that have reached the highest levels of human refinement, sensitivity, and cultural dignity are the ones with a widely accepted and powerful image of God. Such accomplishment may or may not be accompanied by material acquisition and accoutrements, because the ultimate test of Spirit is the achievement of peace and mental well-being without the necessity of material affluence.

The force of the spiritual life has been described as: "a force within you that wants something at the expense of every other force in your body, to work with it to accomplish its goal. It is struggling trying to get everything else in your makeup to agree with it so that it can get something done for you in your lifetime" (Muhammad, 1975). It is the transcendent self that potentially is intended to rule over the lesser human appetites. It restrains hunger from becoming greed, self-perpetuation from becoming lust, knowledge from becoming arrogance and order from becoming tyranny. It is the voice of conscience.

Conscience is the voice of the spirit. We suggest, in line with African philosophy, that moral sense is indigenous to the human being. As the *sunsum* in Akan metaphysics (Abraham 1962) is the basis of character, the conscience is an innate force that also lies at the foundation of the personality. It is, according to the Akan. the educable part of the personality which is the foundation of personal and moral responsibility. This force may be shaped by experience, but, as an instrument of moral awareness, it is innate to the human being. This position stands in sharp contrast to the Western (particularly Freudian) concepts that view moral conscience as a socially imposed entity having no genuine foundation in basic human makeup. Though the actual content of conscience may be acquired through learning and experience, the mechanism of conscience is basic to the human make-up. An individual without this capacity is deformed not unlike an intellectually handicapped person or a person handicapped from birth. The capacity for self-restraint, self-regulation, and perfectible aspiration is actually more basic to human life than physical hunger. In fact, physical hunger operates in the service of raising human life to a higher plane of experience.

The spiritual life is the force in the human being that fights human degradation. It is the voice of frustration that cries out when people become encapsulated by material wishes and preoccupations. It is the force that drives the human being above lustful inundations—the sense of dissatisfaction with sensual pleasure alone. This is the force that pushes the downfallen people to brush themselves off when they spot their humanly degraded appearance in the mirror. It is a force that gives the human being the desire and power to rise above any condition that robs them of their God-given potential for growth and human progress.

The physical life yearns for self-perpetuation. On the mental plane, the same yearning is in communication. And, spiritually, the highest form of this yearning is for oneness and immortality. It is a desire for harmony, fusion, and peace with all things. It has been called "heaven" by the Christians, "paradise" by the Muslims, and "Nirvana" by the Buddhist. Every religious group has an analogous concept that describes this state of universal harmony and peace.

Though it is described in physical allegories, it speaks to a spiritual state beyond the visible world. It has remained the utopian dream of all times and all societies. It represents the highest wish of the human being to be fused into the eternal harmony of the Conductor of creation—the Creator. The desire to know the essential reality versus the illusionary reality prods the intelligence and refines the mental life. The universal oneness is the ultimate recovery from the struggles of diversity, polarity, and conflict that have characterized the lower stages of life.

As the survival forces can become distorted on the physical level with the psychosomatic disorders or on the mental plane in insanity, the spiritual forces can also become similarly perverted. The improperly developed being will seek transcendence in human tyranny or oppression. The voice of conscience will become cruel inhibition, self-flagellation, and elitist self-exaltation. The desire for the universal can be distorted into a mystical superstitious tyranny that locks human beings into a world of fears. This is literally the diabolical. These are the forces that deliberately operate to destroy human life and block human development. The spiritually dead are those who have lost the motivation to be human.

Conclusion

One might characterize the foregoing discussion as a "Metapsychology of Human Personality." It describes the human personality not in terms of its actions, behaviors, or observable dimensions, but in terms of its purpose or teleology. It focuses on the ultimate unity and goal orientation of human life. Though it describes the human being as manifesting life on several planes— physical, mental, and spiritual—it also describes the unity of those strivings.

It presents a model of human life that is absolute. It is culture-free, ethnicity-free, and society-free. It describes the universality of the highest human potential which when subjected to unnatural influences can become corrupt, degraded, oppressive, even subhuman. Many periods in history have shown human life in this lowly condition. Certainly, the conceptions offered here are consistent with the African philosophical view of humans and life. This model offers a yardstick by which the adequacy of human life can be evaluated in any context. Despite the variability of the behavior that may characterize the disorder, insanity and inhumanity can be identified in any cultural context given the criteria of human-life-survival suggested in this discussion.

Unnatural environments and the adaptation to them perverts natural survival mechanisms and leads to bizarre forms of self destruction. By looking for human outcomes reflective of the highest human potential, we can assess the effectiveness of the human environment. Though the human form is potentially quite malleable or subject to assuming almost any form, its nature is to acquire the distinct and quiet dignity reflected in the being whose spiritual being has come to life and stands as a master force over the lower stages of human evolution within the human makeup.

References

Abraham, W.E. (1962) *The Mind of Africa.* Chicago: Univ. of Chicago Press.

Akbar, N. (1986) "Nile Valley origins of the science of the mind." In I. Van Sertima(Ed.) *Nile Valley Civilizations,* New Brunswick, N. J.: Journal of African Civilizations Press.

Erny, P.(1973). *Childhood and Cosmos.* New York: New Perspectives.

Forde, D. (1970). *African Worlds.* New York: Oxford Univ. Press.

Jahn, J. (1961). *Muntu.* New York: Grove Press, Inc.

Mbiti, J.S.(1970). *African Religions and Philosophy.* Garden City, N. Y.: Doubleday.

Muhammad, W. D.(1975) "The Crown of Creation" in *Muhammad Speaks.* Chicago: Nation of Islam Pub. Co.

*This article was previously published in D. Azibo (1996) (Ed.) *African Psychology in Historical Perspective & Related Commentary.* Trenton, NJ: Africa World Press.

Chapter IV

AFRICAN AMERICAN MENTAL HEALTH

OVERVIEW

When the orderly and functional definition of personality has been established, it is then necessary to account for the disordered or dysfunctional personality. Even in the most advanced societal systems such deviation occurs and healing is only possible when the genesis of such disorder has been established. The inevitable next step in the progression of these ideas was to apply the Afrocentric paradigm to the understanding of mental disorder. The universal principle that seemed to be present without deviation was that life forms operated to insure their singular and/or collective survival. This seemed to be an inviolable principle in nature. When any phenomenon sabotaged this process of survival, it was considered to be dis-ease and either the body naturally or some other creative effort was made to attempt healing of this violation of the life principle. It certainly seemed reasonable that a conceptualization of human functioning that found its validation in nature could take this allegory of the biological organism to understand the mental functioning. Therefore, it was assumed that there was mental dis-ease whenever a person did not engage in those processes that affirmed and maintained their mental or cultural survival. Self-maintenance was the hallmark of psychological health. Those who operated in violation of their "self" were in a state of mental disorder.

The two papers in this section define the social manifestation of mental disorders among African Americans who are in violation of their "self-maintenance." The argument is presented that the issue of self-maintenance must be evaluated within a social and cultural context and could not be measured in the isolation of some form of abstract individualism. Under natural circumstances, the social and cultural environment facilitates this effort of self-maintenance and affirmation. The conditions of oppression and captivity seemed to create a deviant environment that facilitated the development of the kind of mental disorder characterized by an affliction of the self-maintenance and affirmation system. This thinking had gained some expression in a signature presentation by Dr. Bobby Wright, who in the mid 1970's had argued that Black people were victims of "mentacide." Dr. Wright argued that this condition was a systematic destruction of a people's mind and the conditions of white supremacy and oppression were a declaration of mentacidal intention against people of color. He saw many of the violations of self-maintenance as being a result of this mentacidal process. Concurrent with Dr. Wright's arguments, the paper "Mental Disorders among African Americans" was presented at the 1976 meeting of the Association of Black Psychologists. A written form of the presentation was published in the periodical *Black Books Bulletin,* by the Chicago based Institute of Positive Education in 1980. This paper caused quite a stir among Black Psychologists, as well as in the Black Nationalist community. The discussion argued in a new way that our mental health as well as our mental disorder must be understood with the context of our own reality and not based on the norms of our oppressors. This thinking was in the tradition of Frantz Fanon's description of the mental disorder of colonized people, but for the first time a culturally appropriate system was introduced to understand the African American person in our unique context. This offered a new level of application of the Afrocentric paradigm.

This work was followed by the writings of Kobi Kambon who elaborated on the concept of "psychological misorientation" that was an extension of "alien self" disorder introduced in this paper. In subsequent years, Daudi Azibo further refined these notions with his formulation of the "Azibo nosology," that was also an extension and elaboration of these concepts. The ideas in this paper ushered in an important new way of understanding African American mental health and mental health in general from the Afrocentric perspective. As the seminal document in this area of conceptualization, it occupies an important place in the evolution of African centered thought in Black Psychology.

The second paper in this section preceded the writing of the mental disorders paper. The concept that "Awareness" was the key to mental health was very much inspired by my understanding of the teachings of Elijah Muhammad. His rather global notion that the ultimate health of a people was rooted in their "knowledge of self," struck a responsive cord in my understanding that the power of mental healing was in consciousness of oneself. This paper that was actually, my very first publication in the area of African Psychology that was initially published in the first edition of the *Journal of Black Psychology* in 1974. The article was subsequently reprinted in the pioneering publication *Reflections in Black Psychology*, edited by William David Smith, et als, in 1979. Interestingly enough, this idea has been the motif in my work over the last thirty years. My most recent book, *Know Thyself*, published in 1999 was an elaboration of this very same notion that the ultimate tool of mental health is rooted in the ancient adage from the Nile Valley in Africa that first articulated the dictum: *"Man, know thyself."*

Mental Disorders of African Americans (1980)

The African American has been the victim of oppression on both the physical and the mental planes. They have endured the atrocities of physical abuse and then their mental efforts to cope have been subjected to intellectual oppression. Intellectual oppression involves the abusive use of ideas, labels and concepts geared toward the mental degradation of a people (or person). There is no area in which mental or intellectual oppression is more clearly illustrated than in the area of mental health judgments or assessments.

Traditional definitions of mental health in the Western world have been normative definitions. In the context of considerable uncertainty as to what constituted a normal human being, a kind of "democratic sanity" has been established. This "democratic sanity" essentially applies the socio-political definition of "majority rule" to the definition of adequate human functioning. As a result, the mental health practitioner determines insane behavior on the basis of the degree to which it deviated from the majority's behavior in a given context. The typical textbook in abnormal psychology such as Coleman (1972) states forth-rightly: "On a psychological level, we have no 'ideal model' or even 'normal' model of man as a base of comparison." "...the concepts of 'normal' and 'abnormal' are meaningful only with reference to a given culture: normal behavior conforms to social expectations, whereas abnormal behavior does not." The consequence of such "democratic sanity" is that entire communities of people with seriously inhuman behaviors can be adjudged sane and competent, even as exemplary human specimens, because the majority of people in that particular context either participated in the questionable behavior or refused to question the dubious behavior.

As a consequence of "democratic sanity" no one has raised a question about the mental competence of a people who enslaved as cattle, thousands of non-hostile human beings. The question of the possible mental incompetence of a people who terrorized and murdered thousands of non-hostile inhabitants in the name of exploration and geographical expansion has never been raised. The persistent oppression and support of oppression of non-hostile human beings simply on the basis of a shared hallucination of color differential has not received consideration by the world's scientists and philosophers who have studied human mental functioning.

Recently, some African American scientists such as Wright (1975), Welsing (1972) and Clark et al., (1976) have suggested the possible pathological origin of such humanly questionable behavior. More commonly, the tendency has been to justify and explain the behavior of the victims of such insanity on the basis of the assumed sanity of the victimizers and the context of the victimization. Such efforts have proven circular in their logic, at best, and have served as the basis for continued intellectual oppression, at worst. The question of emotional disturbance among African Americans has been one of the most frequently addressed issues among many Jewish American and African American social scientists, primarily Clark (1965), Figelman (1968), Grier and Cobbs (1968), Kardiner and Ovesey (1962), Karon (1958), and many others. This preoccupation with the lack of mental health among African Americans has not only presented a distorted image of the American of African descent, but has failed to address the real problems of this substantial constituent of the American community.

The classic work from the early 1960's that tackled the issue of mental health for the African American from a scientific basis was *The Mark of Oppression* (1962) by two Jewish psychoanalysts, Abram Kardiner and Lionel Ovesey. This was the first literature of any great significance that even warrants serious consideration. Previously, the mental health scientists involved themselves in documentation of such dubious notions as "freed slaves showed a much greater proneness to mental disorder because by nature the Negro required a master" (quoted by Thomas and Sillen, 1972).

The conclusion reached by Doctors Kardiner and Ovesey based on their analysis of a select number of "emotionally disturbed" African Americans was that all or most of the personality characteristics of both sane and insane African Americans could be accounted for on the basis of the experience of oppression. There is much to be said for their hypothesis because as we shall discuss below, oppression is an inhuman condition that generates unnatural human behavior. It is ultimately to a source of inhuman conditions that we can trace the roots of mental disorder. At a time when social scientists were acquiring great scholarly renown for documenting the human deficits of African Americans, these observers did attempt to provide a comprehensive psychohistorical analysis of the condition of the "Negro," using slavery as their historical vantage point. The over-riding problem with this book and the subsequent numerous related ones is the reliance on pathological examples and case histories as the basis for their conclusions. All of the case histories presented in the Kardiner and Ovesey (1962) document suffer from some type of sexual and/or aggressive malady, not unlike any human being subjected to the Freudian microscope. The conclusion of incompetent mental functioning is reached based on the norm and the context of the "sanity democracy" standards set by middle class European Americans.

An indication of the severity of intellectual oppression is reflected in the fact that African American scholars have characteristically followed the lead of European American scholars in both conceptualizing and analyzing their problems. (The reader is referred to Baldwin, 1981; Hare, 1969; and Mahdubuti, 1976, for extensive descriptions of the phenomenon). Grier and Cobbs (1968) are probably the supreme examples. Their promising document of 1968 offered the opportunity for an alternative perspective to be offered by African American mental scientists about African American mental health conditions. Instead these accomplished psychiatrists presented a European American social worker's handbook and guide to the neurotic "Negro," on how to understand the justifiable hatred of the "blacks."

The most frequently made criticism of the book *Black Rage* is its tendency to over generalize. This objection is not nearly so disturbing as is the persistence of the scholars to redefine within the traditional context of Western psychology—with its emphasis on pathology—the cause and character of the "limited" mental health and "pervasive" mental disorder facing African American communities. The assumption underlying this study by Grier and Cobbs and related ones (such as *Dark Ghetto* by Kenneth Clark) that to be psychologically healthy is to conduct oneself as much as possible like a middle class European American. They also assume that the behavior that produces problems for European Americans is the same behavior that produces problems for African Americans. It is further assumed that the standards set by "sanity democracy" are in fact reflective of human standards documented by thousands of years of human history.

These writers fail to address the importance of two essential variables in determining the adequacy of human behavior: (1) the historical antecedents or determinants of that behavior and (2) the effects of a functionally inhuman environment and conditions on the human being. As a result of the failure to take account of these variables, there has been a concerted effort to rehabilitate, correct, modify or resocialize many of the behaviors that have been and still are critical to the survival of the African American. There has been a systematic disregard for those special qualities of human sensitivity that have been maintained despite the humanly oppressive conditions of African-Americans, while they have almost disappeared among the historical oppressors. There has also been a failure to address those issues of intellectual oppression that persist even when the more obvious conditions of physical oppression have been reduced.

The classification and description of African American mental health has failed to utilize one of the few "universals" associated with meaningful definitions of mental health. This definition of mental health has its origin in the unalterable laws of physical life, which when transposed to mental life maintains its essential identity. Physical health is characterized by the functioning of the naturally disposed tendency to maintain life and perpetuate the self. Physical illness is identified when forces or processes within the physical body begin to threaten the natural disposition to live. The transposition of this concept would suggest that mental health is reflected in those behaviors that foster mental growth and awareness (i.e., mental life). Mental illness would then be the presence of ideas or forces within the mind that threaten awareness and mental growth. From an ontogenetic or extended concept of self or mind (Nobles, 1972) we could conclude that mental illness is seen in any behavior or ideas which threaten the survival of the collective self (or tribe). With such a definition, we could understand the classification of an entire society as mentally ill if that society were entrenched in a set of ideas geared toward the self-destruction of the people within that society.

On the other hand, we could understand the apparently contradictory behavior of a people who have formulated their survival on the domination and limitation of others. Domination in combination with oppression, though considered insane from the survival perspective of the victim, is the very essence of sanity for the dominating oppressor who requires a victim in order to survive. When two life processes or entities are opposed in such a relationship then one is obligated to assess "health" or "sanity" from the perspective of the life process that you are seeking to understand and/or preserve. Then both processes must be subjected to the universal standard of natural law to determine which is correct in its oppositional force: is it the unprovoked attacker or is it the innocent victim of attack who must seek to define and assure its own survival in defense from such an attack?

The intent of this discussion is to classify the mental disorders of African Americans from the perspective of universal mental health— that which fosters and cultivates survival of itself. This model equips the African American community with a vehicle by which it recognizes "anti-life" forces (Moody, 1971) within itself and threatening from without. Rather than the more typical preoccupation with disorders that threaten the success and effectiveness of the predators, the focus is directed toward those ideas and behaviors that threaten the life of the victims.

The four classifications of disorders from this perspective include (1) the *alien-self disorder*; (2) the *anti-self disorder*; (3) the *self-destructive disorder*; and (4) the *organic disorder*. We accept the basic argument of Thomas Szasz and others that mental "illness" is actually a myth. There is no particular behavior that is sick in and of itself. Therefore, one cannot assume a disease entity being present for the production of certain specific behaviors. We can accept the allegorical relationship between disorders in the body and disorders in the mind since they both signal danger to the life of their separate planes of being. We do submit, however, that there are socially, mentally and spiritually destructive patterns of behavior that we will describe here as disorders in contrast to the self-surviving and perpetuating forces which operate in an ordered mind. "Disorder" is used in this discussion in preference to "mental illness" because we stand opposed to the position of the Western psychologists who assume that man has no natural order. We claim in accord with the African scholars and scientists from the eastern part of the world that there is a "natural order" for man (Akbar, 1977).

The Alien Self Disorder

The alien-self disorder represents that group of individuals who behave contrary to their nature and their survival. They are a group whose predominant behavior patterns represent a rejection of their natural and culturally valid dispositions. They have learned to act in contradiction to their own life and well being and as a consequence they are alienated from themselves. These are the growing numbers of African Americans in recent years that have been socialized in families with primarily materialistic goals. They see themselves as basically material beings and evaluate their worth by the prevalence of material accoutrements which they possess (Braithwaite, et al., 1977). These families are usually preoccupied with materialistic goals, social affluence and rational priorities (to the exclusion of moral objectives).

These alien-self persons have been socialized to deny critical social realities particularly as they relate to issues of race and oppression. They are encouraged to ignore blatant inequities of racism and to view their lives as if slavery, racism and oppression never existed. They have learned to pretend in ways inconsistent with their valid cultural identity and their survival. They are a group characterized by behaviors that represent a rejection of themselves and anyone who is socially or culturally identifiable as being like them. These are individuals whose primary behavioral patterns contradict those things that would insure their cultural well being and the welfare of their socially and culturally appropriate group. They have learned to pretend that there is really no social difference between them and the descendants of their historical oppressors. They live in complete denial that there are forces of injustice threatening their collective survival. They are encouraged to always adopt the perspective of the dominant culture even if it means a condemnation of self.

The outcome for the alien-self disorder is a symptom picture not dissimilar to the rather traditional neurotic in Caucasian society. This is a person who condemns their natural identity and characteristics and attempts, ineffectively, to live in a dream world. Such persons are usually wrought with anxiety, tension and existential stress. They remain in conflict as to their true identity and go from one social charade to another. A typical example is the sorority socialite who becomes the miserable suburbanite playing at happiness in a glass palace. They are burdened with sexual problems and perversions because the natural sexual disposition has either been excessively restrained or accentuated for the purpose of attracting attention to themselves for the wrong reasons.

Certain types of African American homosexuals represent another example of the alien-self disorders. The evidence of this particular type does not suggest biogenetic causes but clearly psychogenic ones. The person's confusion about their identity (ethnic and interpersonal) has generalized to their confusion about their sexual identity. These characteristics are not true of all homosexuals, but they typify the development of a certain form of homosexuality. The critical pattern is the denial of the person's cultural and natural identity. This type of male homosexual has usually been raised to deny his own masculine disposition because the assertiveness that characterizes boyish emergence was viewed as potentially threatening by the dominant culture and by his confused family circle who points to alien (non Black) role models for him to emulate. The feminine pride that rests at the foundation of effective female identity formation becomes associated with Caucasian images of beauty that frustrate the girl's search for identity. Both the male and female in these instances are encouraged to restrain their natural dispositions that merely generalizes to their sexuality resulting in a disorder that perpetuates a pattern disruptive to natural (reproductive) family functioning. The female homosexual has often simply retreated from the field of femininity because the standards of Caucasian "acceptability" were recognizably unattainable for a woman of African descent. Her homosexual lifestyle permits her to find acceptance of herself as a woman by being acceptable to another woman.

Another variation on this theme is the boy who becomes defiantly delinquent because of his refusal to accept the unnatural restraint required of a "good little colored boy," and rather than relinquish his masculine identity as does the homosexual he defines his masculinity by aggressive rebellion, excessive and precocious sexual activity, criminality, etc. Such a revolt is also found in the criminal who rebels by her indulging those feminine drives that she is not "supposed to have" as a young black woman. In a white supremacist society, true manhood and womanhood are inconsistent with being an African-American person. This makes the attainment of manhood and womanhood a struggle for all members of the oppressed group. Forming an *alien self-disorder* is one of the ways that many people resolve this conflict presented by a racist society.

This alien self-disorder is occurring with alarming frequency in middle class and professional African-American communities. The particular manifestation of this disorder in a wide range of unusual and alien forms of sexual conduct (such as molestation of children, or sado-masochistic behaviors) among both heterosexuals and homosexuals is increasingly evident among African-Americans who have adopted the behavioral patterns of the dominant society. The compelling need to assimilate into the dominant society and to deny those factors that have affected us historically and continue to shape us in the contemporary society has succeeded in alienating increasing numbers of African Americans from themselves. Such persons bring the unique contribution of their heritage to these disorders, but the essential problem is that they have assimilated into a lifestyle that is alien to them. They, therefore, are substantially similar to that dominant culture that fosters material acquisition and general carnality rather than the cultivation of the higher self, which is the orientation of most truly civilized societies.

Affectation best describes the person with the alien self-disorder. They speak, walk, dress, act even laugh as they visualize the dominant group. At great pains they live in neighborhoods predominantly or exclusively populated by other ethnic groups; their children attend the same exclusive school of the most elite of the dominant group; they attend exclusive churches and aspire to join exclusive clubs. Their major obsession is to be the *only*, the *first* or one of a precious few of the racially oppressed group to which they belong. The outcome for the alien self person is that they belong to neither group: African American nor certainly not to the European American group. The consequence is loneliness, confusion, and depression. They assume that there is something fundamentally wrong with themselves since they have done all that they can to join the alien group, but have failed to gain acceptance. They have simultaneously alienated themselves from their indigenous cultural group. They often end up living in a no-man's land unwilling to seek the acceptance of others like themselves and unable to be accepted by those whose acceptance they passionately crave.

The Anti-Self Disorder

The *anti-self disorder* adds to the *alien-self disorder* overt and covert hostility towards the group of ones origin and by implications towards oneself. The *anti-self disorder* not only identifies with the dominant oppressor group but also identifies with the projected hostility and negativism towards their group of origin. In the terms of Frantz Fanon (1968), they represent the true "colonized mentality." They have so thoroughly identified with the colonizer or slave-master that they desire to preserve the very social structure and values that accounts for their oppression. Fanon describes the colonized mind as one who seeks to restore the system of white supremacy that existed prior to the actual liberation of that people from their colonizers.

The dangerous aspect of this group is that unlike the alien-self disorder, they feel quite comfortable with their alien identification. Most often, they exemplify the very epitome of mental health according to the standards of the "democratic sanity." They are usually the very model of stability in the context of the dominant group. They are held up as models for how the members of the oppressed group really should act. Dominant group members often compliment them by proclaiming, "you are not like those others." The danger from this group with the anti-self disorder is that they are unlikely to seek help as is the case with the previous group. The alien-self group will often seek assistance because of the discomfort and stress that they experience from trying to fit into a niche that was not made for them. The anti-self group receives such social support and reinforcement because of their rejection of their own people that they experience little of the personal discomfort of the "no man's land" dwelling alien-self person. The anti-self person is unlikely to be coerced into treatment by the legitimized authorities since they represent the real models of legitimate assimilated behavior, from the perspective of the outer group. These persons generating considerable praise and adulation from the members of the oppressor group express the characteristic hostility of the dominant group towards their own kind.

These are the politicians who will join any faction in order to further their careers. They are elected leaders who are more committed to the "system" than to their constituency; the policemen who beat black heads with a vengeance. These are the African American scholars who are more concerned about scientific (i.e. oppressor's) credibility than about community facility. These are the businessmen who are more concerned about their own economic solvency than they are about the communities from which they came. They promote a program of community destruction so long as their profit margin remains impressive. These are the educators and administrators who ask first if they have the approval of the dominant group and secondarily (if at all) if they have provided a service of enlightenment to their group. Included in this group are the African Americans who reach the apex of their self-rejection by carefully and deliberately selecting a marriage partner from the alien group. To the extent that a mate and ones offspring represent the extension of oneself, their statement of who they are is reflected in the identity of that mate. The fact that such blatant betrayal of oneself is done without remorse and with excessive justification reflects the intensity of self-rejection in the *anti-self disorder*. There is nothing implicitly self-destructive in choosing an outer group marriage partner. In fact, we recognize that some of these may be genuine "love" relationships. However, when such partners have historically demonstrated themselves to be in opposition to your group's survival then such choices are clearly self-destructive and are symptomatic of an *anti-self disorder*. This is especially true in instances where the person actively rejects potential partners within their own group in order to select a member of the outer group.

The *anti-self disorder* is more out of contact with reality than the *alien self-disorder*. Therefore, in terms of severity, this person is more disturbed than the alien-self group. When they have fleeting glimpses of their isolation and confusion they merely intensify their efforts for acceptability by the dominant group and become even more hostile and rejecting towards the group of their origin. This personal rejection of self for the purpose of becoming like the aggressor results in a form of psychological perversion that is at best only damaging or derisive to the African American community and at worst could be the instrument of destruction of our communities. Victims of this disorder are most vulnerable to the manipulation of unscrupulous persons who play upon their need for outer group approval and flattery as a means of utilizing them to control the self-affirmative progress of African American communities.

The Self Destructive Disorders

Inhuman and unnatural conditions bring about insanity. Oppression in its varied and sundried manifestations constitutes one of the most severe forms of inhuman conditions. The unnatural pressures exerted on human life by the human abuse of oppression drives human beings away from reality. A system of oppression erects several critical barriers to human growth that foster a retreat from reality: (1) Oppressive systems block access to the oppressed people's awareness of their true identity and worth. (2)The destruction of human dignity and self-respect is a component of oppressive systems. In order to operate effectively in the world of reality, human beings must see themselves as worthy and effective. (3) The systematic barriers to human development such as masculine responsibility, feminine creativity, self-determination and social productivity thwart necessary human effectiveness. (4) Systematic injustice destroys trust and predictability of the social environment fostering the inability to remain in contact with the objective world of so-called "reality."

Victims of the *self-destructive disorders* are the most direct victims of oppression. These disorders represent the self-defeating attempts to survive in a society that systematically frustrates normal efforts for natural human growth. The pimps, pushers, prostitutes, addicts, alcoholics and psychotics and an entire array of conditions that are personally destructive to the individual and equally detrimental to the African American community, typify this group. These are the individuals who have usually found the doors to legitimate self-determination blocked and out of the urgency for survival have chosen personally and socially destructive means to alleviate immediate wants such as pimping, pushing drugs, or prostituting. Black-on-black homicide and crime is an acting-out of the *self-destructive disorder*. The addicts, alcoholics, gang-bangers and psychotics in varying degrees of intensity have retreated from reality into their respective worlds of dreams. The addict and alcoholic find a level of inner peace in the chemically induced world of fantasy that supports the addictions and become victims of the objective problems created by the drug abuse. The psychotic, who for various direct and indirect reasons of oppression never developed sufficient involvement in the "real" world, persists in their world of fantasy, which despite all of its torment often offers greater order than the world of oppression.

These victims have refused to accept (or have not had the opportunity to develop) the alien self-identity. Often as a consequence of great struggle they have acquired an African American identity, which is inconsistent with Caucasian American achievement or success. The pimp has succeeded in maintaining an African disposition of male confidence and flamboyance. In order to do so he had to become a sadistic brute and exploiter in order to actualize these traits in a society that had defined the concept of masculinity as inconsistent with being African American and masculine self-confidence as "nigger arrogance." The junkie, often painfully sensitive to the realities of his environment, retreats from those realities that have defined him as zero even before he picked up a needle.

It takes the most devastating of environments to reverse the most natural trend of life, which is *SURVIVAL*. The conditions experienced by these self-destructive disorders have made them enemy forces to their immediate selves and to their extended selves in the African American community.

The deadliness of human degradation in the American system of human oppression is reflected in the kind of self-destructive minds that are produced. The fact that such self-destructive disorders do not only occur in oppressed communities is indicative of the shared dehumanization that occurs to the oppressor who seeks to dehumanize. We shall discuss elsewhere the nature of disorder in the Western world that makes it the exclusive producer of mass murderers, serial killers, child molesters and other perverse minds that are occurring with increased frequency within Western society. Suffice it to say that there is a universal backlash that brings the human suffering meted out back to the door of the oppressor.

The psychotic is much more complicated than might be suggested by the conciseness of these concepts. For the purpose of my argument that views sane behavior (most basically) as self-preservative and insane behavior as counter self in some form, then the psychotic clearly falls into the category of the self-destructive. Mental life is nourished by awareness of reality. Withdrawal from that reality constitutes the same kind of mental self-destructiveness that exists in physical suicide or drug abuse. Despite the rather dramatic form of many psychotic behaviors we wish to suggest that the psychotic is using mechanisms at their disposal in order to self-destruct reality just as is the alcoholic and the pimp. The alcoholic accomplishes chemically what the pimp accomplishes socially and what the psychotic accomplishes psychologically. The similarity between the psychotic and the addict is further demonstrated by the increased reliance on legal psychotropic drugs to control the mental retreat of the psychotic person. They both come to rely upon chemically induced mechanisms to protect them from their own self-destructive retreat from reality.

Organic Disorders

This group represents those conditions that, insofar as present information suggests, are primarily the result of physiological, neurological or biochemical malfunction. The group includes the severely mentally defective, organic brain disorders and most of the commonly recognized forms of schizophrenia. We are unwilling to accept that all such "organic" disorders are the results

173

of physical defects alone and therefore do not raise questions about the social environment. For one thing, we do not operate under the (mistaken) Western assumption of dualism whereby physical causation occurs in isolation from social and mental influences. Despite the unquestioned predominance of symptoms that suggest physical defect, we are concerned about the potentially correctable contributions made by the social, mental or physical spheres. There is growing evidence that "freaks of nature" may be freaks of society. Each year scientists are increasingly able to isolate the effects of tobacco, commonly dispensed drugs, alcohol and diet on the unborn offspring. The responsibility for life seems to extend far beyond individual survival but for generations ahead. A recent discovery that birth control pills affect the growth of tumors in second-generation female children demonstrates the long-range influence of the folly of meddling with nature's order. The point is that the organic disorder may be the outcome of a disordered society as is the case with the three groups discussed above.

Intellectual defectives seem to be products of poor nutrition, unspecified chemical conditions such as controllable toxic intake and defective environments. Those defective environments seem to result from an increasing neglect and outright abuse of the young. In other words, the self-destructive disorders discussed above are likely to manifest their self-destructive state of mind by abusing their own flesh, in the form of their offspring which gives rise to the organic defectives of this group. Genuine poverty conditions are as much the direct cause of both poor diet and poor environment as is the physical abuse. In such instances the oppressive system remains the essential cause of mental disorder within the African American community.

Another condition that is often classified in this group of organic disorders is senility. This incapacitating disorder of the elderly is on the increase in African American communities as we increasingly adopt the alien life style of the European American. This life style requires the premature burial of our aged in homes that feed mental deterioration. The urgency of the upwardly mobile family to be freed from the inconvenience of elderly parents requires the disposal of this burden to a sanitary field of inactivity—a kind of living death. So an entire population of formerly active, productive and exceedingly valuable members of the community are converted as specimens for organic deterioration. Such conditions of senility don't seem to occur in communities where the elderly remain integral and respected members of the community of Elders.

There is an increasing emphasis on the organic basis for all forms of mental disorders. It is unfortunately an effort to deny the contribution of the society in the shaping of orderly mental life or disordered mental life. It is also an effort to disavow the subtle interaction between social, psychological and physical phenomenon. The African American practitioner must maintain an awareness of the unity of these influences as they attempt to address the cause of conditions affecting all human beings.

Summary

What's the point of another classification system for mental disorders? Why another rehearsal of the disastrous consequences of oppression? Mental disorder is a social, political, economic, philosophical, even spiritual phenomenon. Both the occurrence, its cause and its management is deeply tied into the historical, social and political status of its victims. We do ourselves a disservice to let the psychiatrists, psychologists and other so-called specialists from other cultural persuasions define our mentally disordered people for us. Paradoxical as it may sound, the ability to decide who in your community is sane or insane is one of the ultimate measures of power and community integrity. As long as this definition comes from outside of the community, one's community is controlled by outside influences.

Any type of classification should be not only descriptive and reliable, but also functional. In the case of identifying pathology, the classification system should be able to isolate the generative conditions that give rise to disorder and it should contain implications for correcting that condition. We have attempted in this discussion to classify mental disorders, not as the European American classify them for their convenience and protection, but as African Americans should begin to see it for the preservation of their communities. The classical "bad nigger" is classified as an assaultive paranoid by the European American psychiatrist because he actively combats oppression. The exasperated welfare mother is likely to be classified as psychotically depressed because the caseworkers can more conveniently transfer her to the psychiatric social workers.

Each of the four classifications discussed here represents separate types of danger to African American communities. Each group of disorders emanate as radials from a common axis, i.e., a psychopathic society typified by oppression and racism (See Figure 1). These disorders usually do not endanger the broader European American society. In fact, the alien self-disorder and the anti-self disorder are usually the primary agents for intransigence in the African American community.

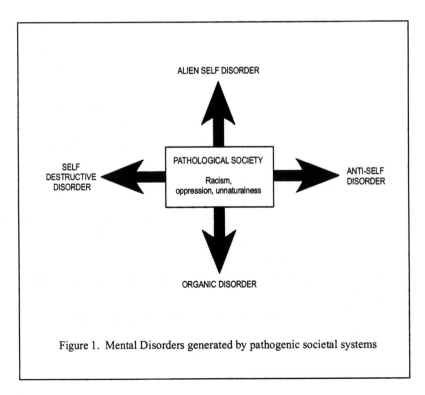

Figure 1. Mental Disorders generated by pathogenic societal systems

Until African Americans are able to effectively define what is normal for our communities, we remain as subjects to an alien authority. Until we recognize the forces that operate to alienate us from ourselves, we will continue to lose our mental power and collaborate with anti-community forces. The definition of normality and abnormality is one of the most powerful indications of community power. So long as these definitions come from outside of the community, the community has no ability to grow nor can human beings within those communities realize the full power of their human potential.

References

Akbar, N. (1974) Awareness: The key to black mental health. *Journal of Black Psychology*, 1(1).

Akbar, N. (1995). *Natural Psychology and Human Transformation. Tallahassee, FL*: Mind Productions and Associates.

Braithwaite, H., Taylor, K., & Black H. (1977). "Materialistic depression". Unpublished manuscript.

Clark, C. (1972). Black studies or the study of black people. In R. Jones (Ed.), *Black Psychology*. New York: Harper & Row.

(Clark) X, C. (1975). Voodoo or IQ: An introduction to African psychology. *Journal of Black Psychology, 1(2)*, 9-29.

Coleman, J. (1972). *Abnormal Psychology and Modern life* (4th ed.). Glenview, Ill.: Scott & Foresman.

Fanon, F. (1968). *The Wretched of th eEarth*. New York: Grove Press.

Figelman, M. (1968). A comparison of affective and paranoid disorders in Negroes and Jews. *International Journal of Social Psychiatry, 14*.

Grier, W., & Cobbs, P. (1968). *Black Rage*. New York: Basic Books.

Hare, N. (1969). A challenge to the black scholar. *Black Scholar*, 2-7.

Kardiner, A., & Ovesey, L. (1962). *The Mark of Oppression.* Cleveland, OH: World Publishing Company.

Karon, B. (1958). *Negro personality: A rigorous investigation of the effect of culture.* New York: Springer.

Lee, D. (aka Mahdubuti, H.) (1976). *From Plan to Planet.* Chicago: Third World Press.

Moody, L. (1977). "The white man as anti-life force". Unpublished manuscript. Norfolk State University.

Nobles, W. (1972). African philosophy: Foundations for black psychology. In R. Jones (Ed.), *Black psychology.* New York: Harper & Row.

Szasz, T. (1960). Myth of mental illness, *American Psychologist, 15,* 113-118.

Thomas, A., & Sillen, S. (1972). *Racism and Psychiatry.* New York: Bruner/Mazel Publishers.

Welsing, F.C. (1970). *The Cress Theory of Color Confrontation.* Washington, D.C.: C-R Publishers.

Wright, B. (1975). *The psychopathic racial personality.* Chicago: Third World Press.

***This article was originally published in *Black Books Bulletin,* Vol. 8. Chicago: Third World Press (1981) and subsequently reprinted in R. Jones (Ed.) *Black Psychology* (3rded.): Cobb & Henry Pub. (1991*).* Only editorial and some reference modifications have been made in this form by the author.

Awareness: Key to Black Mental Health (1974)

An increasing amount of rhetoric and discussion accompanied by a decrease in effective programs have come to characterize our orientation and attack on the economic, social, political, and psychological problems of African people within the confines of the United States of America. Unfortunately, it has become more fashionable to offer extensive Marxian or other such esoteric but distant theoretical descriptions of the problems confronting our people than it has been to provide relief from the economic, social and psychological blight still faced by a growing (yes, growing!) number of black people. Drug use, Black-on-Black crime, suicide and other symptoms of social and emotional unrest increase despite the resounding cries of "Beautiful Black," how "together" we are, what the "honky" has done, is doing, or will be doing to us. The essential problem is that we have not followed through logically or practically on the awakening of the sixties during which an awareness began to surface of the dynamics of our condition in this country and in other parts of the world.

Black psychologists and professionals in other mental health fields have decried the application of inappropriate norms to the assessment of our problems. With few dissenting votes, we have condemned things such as IQ tests, personality inventories and other measures of psychological characteristics as inappropriate and destructive to our well—being. We have condemned white researchers and mental health workers as unqualified to define and provide solutions for the morass of problems that confront us. At the same time, we have so far failed to come forth with viable alternative solutions, which take into account our increased awareness of our condition in this country along with our true and historically legitimate characteristics as African people.

Let me assume that all of us have heard the basic arguments

179

that have been put forth against the traditional conception of mental health problems. For those who are not aware let me recommend *Black Rage* by Grier and Cobbs, and *Dark Ghetto* by Kenneth Clark as early attempts to analyze the mental condition of the black people of this country. The error made by these accomplished black scholars is that they redefine the cause and character of the mental health problems confronting our communities within the traditional context of Western psychology including its emphasis on pathology in their assessments. These social scientists fail to fully accept a proposition implicit in their works—that most of the basic tenets of psychology have grown out of the attempts that Western people have made to understand the mental problems that occur within and as a consequence of their environment. The two premises that render such notions inappropriate to the problems of Blacks are:

(1) We are Africans (i.e., non-Western) in our basic dispositions; and (2) the quality of our environment (by the mere factor of oppression) is systematically different from the environment which Western writers use as the point of reference for understanding their condition.

John Orley in *Culture and Mental Illness*, Freud in *Civilization and its Discontents*, and many other Western theoreticians have espoused the notion that mental illness is the price paid for "social development" or increased "civilization." The assumption here again is that increasing civilization and meaningful social development are directly proportionate to the degree to which a people come to resemble the people of the Western world in their interactions, manners and concerns. In fact, these writers unwittingly provide a warning to people of the world that a pervasive backdrop of real pathology lies within the constructs of what is revered as Western culture. American racism in its most insidious and sundry forms is only one of many symptoms underlying the insanity that characterizes the Western world. This fact alone represents the certainty of mental disorder for African people who find themselves in a social setting controlled and maintained directly or implicitly by Western people.

This particular form of black disorder is what I have referred to in a paper on "mental disorders of African Americans" as an "alien-self" disorder. African Americans with an "alien-self" disorder are persons whose familial and cultural experiences have so duplicated the modal white experience in this country that they have in fact developed a Western consciousness that disposes them to markedly similar disorders as those experienced by Euro-Americans within their cultures. Most of the neuroses as we know them in America are unknown in cultures with limited contact with European values. Disorders such as female frigidity, bizarre sexual perversions, and extreme anxiety are essentially unknown in cultures with drastically different value systems and social organizations. The primary characteristic of the "alien-self disorder," however, is the person's desire to be other than himself or herself.

The treatment implication for Blacks with emotional problems of this nature is two-fold. This systematic denial of themselves as African people is the fundamental basis of the disorder. It is not dissimilar to the self-denial of people in other cultural groups who become preoccupied with being someone other than himself or herself. Secondly, the people with the "alien-self disorder" have overly identified with the dominant culture to the extent that within their minds they have become Euro-Americans. To assist people suffering from such problems, it is necessary that we understand the nature of the Western mind that they have identified with that makes them vulnerable to such disorders and the characteristics that African people have assimilated leading them to the development of such disorders. Two examples of these characteristics are the Western preoccupation with individualism and the focus on materialism. On the one hand these western values and psychological orientations deny the interdependence of self and others.

The idea that people should "do your own thing" is an attitudinal construct that frees us from our responsibility to the communities and people who constitute the extension of who we are.

181

It also robs us of the necessary control of our behavior by our own communities. We are never without control and if we do not recognize our proper reference group and submit to the collective control that advances our humanity, then by default we surrender to some other community's control over us for the advancement of their agenda.

There is no doubt that much of the distress experienced by black people today has to do with their passionate attempt "to do their own thing" and their discovery (often too late) that they have no "thing" to do. The priority value for any social group is the "thing" that assures the survival of that group *first* and secondarily the individual as a member of that group. It is no wonder that a growing group of middle-class black women have lost the innate disposition of sexual responsiveness. Many of these women have defined their "own thing" as the degree to which they can look, act, and feel like a European-American actress, model or some other image of white aesthetics.

Materialism is another Western value that robs people of the recognition of their true essence. The European-American preoccupation of defining themselves by what they own, wear, drive or where they live affects them with confusion and obsession with the question of who they are and leads them to anxiety arousing preoccupations because of these superficial bases for self-definition. If there is a growing preoccupation with comparing ourselves and our things with our neighbors' things, then there is no wonder that African Americans become depressed to the point of suicide. There is growing evidence that the increase of inter-group hostilities (both suicide and homicide) among black people is directly proportional to the extent to which those people have identified with the European-American value system that emphasizes the autonomy of the individual and materialistic definitions of the human being.

Treatment for disorders such as these must rely on expanding the individual or personal consciousness. The concept of consciousness is derived from the Latin phrase *con scio*, which means "with knowledge." The helping person must concentrate on expanding the personal awareness and knowledge of the individual to better appreciate the aspects of the self that are being denied in their attempt to follow alien models. Those who are familiar with traditional methods of counseling and psychotherapy will recognize the proposition presented here as similar to the goal of most traditional counseling.. Implicit in the notions thus far presented is the idea that to the extent to which African-Americans have identified with Western people (even their mental disorders) they are also subject to some of the same influences and interventions.

Some of the methods that have proved "effective" in the alleviation of the European-American disorders may, with appropriate modifications, be used in the alleviation of problems that we have developed because of our "successful assimilation into the culturally alien values. An example of this proposition lies in the analogous introduction of venereal disease on the African continent by Europeans. Antibiotics are the treatment of choice for such a condition despite the fact that the presence of these diseases among Africans was based on the cohabitation of Africans and Europeans. We might extend the analogy by suggesting that although antibiotics may be effective in alleviating this unfortunate physical malady, Africans might have been protected from this disease had they the knowledge and been able or willing to protect themselves from the kind of contacts which led to the initial development of these disease conditions.

The traditional methods of increasing self-awareness by psychotherapy and counseling must be supplemented by systematic and structural instruction about the nature and acceptance of self. The parroting of European values and behaviors must be replaced by what a close friend and distinguished colleague, Dr. D. Phillip McGee of Stanford University, has called the " restoration of African consciousness." The limitation of the scope of this discussion will not permit a full elaboration of this concept but it essentially challenges us to better understand and adopt those communal values and self-definitions that undergirded African people and insured their survival when, by all Western notions of physical and mental strength and endurance, should not have survived - but did!

Oppression Disorder

A second general classification of mental health problems of African people includes those disorders that are direct extensions of the alien-self condition. All of these disorders have their origin in a system of oppression and result in *anti-self* or *self-destructive* behaviors. Frantz Fanon (1963, 1967) offers an extensive description of how systems of oppression and colonialism create their own array of mental disorders. These disorders represent the self-defeating but adaptive attempts to survive in a society that maintains a system of contradictions between ones self-affirming efforts and the conditions for survival in an antagonistic environment. As we have described elsewhere ("Mental Disorders among African-Americans") the anti-self disorder is characterized by active hostility towards ones own cultural group. They have internalized the antagonism that comes from the dominant group and treat their communities or themselves as if they are the oppressors. The drug addict sees him or herself as worthless and incapable of managing their lives. In addition they have been thrust into environments of perpetual stress and discomfort that results in a constant search for relief. Drugs serve as a palliative for the psycho-emotional pain created by oppressive environments. Such relief actually reinforces the self-destruction implicit in drug abuse. Drugs manage to achieve precisely the opposite need for the addicted person, that is they restrict awareness rather than expanding it. Drug substitutes that curtail the craving merely substitute one form of addiction with another.

The people who delight in various forms of attacks against their communities or themselves have become Trojan horses of the oppressive system. They become policemen, politicians, educators, lawyers or even entertainers whose primary objective is to further denigrate the people who constitute their cultural group. They tear down their constituency, often with greater venom, hostility and predictability than the actual oppressors themselves. The anti-self disorder drives them to destroy any semblance of the mirror that is their own people. They perform on a social and collective scale what the drug abuser, alcoholic, mate or child abuser, even the psychotic does by engaging in acts of self-destruction on a personal level.

There is much to be learned by a critical analysis of the work of one of the most effective social change and therapeutic agencies for Blacks in this country, i.e., the leadership and organization of the Honorable Elijah Muhammad. Regardless of the philosophical or ideological differences one might have with the Nation of Islam, it is important to recognize that Elijah Muhammad was able to accomplish with his followers what the "sophistication" of all Western technology, psychology and theology had failed to accomplish. In their most basic form, Elijah Muhammad's teachings for the resolution of mental health problems within this category have to do with the relationship of self-knowledge and it's extension into self-help. The Muslim woman who recognizes and receives respect commensurate with the worth of a glorious black woman is incapable of becoming a prostitute. A junkie who has committed himself to the building of a nation based on equality, freedom and justice for himself and his kind (even by such a simple act as selling newspapers on a street corner) has no place for the "sleep" afforded by drug addiction. The alcoholic is unable to flood his body with poison when he or she believes in the essential beauty and worth of that body.

In other words, I am suggesting that the key to treatment of this wide range of disorders (which represent attempts to destroy the self) lies in the basic acceptance of self and vehicles for the maintenance of self. Understanding ones authentic identity not only resolves the issues of personal self-destruction, but also arrests the tendency of collective self-destruction manifested by the anti-self disorder. Giving methadone to an addict with no job or job skills to provide for himself and those he loves is like putting out a fire with gasoline. Let's be very clear that I am not referring to token programs that seek to rehabilitate by teaching basket weaving when everyone uses plastic bowls. We are suggesting here that clear-cut procedures for the development of self-reliance must be cultivated in response to the self-destructive and anti-self behaviors that characterize these disorders.

It is important to recognize the service needs of the communities where we live and understand that the best cure for anti-self and self-destructive behaviors is to replace those behaviors with self-help behaviors. If people are prepared to fulfill the service needs of their communities and to become acquainted with their own human needs then self-help can replace anti-self and self-destructive conduct.

There are basic necessities from the provision of food and shelter to the manufacture and maintenance of technology that we must learn to depend upon ourselves as a community to provide. From entertainment to the reeducation of our children, after they have been subjected to a day's worth of programming from the public schools, can be provided by the systematic retraining of many people who we have given up because of their attempted escape by the use of drugs, prostitution, alcohol or other methods of self-destruction.

The key here is that people who know themselves accurately will love themselves and, if permitted, take excellent care of themselves. Preparing people for self-help is the most effective therapeutic device to remedy the consequences of oppression neurosis. This is done through reeducation at the personal level or restructuring communities as a whole to convey the realities of their self-knowledge and the inspiration for self-help.

Organic Disorders

I shall not spend extensive time on these conditions of universal occurrence. These disorders are primarily caused by physiological disorders within the occasional biochemical mutations of nature. We must, however, be ever cognizant of the interaction of the physiological with the psychological and of the psychological with the social. High blood pressure has been shown to have a markedly low rate of occurrence among people who have control over their basic life processes and who effectively manage their diets. As the pressures of urban living increase and the vehicles for alleviation of these pressures (such as the availability of jobs) decrease, the hypertension and many similar disorders show a marked increase. Many of the psychoses and especially "true" schizophrenia are increasingly being demonstrated to have biochemical bases. (I make a distinction here between what is in fact a basic disturbance in organizational and perceptual processes based on a biochemical imbalance and the unique behavioral patterns—such as paranoid adaptation based on attempts to cope with an untenable and hostile environment). In such instances let us be made aware that most of the chemicals for the alteration of consciousness came out of African Science (including spiritual and herbal interventions) practiced by many of the older traditional people of the Earth.

The difference between African administration of these drugs and the indiscriminate use of drugs by the Western medicine man is the Western emphasis on behavioral modifications rather than alterations of consciousness. The "witch doctor" applied his chemicals along with systematic re-education and community involvement as the treatment of choice for disorders of this nature. Family therapy is a recent arrival in the Western package of treatment for mental illnesses. Traditional African healers always engaged the entire milieu of the identified "patient" in the treatment process. Consequently, even in instances where the disorder can be identified within the somatic make-up of the individual, the person's re-involvement with their social group involves not only their individual treatment but also a cooperative re-socialization within the known and identified social group.

One additional example may further substantiate the point being made here. Senile psychosis and depression are described as natural deterioration of the nervous system —a function of the aging process. It is interesting to note that these disorders among African Americans have increased in incidence as the treatment of our Elders has come to parallel the Western people's treatment of their aged. As we remove our old people from the ongoing living process by depositing them in tombs for the living (called "old folks homes"), we also initiate the deterioration processes that take on physiological characteristics. With the loss of meaning and activity of the mind, the body succumbs to death.

Even in situations where the available knowledge suggests that the disorder is one of physiological origin, we must be respectful of the holistic conception of life that understands that mind body and spirit are all connected and there is no occurrence in one dimension that doesn't impact the other dimensions of the self. It is important to avoid the flaw of Western knowledge that assumes that things are *either* physical or mental or spiritual. The healing process requires us to attend to all dimensions of the self.

An underlying assumption throughout this discussion is the importance of sensitive diagnostic differentiation. Essential to understanding and treating mental disorders of African people (and all other people for that matter) is the sensitive ability to differentiate what are the differential roles of the environment, the mind and the culture and the genetic make-up of the person.. This is the first step toward the classification and consequent application of treatment procedures to a particular disorder. The implication here is that mental health workers must begin with sensitive self-knowledge that frees them from the biases of imposing an irrelevant theoretical conception on a reality that they do not understand.

The Healing Dimensions of Awareness

The focus of this discussion has been on the role that consciousness (particularly a person's conscious identity) plays in effective mental functioning. The underlying assumption is that it is through this conscious identity that people are able to mobilize their human faculties to engage in the process of growth and development.

Societies and cultures enhance such awareness because of the benefit that it brings to the collective community. When a process of captivity or oppression intrude on the natural processes of culture, then people begin to lose the conscious identity of who they are and as a consequence, they lose access to their natural human motivations that insure their continued, survival and advancement. When oppression causes the type of mental disorder that alienates people from their own self-interest because of their loss of self-knowledge, then there is a full array of behaviors that are inconsistent with the collective advancement of the group as well as the individual. This is certainly evident in so much of the behavior of African Americans and in this discussion such disordered conduct is attributed to the conditions of slavery, colonization and oppression that has characterized the African experience over the last 400 years.

The intention is neither to blame nor excuse these behaviors that are not only deleterious to the dominant society, but even more harmful to the affected group. Human beings who have survived physically what African people have endured through the last millennium certainly have the capacity to overcome the residue of that collective and cultural trauma. We propose that the unique and special human quality of "self consciousness" is the "key to Black mental health" as it is the tool of advancement for all human beings.

What is achieved through "awareness" or "self-knowledge?" This fundamental recognition of who you are as a human being personally, tribally and universally is the foundation for all constructive human activity. There are four major drives that are generated by "self-knowledge": 1) self-acceptance or self-respect; (2) self-preservation; 3) self-help or self-determination and (4) self-discovery. Each of these drives has contained within it the energy and objective that guides most of constructive human activity. When we address the issue of healing African Americans from our captivity and oppression, then the reactivation of these essential processes is the natural goal of therapy.

Of course *self-acceptance* is fundamental for any constructive human conduct. Self-knowledge ultimately generates a message of such acceptance. This is not because everything about a human community (or tribe) is perfect, but we all have a history of success. Our very survival is success and those who preceded us are the proof of our resilience. Regardless of our shortcomings, this ultimate declaration of victory is what communicates to the human spirit that we are made of worthwhile material. We find in that recognition a new level of self-respect and self-love. Such self-respect is not narcissism, arrogance or self-righteousness, but it is the kind of calm self-confidence that attracts you to yourself. It lets you know that no matter what else may be wrong, you and those like you are fundamentally all right. In the above discussion, we described the consequence of people becoming alienated from themselves and the path of decline that such self-rejection precipitated.

The healing process begins when the person is able to access information that tells them who they are historically, cosmically, socially and culturally. This is the implicit process of educational and cultural systems. They are structured to communicate this kind of fundamental understanding of self for the people that set up and maintained that particular culture and educational system. Obviously, the European-American educational and cultural system has evolved as the effective method to communicate such self-knowledge to the future heirs of European-American culture. Built into the rituals, heroes and heroines, and even myths of the culture is the objective of teaching young European-Americans how to maintain their influence on the environment of the world. African culture had built-in mechanisms to insure the continued perpetuation of African culture. The loss of those systems also deprived African people of their birthright to engage in human activity at the highest and most effective levels as they had in earlier generations. So this self-acceptance becomes the catalyst for all of the activities that feed human growth and transformation. The attraction or attachment to ones self is the outcome that repels the alien-self disorder and it's off-shoots. When you love and respect yourself, you engage in those processes that insure the very best consequences for that person and their community.

Self-acceptance generates the powerful urge of "self-preservation" (referred to by some as the 1st Law of Nature.) *Self-preservation* is that critical human drive that activates in us the effective struggle to survive. We do what is necessary to insure our continued life and the life of our kind. Just like the automatic responses of the autonomic nervous system and immune system watches over our physical survival, this consciousness is a sentry over our mental survival. Human beings build mighty structures, engage in bloody wars and write beautiful songs of the spirit driven by this need to survive, maintain and extend our existence. One of clearest indicators that a life is out of order is when that life does not seek to preserve itself. The self-destructiveness of the oppression disorders discussed above is an indication of a very severe mental disorder because these are human beings who have abdicated their desire to survive. Self-murder stands as the ultimate contradiction to human consciousness and life. Everything in our human constitution is geared towards preserving life. When a human consciousness robbed of its self-knowledge either chooses not to survive or passively fails to maintain its survival, this is the ultimate disorder of our humanness. Self-preservation that comes from self-knowledge as well as through self-acceptance is the dimension of consciousness that must be activated in order to heal "anti-self" and "self-destructive" conduct.

A natural outgrowth of *self-preservation* is *self-help*. As we noted above, the engagement in self-help activity is the healing elixir for anti-self and self-destructive activities. From the model of the behaviorist, we are confronted with two competing behaviors. The person cannot be engaged in self-help activities that advance and insure their survival while simultaneously engaging in behaviors that are anti-self and self-destructive. The contradictory behaviors are incompatible. In addition, there is a feedback mechanism whereby self-help not only diminishes the anti-self and self-destructive tendency it also expands the self-knowledge. There is a reciprocal enhancement of the positive forces or mental health and a reduction of the negative forces.

Self-discovery is the final dimension of Awareness for the purposes of this discussion. This dimension is not simply a restatement of the idea of self-knowledge. This is the actual mechanism in the separate and collective self that fuels and energizes the drive for research and exploration. This is the fuel of the scholar and researcher alike because the objective of this drive is to further expand the arena of self-knowledge and self-aware-

ness. This drive sends the anthropologists to their digs, the ge-
neticist to their laboratories and each person is sent to explore
the family tree as they seek to satisfy this insatiable desire to
know more of what brought them into being and what were the
struggles that were mastered in order to insure their existence.
As we have already noted, the expansion of self-knowledge activates the other four dimensions that insure the continued development of the self. These attitudes, orientations and behaviors
that follow are the healing forces that counteract the alien self
deviations that occur as a result of being robbed of the knowledge of self through subjugation by an alien culture and people.

Healing through awareness is a form of cognitive restructuring, but it is much more. It's about developing insights into the
mechanisms that have misdirected your conduct as well as rediscovering the spiritual center that is universally accepted as the
core of being by African and most of the worlds' cultures. The
expansion of awareness and self-knowledge is also a reeducation process. If the core of mental disorder is the loss of self-
knowledge through "miseducation," the healing must, of course,
involve re-education. The creative therapist, teacher, parent or
politician can operate from this model and create mechanisms
that ultimately expand the knowledge base of the population with
whom they interact.

Conclusion

This discussion was formed on three basic assumptions about
the mental and social problems of African people within the
U.S.A. and in most parts of the Diaspora:

(1) The basic dispositions of African people differ from the
basic dispositions and values of Europeans;

(2) The condition of oppression accounts for a wide range
of mental disorders among African people; and

(3) Deliberate attempts to hamper knowledge of self (i.e., of ones cultural group and "tribe") are the dynamic bases of mental problems among African people.

Based on these assumptions, from a sensitive understanding and diagnosis of mental disorders, the treatment of choice becomes an initial effort to increase the individual's knowledge of who they are in the full dimensions of the self. An understanding of the system of oppression (awareness) is the hallmark of making systematic attempts to alleviate the condition of oppression and in turn, the behavioral consequences thereof.

The most insidious device working against effective correction of mental disorders is the naïveté of the mental health practitioner. Again let me refer to traditional African society where the healers were widely informed members of the tribe, not only in terms of the secrets of healing but in self-understanding and knowledge of the philosophical underpinnings of the culture and the community. This is a training that was passed down from father-to-son or mother-to-daughter, implying a need for life-long skill and personal development. The ineptness of most contemporary mental health workers in understanding themselves and the culture of the African person is a greater cause of ineffective treatment than any other single force.

*This article was originally published in *The Journal of Black Psychology* 1(1)1974. It was reprinted in Smith, W.D., Burlew, K., and Whitney, W. *Reflections in Black Psychology.* Washington: Univ. Press of America.

Chapter V

NILE VALLEY ORIGINS OF THE SCIENCE OF THE MIND

OVERVIEW

The paper in this chapter stands alone. When Dr. Ivan Van Sertima called together a conference at Morehouse College in 1984 on Nile Valley Civilization, he asked me to do a paper on Kemitic (Egyptian) origins of psychology. I had done some limited research on Kemitic conceptions of the human being and had made a couple of trips to Egypt when I was given this assignment. From my very limited studies into the very complex Kemitic cosmology, I had discovered that many of the basic assumptions about the functioning of the human being that we had found in looking at West African philosophy and psychology already had their precedent in Nile Valley conceptions of the human mind.

This paper required me to do some additional research and identify some important similarities in the conceptions that we were developing in African Psychology and what we discovered had already been well-developed in Ancient African society along the Nile Valley. These discoveries were exciting because it gave additional validation to our assumption that prior to the rise of Greek philosophy, Africans had already evolved an impressive and more complete notion of the human being than the more fragmented assumptions about the nature of the human being that Western psychologists had evolved from Greek and later European philosophy.

The very critical distinction that we had discovered in the African conceptions of the human personality (described in the previous two chapters) was the recognition of the soul as the core of the human make up. This idea that was present in the cosmology of all of the African systems that we researched was also found in the Kemitic system The most fascinating discovery of all was that the term from Ancient Kemit that was used to designate the "soul" was "sakhu" which was the etymological origin of the Greek word "psyche" that was actually root of the later designation of "psychology." We discovered, not only the

African origins of European psychology but also the source of the early European distortions that began to fragment the more holistic conceptions from Ancient Africa.

The ideas in this paper served to summarize and reiterate with added evidence the idea that there was a better paradigm by which to understand the human personality.

The founding of the "Association for the Study of Classical African Civilization" (ASCAC) in the mid 1980's and its continued work served to enhance this recognition of Ancient Kemit as the foundation of all systems of thought. The ideas in this paper were inspired by the remarkable research and work of Dr. Maulana Karenga, Dr. Yosef Ben Jochannon, Dr. John Henrik Clarke, Dr. Asa Hilliard, Dr. Ivan Van Sertima, Dr. Cheikh Anta Diop, Professor John G. Jackson, Dr. Jacob Carruthers and the other luminary scholars. Their work and that of their students has continued to expand the preliminary notions that I identify in this paper.

The critical conversion of history, culture and science as the tools of African Psychology is the main significance of this paper. The establishment of African Psychology as a "perspective" rooted in the Classical conceptions of the African world remains a compelling part of this work.

Nile Valley Origins of the Science of the Mind (1985)

Despite the impressive technological advancement of modern Western man relative to his own history, he ranks far behind the Ancient African people of KMT (Egypt) both technologically and spiritually. Part of the reason for this scientific devolution is the limited conception of human potential that one finds in Western science. Western man's limitation is a disaster for his captives, who are the descendants of the people of Ancient Kemit. The possible advancement of Western humanity and the redemption or "renaissance" of the African mind is contingent upon rediscovering those concepts of human development that inspired the ascension of the people of Ancient Africa.

The originators of modern thought, as it emerged from its genesis in the Nile Valley, were the early and indigenous people of Northern Africa: Black people! It is important to be explicit about the race of these fathers of civilization, not because they emphasized race as the basis of their greatness, but because the subsequent thieves of Kemitic civilization intentionally concealed the racial identity of their teachers in order to take credit for Africa's accomplishments and we affirm the Blackness of those Ancient Masters in order to redeem the orphans of these authors of civilization. The certainty of the origin of those authors of civilization has been well-documented by Diop (1967), Garvey (1923), James (1976) Ben Jochannan (1971), Muhammad (1965), Rogers (1961), Williams (1976), and many others. Beginning to assert the source of this higher knowledge of humanity and of the universe becomes for African People what James (1976) referred to as a "philosophy of redemption." Just an awareness of the source is redemptive, not to mention the knowledge itself, which is transformative. James (1976) observed:

> This proposition (Greeks were not the authors
> of Greek philosophy, but the Black people of North

Africa, the Egyptians) will become a philosophy of redemption to all Black people, when they accept it as a belief and live up to it....Our philosophy of redemption is a psychological process involving a change in behaviors. It really signifies a mental emancipation in which the Black people will be liberated from the chains of traditional falsehood, which for centuries has incarcerated them in the prison of inferiority complex and world humiliation and insult.

Western Psychology

Psychology is a Greek word revealing its most recent origins among the Greek students of the Ancient African masters as "Psyche" frequently identified with a Greek goddess of the same name actually means "soul". According to Massey (1974) the word *Psyche* is actually derived from the Egyptian in which *Khe* is the soul and Su is she; hence the feminine nature of the Greek *Psu-khe*. Without the article "P", *Sakhu* means the "understanding, the illuminator, the eye and soul of being, that which inspires." Not only is the study of the mind derived from ancient Egypt, but even the word used to characterize that study has a Kemitic origin.

The serious handicap of this Western development is the devastation wrought by the distortions of the Divine Sciences as they were taken from their original teachers and forms. We will not review the steps in the devolution of Western conceptions of Ancient African science as this has been well-documented by Diop (1967), James (1976), Ben Jochannan (1971), and Williams (1976). A recent review by Wade Nobles (1982) is particularly relevant to understanding how psychology has suffered from this distortion by the Western mind.

For purposes of contrast, let us briefly review some of the Western assumptions about the study of the human being as he is currently defined in the Judeo-Christian, Euro-American psychology. We are aware of wide diversity among the various "schools" of Western psychology and our description merely summarizes the pervading ethos. We are aware that increasing numbers of Western-trained scientists are raising similar concerns about the limitations of Western mental science. Euro-American psychology approaches its study of man in the following ways:

1. Man is viewed as an object and the emphasis is upon objective methods for studying him.
2. Quantification is the only acceptable measure of reality.
3. The material world is viewed as essential and the essence of man is material.
4. There is no superior power or purpose beyond man.
5. The observable activities of a person are the critical dimensions of his being.
6. Concepts such as soul, spirits, revelations or any non-observable phenomena is viewed as superstition or delusion and has no relevance to understanding humanity.
7. Life and consciousness are identical with physical processes.
8. Man's individuality is paramount and there is no transpersonal awareness.
9. Man is a product of biological determinants, personal experiences and chance.
10. There is no "correct" order for man's development; he survives against odds by adaptation to his environment.
11. Morality and values have no meaning outside of personal experience.
12. Death of the body is death of the mind and one need not attend to life before or after the body.

Such an orientation to the study of the human being results in what Schwaller de Lubicz (1978) calls "a research without illumination." He observes: "this indecision colors everything, art as well as social organization, and even in many cases, faith."

In addition to these characteristics, which, as we shall see, stand in stark contrast to the Ancient conception of humanity, there is another problem that has served to distort the Western study of mind (man). This problem is rooted in the need of Western scholars to dichotomize reality and assert their superiority and to discredit the source of their knowledge. This distortion resulted in two rather serious problems for the Western scholar. One problem was his fear of the matriarchy and the need to inferiorize women. This is a problem with deep and ancient roots in Western culture, but this fear of women and feminine power resulted in the need to sharply delineate themselves from characteristics identified as feminine. The further need to control those forces led to a derogation of femininity and feminine characteristics that resulted in a limited view of the whole human form that was always present in the masculine and feminine *neters* or principles constantly interacting in the Kemitic Cosmos.

The other problem affecting the European distortion of mental science was a pervasive racism that has permeated the interaction of Europeans with African people and African knowledge. As Diop (1967) has pointed out: "the common denominator which characterizes the mindset of Egypt has been summarily lifted from the African continent in the intellectual view of most scholars. Egypt in modern parlance is identified as the "Middle East" and rarely in Africa. What's even worse, the effort to displace the origin of Egypt's genius outside of Egypt altogether, has served to further the conspiracy of exclusion. Diop (1967) observes:

> As Egypt is a Negro Country, with a civilization created by Blacks, any thesis tended to prove the contrary would have no future. The protagonists of such theories are not unaware of this. So it is wiser and safer to strip Egypt, simply and most discretely of all its creations in favor of a really White nation (Greece).

Such racist intention by Aryan scholars led to the need to dissociate themselves from any qualities which were undeniably Black. The fundamental error of dichotomizing man's make-up in to mind and body eliminating the sprit altogether was done in glory of the material or the physical. Therefore, the spiritual or non-material world was relegated to the practitioners of the "Dark Sciences" and essentially given to the dark races, but not without degrading such involvements as superstitious, primitive (in the sense of uncivilized) and unscientific (i.e. ignorant). On the other hand, the physical and material was the source of thought, action, intellect and science.

Therefore, the material was superior and its practitioners (The Aryan races) were a superior people. (Again, a lengthy review of this development in a 1983 paper by Wade Nobles entitled "Standing in the River, Transformed and transforming: (The Re) Ascension of Black Psychology" is recommended for more detail on this issue.) Suffice it to say that the racist motive to distinguish themselves from the African teachers and to place themselves above their conquered mentors were fundamental in fueling the distortions that came to characterize Western Psychology. Many reviews of the distinctions between Western and African Psychology over the last two decades are recommended as an extension of this discussion which space will not currently accommodate. See: Akbar (1981, 1984), Asante (1980), Baldwin (1976), Clark (1972), Jackson (1979), King (1976), and Nobles (1980).

The Psychology of Ancient Kemit

The wisdom of Ancient Kemit is like a vast tapestry of amazing complexity. Each thread of the tapestry has been carefully woven such that every thread is defined by every other and the tapestry holds together in its wholeness only because every thread is present. No thread can be unraveled meaningfully without destroying the tapestry. Such is the task, which faces anyone who seeks to explore any "thread" of the knowledge of Ancient

Egypt. As Schwaller de Lubicz (1977) observes:

> Excavations and philological studies supply the
> Egyptologists with abundant material for knowl-
> edge of the life, beliefs and theology of Ancient
> Egypt. An encyclopedic amount of work is avail-
> able to the researcher. Nevertheless, Pharaonic
> Egypt remains unknown in terms of its true sci-
> ence, its contingent psychospiritual knowledge and
> its philosophical mentality.

In short, the task that we have set for ourselves is an impossible one for even the Egyptologist of advanced knowledge and
experience. The other confounding factor is that our approach to
knowledge within the Western context, is fragmentary and rational which automatically eliminates the holistic, suprarational and
symbolic knowledge that typifies Egyptian thought. The most
that we can hope to accomplish is to focus on a small design in
this massive tapestry and hope that by analogy and induction we
may begin to glimpse this Egyptian understanding of the mind.

Let us be clear, though a psychology of Ancient Egypt does
not exist in any explicitly identifiable sense, it is important to
realize that the human being was viewed as the fundamental
metaphor for all higher Truth. The gods (*neters*) and most importantly the pharaoh all stood as symbols of profound truth.
So, clearly the understanding of man (mind) was viewed as paramount in the science, the wisdom and the theology of Ancient
Egypt. The study of religion, science (principles of nature),
mathematics, psychology and government was the study of man.
Contrariwise, the study of man (mind) was the study of religion,
etc. The threads of the tapestry are inseparable. Schwaller de
Lubicz (1967) describes the Egyptian view of the man as microcosm:

> Man is a microcosm in the sense of a tree in
> relation to the seed potentially containing it; the
> potentiality is its macrocosm, since the seed in-

cludes all the possibilities of the tree... The seed
will develop these possibilities, however, only if
it receives corresponding energies from the earth
and sky. Even more so, man – who bears within
him the total seed of the universe, including the
seed of spiritual states – can identify with the totality and gain nourishment from it. The relationship of this microcosm with the macrocosm is...
a unity depending only upon his degree of perfection as a human being relative to man as the final
achievement foreseen by the cause.

The dictum (now currently identified with its source) of "man
know thyself," is the fundamental principle of the psychology of
Kemit. James (1976) observes:

The doctrine of self-knowledge, for centuries
attributed to Socrates is now definitely known to
have originated from Egyptian Temples, on the
outside of which the words "man know thyself,"
were written.

James goes on the describe the Ancient Egyptian doctrine of
self-knowledge by observing:

Self-knowledge is the basis of all true knowledge. The mysteries required as a first step, the
mastery of the passions, which made room for the
occupation of unlimited powers. Hence as a second step, the neophyte was required to search
within himself for the new powers which had taken
possession of him.

Essentially, we find in this doctrine of self-knowledge, a sim-
plified description of the initial psychology of consciousness.
Man's capacity to know himself was established as a fundamental human characteristic and in pursuit of that knowledge of one-

self one was in pursuit of knowledge of all things. Again, in her description of Kemitic thought, Schwaller de Lubicz (1967) observes:

> ...the universe is only consciousness and presents only an evolution of consciousness from beginning to the end—the end being a return to its cause. This implies evolution of an innate consciousness toward the psychological consciousness that is consciousness of the innate consciousness, the first step towards the liberated consciousness of physical contingencies.

The question of consciousness is fundamental for understanding the Ancient Egyptian conception of human psychology. Initiation into the mysteries was not only a system of education but a metaphor for the total development of the human soul throughout life and death. This system of education (or more appropriately, "initiation") was a formalized system of evolving consciousness of the person, which was the nation (symbolized in the Pharaoh), which was the entire cosmos.

What was to be known in this pursuit of consciousness? The initiate was instructed that he must know "self:" and self in the conception of the Ancients (as well as modern) Africans meant "soul." The kind of consciousness that had to be developed was, therefore, of much greater depth than the "brain consciousness" which most Westerners have reference to when they speak of "consciousness of self." Such consciousness, Schwaller de Lubicz (1981) describes as no more than a "a mental projection of what a man believes himself to want and do." The soul in its various dimensions as conceived by the Ancients is the most explicit description of the Egyptian conceptualization of human psychology.

Therefore, a description of these components of the psyche (soul) will constitute the core of this discussion with its implications for the "natural" form of the human being.

Ancient Kemitic Dimensions of Self (Soul)

The soul is the fundamental subject of study for these wise men of Ancient Kemit. As Schwaller de Lubicz (1978) observes:

> The tombs of the leaders of this people (from Ancient Egypt) are consecrated to their profession of faith in the survival of the soul... The West labels this attitude of wisdom a state of science that is 'still mystical.' But the Egyptian technique and their symbolic attest to a realistic sense and to faculties of reasoning, contradicting the view held that this epoch is a "primitive, mystical" age.

Unfortunately, any science that delves into understanding the real "psyche" (soul) has come to be seen as "mystical" in Western scholarship. It was precisely these components of the person that have been discredited and excluded from the Western study of the mind that has resulted in its limitations. It is the inclusion of these elements in the studies of the Ancients that has given that science its power of permanence.

There is some inconsistency in the translation and identification of the components of the soul among various Egyptologists. Table 1 presents a comparison of how various writers have described the way that the world's earliest psychologists characterized the dimensions of the human mind. Generally the dimensions that are identified are all similar to Massey's (1974) list: (1) *Ka (Kha)*, (2) *Ba, (3) Khaba, (4) Akhu, (5) Seb, (6) Putah, (7) Atmu*. These seven souls constituted the natural form of the human being's psychology as well as the course of his evolution. The challenge to man was to become knowledgeable of these souls and achieve a crystallization of them into an Eighth of Divinely permanent form.

Table 1
Comparison of the Ancient Kemitic Conception of the Soul (Self)
as identified by Four prominent Egyptologists

Massey (1974)	James (1954-71)	Budge (1960)	Schwaller de Lubicz (1981)
Ka - a formal structure that would return to the elements; soul of blood	Ka - abstract personality of the man to whom it belongs possessing the form and attributes of a man with power of locomotion.	Ka - double or inner self which comes into being with each person and follows him throughout life. It is the thread of connection between man's tangible and intangible being.	Ka - Formal element which gives form to substance and creates matter. 1. original Ka - Creator of all the others. Divine Ka. 2. Kas of nature, mineral, vegetable and animal. Imtermediate Ka - personal consciousness; Inferior Ka. 3. Individualized Ka, inherited characteristics of psychological consciousness; Inferior
Ba - Breath of life; Eternal, invisible energy that runs through all visible functions. Essence of all things.	Ba - heart-soul dwells in the Ka. It has the power of metamorphosis and changes its form at will.	Ba - a combination of intelligence and spirit which leaves the body at death.	Ba - most spiritual element in man; it is his link with the Creator. It is free, unfixed and unaffected by the human being whose only with it is a link of consciousness. 1. Ba is the cosmic soul in all constituents of the world (Universal soul) 2. Ba - the natural soul stabilized in the bodily form; 3. Ba - represented by bird with human soul, which comes and goes between heaven and earth.
Khaba - veil of the vital principle produced emotion and motion; sustains the sensory perceptions, total harmony and circulation of the blood shade soul	Khaibit - Shadow, associated with Ba. It has the power of locomotion and omnipresence.	Khaibit - the shadow or soul of the blood.	Khaibit - astral or etheric body, ghost or shadow. Holds the records of all pictures or imaginings in our universe.

Table 1(continued)

Comparison of the Ancient Kemitic Conception of the Soul (Self)
as identified by Four prominent Egyptologists

Massey (1974)	James (1954-71)	Budge (1960)	Schwaller de Lubicz (1981)
Akhu - Seat of intelligence and "mental perception." Attributes of judgment, analysis, and mental reflection all of which could be dedicated to service of higher being.	Ab - The heart, the animal life in man that is rational, spiritual and ethical. Associated with the Ba and undergoes examination in the Judgment.	Hati - represents the heart or conscience and understanding.	Inferior Ka (see above)
Seb - manifested at puberty; selfcreative power of the human being. Ancestral soul. Procreational soul.	Khat - the concrete personality, the physical body which is mortal.		Inferior Ka
Putah - "first intellectual father," marked the union of the brain with the mind. From its attainment the intellect governs conduct. intellectual soul.	Sahu - body in which the khu or spiritual self dwells. All mental and spiritual attributes of the natural body are united to the new powers of its own nature.	Sahu - the spiritual body.	Ba - natural soul
Atmu - the Divine or eternal soul. Represented as parenthood, which symbolized the full creative power and perpetual continuation.	Khy - spiritual soul which is immortal. It is immortal. it is closely associated with the Ba (heart-soul),which is immortal.	Khu - the pure spirit or Horus - the highest expression of the personality, the perfect spirit of Christ consciousness.	Divine ka - "Father of the father of the Neters" (Spiritual Witness)

The Ka is described by Massey (1974) as "the soul of Blood." This psychic dimension is the formal element of the person, which gives form to substance and creates matter It is formative or of the abstract personality structure which has a formal structure capable of ultimate disintegration and return to the elements from which it came unless it is Osirified or mummified. The structure would have to become Divinely or permanently set (which is the symbol of the Mummy) as an eternally preserved form of the person (which is a symbol of Osiris.) The body is usually identified as the symbol of the Ka though the Ka soul was certainly transcendent. Budge (1960) describes the Ka as "the thread of connection between man's tangible and intangible being."

The Ka is refined through the other dimensions of the soul, but it has a multiple expression of its own. Schwaller de Lubicz (1981) identifies these three manifestations of the Ka as:

1. Divine Ka—the original Ka, which is the creator of all the others.
2. Intermediate Ka—Kas of nature, mineral, vegetable and animal.
3. Inferior Ka—individualized Ka; inherited characteristics of psychological consciousness. Consciousness of the Ka evolved from the Inferior to the Divine Ka.

Schwaller de Lubicz (1981) observes:

> A man ignorant of his own spiritual world has little or no contact with his Divine Ka. His personal Ka is brought down to the whole of his lower Ka; therefore after death, he will become his own shade or ghost...the quest for spiritual springs of action and the enlargement of consciousness, can modify the character of his "personal" Ka until the spiritual faculties are awakened and it makes contact with the Divine Ka.

The Ba called the "Soul of breath" by Massey (1974) is the second division of the psychic nature. It represented the transmission of the invisible energy source (like electricity), which runs through all visible functions. The Ancients believed that there was only one power, which was symbolically represented as "the breath," and, that this power or breath was transmitted from the ancestors to the descendants. They believed that this power or energy has always existed and will always exist. The Ba was in effect the vital principle that represented the essence of all things.

The *Ba* as represented by a bird with a human head as the symbol of the "human soul" which comes and goes between heaven and earth. It is the most spiritual element in man for by its divine nature it is linked with the Creator. It is incommensurable, and indivisible, free, unfixed and unaffected by the vicissitudes of the human being whose only link with it is a link of consciousness. Schwaller de Lubicz (1981) also divides the *Ba* into three aspects:

1. *Ba* (universal soul) the spirit of fire which gives life to the world in all its parts. The spirit of *Ba* is in all constituents of the world and in its final perfection.
2. *Ba* (natural soul) stabilized the bodily form (*Ka*), and its character is Osirian, that is, it is subject to cyclic renewal.
3. *Ba* as the human soul described above as represented by the bird.

The K*a* by assimilating the universal *Ba* generates a new being which is the individualized soul that remains divine, incorruptible and therefore immortal. In fact the definitions of *Ba* and *Ka* must always be relative to each other, since they can only refer to one aspect in its relation to the other.

The *Khaba* is the shade or covering soul, corresponding to the popular notion of the ghost. It is the astral or "etheric" body. It is related to the *Akasha*, the world or state which holds the records of all the pictures or imaginings in our universe. The *Khaba* (call *Khabit* of *Kaibit* by some writers) produced emotion and motion. It was further thought to be responsible for sustaining the sensory perceptions and the phenomena of color, total harmony and the circulation of blood.

The *Akhu* is the fourth division of the psychic nature and is described as the seat of intelligence and mental perception. It was in the area of the *Akhu*, the Ancients believed, that the whole mystery of the human mind was to be comprehended. The mind was in fact, an entity in and of itself and only during physical life was the mind the instrument of the human spirit. The concerns of the mind were primarily the survival of its own thinking processes. The *Akhu* was characterized by attributes like judgment, analysis and mental reflection, all of which could be trained and disciplined so as to be dedicated to the service of the higher being. The intelligence was considered to be located in the heart and it was considered to be not only rational but also spiritual and ethical. In the Ancient Kemitic Judgment drama it undergoes examination and is weighed on the scale of justice against a feather (*Ma'at*) in the presence of Osiris, the great judge of the unseen world.

The *Seb* is the soul of pubescence in that it doesn't manifest itself in humans until puberty or adolescence. The evidence of the presence of the *Seb* was the power of the human being to generate his own kind. The *Seb* is in effect the self-creative power of Being.

The *Putah* was the intellectual soul or the "first intellectual father." Unlike the *Akhu*, the *Putah* was associated with the mental maturity of the individual and marked by the union of the brain with the mind. It was the *Putah* that established the fact of the person and form the moment of its manifestation or attainment it was believed that intellect (i.e., will and intent) alone governed conduct. The maturity of the *Putah* represents the person's ability to reproduce intellectually.

The *Atmu* as the seventh division of the psyche was considered the divine or eternal soul. In some texts it is identified with the seventh creation, the god *Atmu* who inspired the breath of life everlasting. In ritual this division of the soul is represented as parenthood, which symbolically stood for the presence of full creative powers and perpetual continuation.

Some writers, such as Massey, identify an eighth form of the soul, which represents a synthesis or crystallization of the other seven. Massey (1974) refers to it as "Horus" or the Christ." It is the same as the "*Divine Ka*, " described above by Schwaller de Lubicz (1981) and by Frankfort (1946). This component is described as enwrapping and serving as the essence of all the divisions of the soul and was the *Ka* of God. The *Ka* was the divine spirit which endowed all things and which survived past the physical life of the individual.

The *Ka*, it was thought, had magical powers and could cause the dead to live again (the resurrected Christ) and could even enter a mummified being, animate it internally and cause it to have a continued inner life or existence.

Conclusion

This discussion has focused on just one aspect of a multi-faceted and complex system that describes the human psyche according to Ancient Kemitic tradition. As we cautioned from the outset, the entirety of the Kemitic cosmology actually is a comprehensive description of the Psyche of the human being. The amazingly complex theology of Ancient Kemit represents a series of allegories that define the workings of nature and most importantly the genesis and implied potentialities of man. These myths and symbols actually transcend the empirical conclusions of Western Science and describe man, not only on the basis of what he does but what he is.

We chose to look at the psychic dimensions as the Ancients described it because in that system we find a summary of what the human being is. By implication we can more effectively describe the properly functioning human being and can actually see the distinctions from the African perspective. Each of the components of the septenary soul, which we have described, has implications for understanding the nature of the human being.

The fundamental conclusion about human nature as implied by the description of the *Ba* and the *Atmu,* as well as the *Divine Ka* is that the human being is essentially connected with the Divine and with everything else in nature. There is continuity in all that is, having its origin in the Creator. This is consistent with the African psychologists (Akbar 1976; Baldwin, 1976; Jackson. 1979; Nobles 1980 and X. et al. 1976) who have suggested the principle of consubstantiation as expressed in the idea "I am because we are and because we are, therefore I am," (Mbiti, 1970) as fundamental to understanding the African psyche. We have identified that this same concept called *Ba* in Ancient Africa is called *dya* by the Bambara people and the *Okra* by the Akan people of Ghana and more generally 'soul by African -American people, showing a continuity in this Ancient Kemitic conception of the human being among African people. This is in contrast with the dualistic and materialistic conception of the Euro-American psychologists who would be appalled at even admitting that 'psyche'' once meant soul even to them.

The *Ka* on the other hand brings balance to the picture of the human being and shows that the human being is not only of 'heavenly'' material but also of 'earthly' material. There is implicit in this system, recognition that the human being has a connection and an involvement in the earthly sphere. He has a physical component that is tangible, but this is a dimension and not an exclusive view of the person. The Ancients were able to construct impressive physical structures, feed their citizenry with advanced technology, master physics and physical medicine while understanding that all of those structures were transient in comparison with the higher being.

The *Kaibit* suggests that man has access to Universal knowledge from the so called "Akashic records." Man can reach into the recesses of his own consciousness and retrieve the world's most valuable knowledge. This eliminates the apparent inequity in knowledge when it is assumed to emanate from outside.

Intelligence is multiple in its dimensions: rational, spiritual and ethical. The intelligent person is not simply one who has mastered a technique but is prudent enough to know when and how to apply that technique. The intelligent person is not one who is capable of performing independent of his moral and spiritual obligation to the rest of humanity. The *Akhu* and *Putah* give a conception of intelligence, which requires self-mastery, and service to ones higher being in order to be considered intelligent.

Seb reminds the person that his nature is not only one which permits reproduction, but is procreative and self-creative, The human being is equipped not just to reproduce himself, but to re-create and then perpetuate his creation.

Ultimately, the human being becomes the fullness of what he is from his inception and that is a Divine form reunited with his Divine genesis. Through realization of one of Ancient Kemit's most consistent motifs (that is) transformation. The person transforms the raw material of his transient form and self-consciously forms and is transformed to the higher being from which he sprang.

> *The deceased cries. 'Do not take my soul!' (Ba) "Do not detain my shade!" (Khaba) "Open the path to my shade, and my soul, and my intelligence (Akhu) to see the great God on the day of reckoning souls."*
> —From the Coffin Text—

References

Akbar, N. (1984). Africentric social sciences for human liberation. *J. of Black Studies,* 14 (4), 395-414.

Akbar, N. (1981, 1985)) Our destiny: Authors of a scientific revolution. *The Fifth Conference on Empirical Research in Black Psychology.* Washington. D.C.: Howard University Institute for Urban Affairs. 1981.Reprinted in H. McAdoo and J. McAdoo (Eds.)(1985), *Black Children.* Beverly Hills: Sage Publications.

Asante, M. & Vandi, A. (Eds.)(1980). *Contemporary Black Thought.* Beverly Hills: Sage.

Baldwin. J. (1976). Black psychology and black personality. *Black Books Bulletin.* 4(3). 19.

Budge, E.A.W. (1960). *The Book of the Dead:* An English translation of the *Papyrus of Ani.* New Hyde Park, New York: University Books.

Ben-Jochannan, Y. (1971). *Africa: Mother of Western Civilization.* New York: Alkebu-Lan Books Assoc.

Clark. C. (1972). Black Studies or the study of black people, in Jones, R. (Ed.) *Black Psychology* (1st edition). New York: Harper & Row.

Diop, C.A. (1967). *The African Origin of Civilization: Myth or Reality.* Westport: Lawrence Hill & Co.

Frankfort, H., et al. (1946). *The Intellectual Adventure of Ancient Man.* Chicago: University of Chicago Press,

Jackson, G. (1979). The origins and development of Black Psychology: implications for Black Studies and human behavior. *Studia Africana,* 1(3), 1979. 270-293.

James, G.G.M. (1954,1976). *Stolen Legacy.* San Francisco: Julian Richardson Assoc.,

King, L. et al. (1976). *African Philosophy: Assumptions and Paradigms for Research on Black Persons.* Los Angeles: Fanon Center Publication.

Massey, G. (1974). A Book of the Beginnings, Vol. 1. Secaucus, N.J.: University Books, Inc.

Massey, G. (1974). *Gerald Massey's Lectures.* New York: Samuel Weiser, Inc.

Mbiti, J. (1970). *African Religion and Philosophy.* Garden City: Doubleday and Co.

Muhammad, E. (1965). *Message to the Black Man.* Chicago: Muhammad Mosque of Islam.

Nobles, W.W. (1972,1980). African Philosophy: Foundations for Black Psychology in Jones, R. *Black Psychology* (1st. & 2nd eds.) New York: Harper and Row.

Nobles, W.W. (1984). Ancient Egyptian thought and the development of Afrikan (Black) psychology Presented to "The First Annual Ancient Egyptian Studies Conference: The Social Life. Los Angeles, February 24-26, 1984.

Nobles, W.W. (1984). Standing in the river, transformed and transforming: The re (ascension) of psychology in Nobles, W.W. *African Psychology.* Oakland, CA: A Black Family Institute Publication.

Rogers, J.A. (1961) *Africa's Gift to America.* New York: Hula M. Rogers.

Schwaller de Lubicz, I. (1978). *Her-Bak: Egyptian Initiate.* New York: Inner Traditions International.

Schwaller de Lubicz, I. (1981). *The Opening of the Way:* New York: Inner Traditions International, 1981.

Schwaller de Lubicz, RA.(1977). *The Temple in Man.* New York: Inner Traditions International.

Schwaller de Lubicz. RA. (1978). *Symbol and the Symbolic.* New York: Inner Traditional International.

Williams, C. (1976). *The Destruction of Black Civilization.* Chicago: Third World Press.

**This paper was originally published in I. Van Sertima (Ed.) *Journal of African Civilization.* 6(2), November 1984.

Epilogue

OVERVIEW

Of course, this work has just begun and these papers reflect the musings of one small piece of a mighty system that is making this happen. My small part in articulating this reality that has grown to be known as "Afrocentricity" must be understood in the context of a progression that began thousands of years ago in the Nile Valley, has experienced numerous renaissances in Zimbabwe, Mali, Ife, Kumasi, in Harlem and many other parts of the world. It is the same voice of Rev. Henry McNeil Turner, Marcus Garvey, Elijah Muhammad, Mary McCleod Bethune, W.E.B. DuBois, Cheikh Anta Diop, Ida B. Wells, Frantz Fanon, Edward Blyden , Fannie Lou Hamer, David Walker, Martin Luther King, Jr., John G. Jackson, Chancellor Williams, John Henrik Clarke, Malcolm Shabazz and so many others who are already a part of our ancestral family. It is not a new voice, but the continuity of a very old and ancient voice that has been persistent in its call to a realization of our authentic identity as African people. As that voice has not been quieted with the transition of these brilliant minds, neither is our contribution the completion of this work.

This final selection in these papers is a more recent writing and it is outside of the context of the 1970-1989 range of these papers. It is included because as an epilogue, it challenges the next generation of young scholars to proceed with this work. It calls those new thinkers who have been students of this work to continue along the path of articulating the meaning of the African perspective. It encourages the young African psychologists such as Cheryl Tawede Grills, Adisa Ajamu, T. Owens Moore, Edward Bynum, Leon Caldwell, Anthony Smith, Shawn Thompson, Shawn Utsey, Ezemenari Obasi, Daryl Rowe and many others to continue with the expanding research and practice of these concepts. We encourage young African scholars such as Jerome Schiele, Erriel Roberson, Janice Hamlet and many others in allied fields who have taken these concepts into new dimensions and new arenas.

Though these papers represent the *beginnings* of my work,

my work in this area continues. The work of the stalwarts such as Nobles, Parham, Kambon, Myers, Azibo and so many others heavily referenced in these papers also continues. The challenge that is issued in this closing paper is as much a prologue to the work yet to come, as it is an epilogue to the work that we have begun.

A luta continua (The struggle continues . . .).

Afrocentricity: The Challenge of Implementation (1998)

The African-American students and scholars who will usher us into the dawn of the 21st century will be greeted by many of the paradoxes which have confronted African people since our entrance of bondage into North America. These paradoxes will be no less problematic than before, and challenges facing our people over the next century will continue to be of the incredible magnitude that we, as a community of Africans in America, have come to know. As has been the case with each previous generation, this new generation will be called upon to reap the harvest of those who have sown before them and to carry on the process of plowing the fields of time for those yet unborn.

The last 20 years in America have generated a remarkable new crop in the intellectual fields of African-American life. The new crop has been described in the popular language of "Afrocentricity," which has unfortunately come to mean a wide variety of things from the wearing of Kente cloth shawls to a radical reinterpretation of world history. In any event, the new concept has heralded a massively important paradigm shift in African thought specifically and American scholarship in general. As the previous generation of African-American freedom fighters ignited the redefinition of freedom for all Americans (e.g., women's rights, handicapped rights, etc.) this new conceptual analysis identified as Afrocentricity will no doubt usher in a universal reanalysis of Western scholarship in which people will boldly bring the particular perspective of their diversity to the table of human commonality.

Contrary to the claim of its critics, Afrocentricity is no more than the description of a perspective for the purpose of analysis. The so-called "Scientific method" (which is in fact only a method of science) is a perspective which takes objectivity as its stance for analysis. This method suspends the reality of subjective factors only in creating an objective illusion. This is a valid suspension of belief not unlike that of the fiction writer who suspends disbelief to create a fantasy. It is a valid perspective for the purpose of a particular type of analysis.

The Afrocentric scholar claims that the perspectives of other experiences have been willfully suspended in the Eurocentric analysis of reality. This suspension has tremendously benefited the ascension of European people and those capable of identifying with their experiences. This same suspension has massively handicapped people who negated their own reality and sought to identify with a reality and an experience that was not their own.

No one can legitimately claim that the Eurocentric reality is not correct for Europeans in the same way that one cannot argue that the conditions of a genuine vacuum are not correct if we were capable of producing such an objective reality. We do argue that each people must enter the world of scientific and scholarly analysis from the path of their historically and culturally developed perspectives. These perspectives are not counter to universal reality and truth, but simply access the universal through the window of one's particular worldview. Such a perspective can only enhance human understanding in general.

The real challenge for our young thinkers here at the dawn of the 21st century is how to execute the next step in the progression of this paradigm shift. Thanks to Diop, Van Sertima, John Henrik Clarke, and others, we now know that history is not only what we have been taught from the Eurocentric perspective. Thanks to Nobles, Hilliard, Welsing, King, and others, we now know that psychology is not only what the European behavioral scientists have taught. We have a new grasp on the concept that Africans view the world differently, thanks to the work of Asante, Karenga, Carruthers, Jeffries, and others. We now need a new implementation, both in social construction and in technology.

Those coming from the Afrocentric perspectives are to be the vanguard in developing a technology that is compatible with the Afrocentric concept of harmony with nature. They are obligated to develop systems of technology which are respectful of a much abused environment which Africans, from their perspective, view as a divinely given gift which requires humans to interact with it harmoniously. We need Afrocentric architects who construct buildings that are not only efficient, but also maintain human ties and facilitate human interaction. We need Afrocentric organization developers who build organizations sensitive to the human ties and the spiritual aspirations that the Afrocentric orientation teaches us. We must have educators who structure learning systems in such a way that children learn to respect who they are and see themselves as allies with the environment rather than oppressive conquerors. We must have social organizers who develop social systems that respect gender difference while facilitating the expressions and genius of all people.

The values and philosophical basis for the development of such systems are implicit in the Afrocentric system. The prophetic thinkers who have helped to reveal this system are neither capable nor have the longevity to implement the structures which must stand on the foundation that they have built. Those who opened the doors to greater civic freedoms could not simultaneously become the political brokers who developed a Harold Washington or empowered a Maynard Jackson.

In the same vein, it is overly messianic for us to expect that those who have revolutionized our thinking about ourselves can also implement the new techniques, structures, and systems which that new thinking will necessarily produce. Already, many of our young students are growing impatient with what they describe as too much "theory" and "rhetoric". They don't realize that this theory and rhetoric account for the re-energizing of themselves with a kind of vision and motivation for the rebuilding of African reality such as we have not seen since the Civil Rights Movement and the Harlem Renaissance. They must understand that they are having the baton passed to them and they must now implement the structures that demonstrate this great power of the African genius which the Afrocentric paradigm shift has revealed to us.

We now know what we have done and what we can do. The challenge for the carriers at the dawn of the 21st century is to demonstrate to the world that not only have we done the impossible in charting the course for all humanity, repeatedly in the past, but also we are now taking it as our imperative for the people of Africa to once again bring a renaissance to all humanity.

*This article originally appeared in *Black Collegian*, September/ October, 1991. It was later published as a chapter in Janice Hamlet (Ed.) (1998*), Afrocentric Visions - Studies in Culture and Communication*. Thousand Oaks, CA: Sage Publications, Inc.

Bibliography

Akbar, N. (1999). *Know Thyself.* Tallahassee, FL: Mind Productions and Associates.

Akbar, N. (1980). The evolution of human psychology for African Americans. Unpublished manuscript presented to SREB Student Conference, Atlanta

Akbar, N. (1981). Our destiny: Authors of a scientific revolution. The Fifth Conference on Empirical Research in Black Psychology, Washington: NIMH.

Akbar, N. (1981). "Mental disorders among African Americans," *Black Books Bulletin*, Vol. 8. Chicago: Third World Press.

Akbar, N. (1984). Africentric social sciences for human liberation. *J. of Black Studies,* 14 (4), 395-414.

Baldwin, J. (1976). Black psychology and black personality. *Black Books Bulletin*, 4(3), 6-11.

Baldwin, J. (1980). The psychology of Oppression. In M. Asante, & A. Vandi (Eds.), *Contemporary black thought.* Beverly Hills: Sage Publishers.

Banks, W.C. (1980). Theory in black psychology. Paper presented at the Thirteenth Annual National Convention of the Association of Black Psychologist, Cherry Hill, NJ.

Ben-Jochannan, Y. (1971). *Africa: Mother of Western Civilization.* New York: Alkebu-Lan Books Assoc.

Braithwaite, H., Taylor, K., & Black H. (1977). "Materialistic depression". Unpublished manuscript.

Bridgman, C. (1923). *A study of American intelligence.* Princeton: Princeton University Press.

Budge, E.A.W. (1960). *The Book of the Dead:* An English translation of the *Papyrus of Ani.* New Hyde Park, New York: University Books.

Carruthers, J. (1972). Science and Oppression. Chicago: Northeastern Illinois University's Center for Inner City Studies.

Clark. C. (1972). Black Studies or the study of black people, in Jones, R. (Ed.) *Black Psychology* (1st edition). New York: Harper & Row.

(Clark) X, C., et als (1975). Voodoo or IQ: An introduction to African psychology. *Journal of Black Psychology* 1(2), 9-29

Clark, K. (1965). *Dark Ghetto: Dilemmas of Power*. New York: Harper & Row.

Coleman, J. (1972). *Abnormal psychology and modern life* (4th ed.). Glenview, Ill.: Scott & Foresman.

Diop, C.A. (1967). *The African Origin of Civilization: Myth or Reality*. Westport: Lawrence Hill & Co.

Dixon, V. (1976). Worldviews and research methodology. In L. King, et al. (Eds.), *African philosophy: Assumptions and paradigms for research on black persons*. Los Angeles: Fanon Center.

Fanon, F. (1963). *The Wretched of the Earth*. New York: Grove Press.

Fanon, F. (1967). *Black Skin, White Masks*. New York: Grove Press.

Figelman, M. (1968). A comparison of affective and paranoid disorders in Negroes and Jews. *International Journal of Social Psychiatry, 14.*

Frankfort, H., et al. (1946). *The Intellectual Adventure of Ancient Man.* Chicago: University of Chicago Press,

Freud, S. (1930). *Civilization and its Discontents*. London: Hogarth Press.

Glazer, N., & Moynihan, D. (1963). *Beyond the melting pot.* Cambridge: M.I.T. Press.

Grier, W. & Cobbs, P. (1968). *Black Rage*. New York: Basic Books.

Hare, N. (1969). A challenge to the black scholar. *Black Scholar, 2-7.*

Jackson, G. (1979). The origins and development of Black Psychology: implications for Black Studies and human behavior. *Studia Africana,* 1(3), 1979. 270-293.

Jacob, J. (1963). *Psychology of C.G. Jung.* (New Haven: Yale University Press.

James, G.G.M. (1954,1976). *Stolen Legacy.* San Francisco: Julian Richardson Assoc.

Jensen, A. (1969) How much can we boost IQ and Scholastic Achievement? *Harvard Educational Review* 39, 1-123.

Jones, R. (Ed.) (1991). *Black Psychology* (3rd ed.). Berkeley: Cobb & Henry Publications.

Jung. C. (1968). *Analytical psychology: Its theory and practice.* New York: Vintage Books.

Kardiner, A. & Ovesey, L. (1951). *The Mark of Oppression.* Cleveland, OH: World Publishing Co.

Karon, B. (1958). *Negro personality: A rigorous investigation of the effect of culture.* New York: Springer.

King, L. et al. (1976). *African Philosophy: Assumptions and Paradigms for Research on Black Persons.* Los Angeles: Fanon Center Publication.

Kuhn, T. (1970). The structure of scientific revolutions. International Encyclopedia of Unified Science, 2(2). Chicago: University of Chicago Press.

Ladner, J. (Ed.), (1973). *The Death of White Sociology.* New York: Vintage Books.

Lee, D. (aka Mahdubuti, H.) (1976). *From Plan to Planet.* Chicago: Third World Press.

Majors, R. (1989). Cool pose: The proud signature of Black Survival. In M. Messner, & M. Kimmel (Eds.), *Men's Lives: Readings in the Sociology of Men and Masculinity.* New York: Macmillan.

Massey, G. (1974). A Book of the Beginnings, Vol. 1. Secaucus, N.J.: University Books, Inc.

Massey, G. (1974). *Gerald Massey's Lectures.* New York: Samuel Weiser, Inc.

Mayers, S. (1976). "Intuitive Synthesis in Ebonics: Implications for a Developing African Science." In L. King, et al. (Eds.) *African Philosophy: Assumptions and Paradigms for Research on Black Persons.* Los Angeles, CA: Fanon Center Publication, C.R. Drew Postgraduate Medical School, pp 190-214.

Mbiti, J.S. (1970). *African Religions and Philosophy.* New York: Anchor Books.

McClelland, D. (1965). Achievement motivation can be Developed. *Harvard Business Review,* 43(6), 6-18.

McGee, D.P. (1976) "Melanin: The Physiological Basis for Psychological Oneness," *African Philosophy: Assumptions and Paradigms for Research on Black Persons,* L. King et al (Eds.) Los Angeles, CA: Fanon Center Publication, C. R. Drew Postgraduate Medical School, pp. 215-222.

McGee, D.P., & X (Clark), C. (1973). Genetic Research and Black Intelligence. Los Gatos, CA: Nefertiti Publishers

Moynihan, D. (1965). Employment income and the ordeal of the Negro family. *Daedulus,* 94, 745-770

Muhammad, E. (1965). *Message to the Black Man.* Chicago: Muhammad Mosque of Islam.

Nobles, W.W. (1972,1980). African Philosophy: Foundations for Black Psychology in Jones, R. *Black Psychology* (1st. & 2nd eds.) New York: Harper and Row.

Nobles, W. W. (1974). "Africanity: Its Role in Black Families," Black *Scholar,* Vol. 5, No. 9 (June 1974), pp.10-17.

Nobles, W. W. (1978). "The Black Family and its Children: The Survival of Humanness," Black *Books Bulletin,* Vol. 6, No. 2, pp. 7-16.

Nobles, W.W. (1984). Standing in the river, transformed and transforming: The re (ascension) of psychology in Nobles, W.W. *African Psychology.* Oakland, CA: A Black Family Institute Publication.

Nobles, W.W. (1984). Ancient Egyptian thought and the development of Afrikan (Black) psychology Presented to "The First Annual Ancient Egyptian Studies Conference: The Social Life. Los Angeles, February 24-26, 1984.

Orley, J. (1973). *Culture and Mental Illness: A Study from Uganda.* International Publishing Service.

Richards, D. (1980). European mythology: The ideology of progress. In M. Asante, & A. Vandi (Eds.), *Contemporary black thought.* Beverly Hills: Sage Publishers.

Rogers, J.A. (1961) *Africa's Gift to America.* New York: Hula M. Rogers.

Thomas, C. (1971). *Boys No More.* Beverly Hills: Glencoe Press, 1971.

Schwaller de Lubicz, I. (1978). *Her-Bak: Egyptian Initiate.* New York: Inner Traditions International.

Szasz, T. (1960). Myth of mental illness, *American Psychologist, 15,* 113-118.

Schwaller de Lubicz, I. (1981). *The Opening of the Way*: New York: Inner Traditions International, 1981.

Schwaller de Lubicz, RA.(1977). *The Temple in Man.* New York: Inner Traditions International.

Schwaller de Lubicz. RA. (1978). *Symbol and the Symbolic.* New York: Inner Traditional International.

Shockley, W. (1972). Possible transfer of metallurgical and astronomical approaches to the problem of environment versus ethnic heredity. Quoted by Thomas, A., & Sillen, S. in *Racism and psychiatry.* Secaucus, NJ: Citadel.

Smitherman, G. (1977). *Talkin' and Testifyin': The Language of Black America.* Boston: Houghton Mifflin.

Stanton, W. (1960). *The Leopard's Spots: Scientific Attitudes Toward Race in America*, 18 15-1819. Chicago: University of Chicago Press.

Weems, L. (1969). "Relevance of power themes among male, Negro and White Paranoid Schizophrenics". *Int. J. of Social Psychiatry*, 15(3).

Welsing, F.C. (1970). *The Cress Theory of Color Confrontation.* Washington, D.C.: C-R Publishers.

Wright, B. (1975). *The Psychopathic Racial Personality.* Chicago: Third World Press.

Williams, C. (1976). *The Destruction of Black Civilization.* Chicago: Third World Press.

Williams, R.L. (Ed.)(1975). *Ebonics: The True Language of Black Folks.* St. Louis: Williams & Associates.

Wilson, A. (1978). *Psychological Development of the Black Child.* New York: United Brothers Communications Systems.

Acknowledgements

An accurate and comprehensive listing of all of those deserving acknowledgement for making this work possible would result in a rather voluminous document. So many people have taught, inspired, encouraged, supported and loved me in order to make this work possible. The papers in this volume capture most of my scholarly writings for the vast majority of my career. From that perspective almost everyone I have known over the last thirty years has in someway contributed to this work. To all of those who know that I know you, I must first extend my gratitude to you for being in my life.

In a more particular way, there are some specific people who shared early on in the conversations and discussions that gave birth to these ideas. In this regard, I must celebrate and thank my dear friend, now transitioned, D. Phillip McGee who began these conversations with me about African Psychology. The dedication of this volume to his memory is an acknowledgement of his very special contributions to the unshackling of my mind permitting the development of these ideas.

Wade Nobles, has remained a wonderful friend and a twin mind for over thirty years and we seem to maintain an on-going mental dialogue, ending up at the same place at the same time whether we see each other or not. Syed Khatib was an early and influential guide to so many of these ideas and I thank him for his audacity.

Adib Shakir, Kobi Kambon, Charlyn Harper Brown, and Asa Hilliard have been long-term colleagues who have inspired and stimulated so many of the ideas that are shared in this volume. In more recent years, conversations with the brilliant minds of Cheryl (Tawede) Grills, Marimba Ani, Thomas Parham, Morris F.X. Jeff, Jr., Tony Browder, Leon Caldwell, Jeremiah Wright, Willie Wilson, Nathan McCall and Iyanla Vanzant have continued to feed and stimulate my mental growth in grasping and communicating these ideas.

Alvin Turner who did the preface for this volume is a long time confidant and colleague who has been a shoulder of support and a stimulating mind. Jerome Schiele who did the Foreword is an important friend, colleague and comrade in the struggle for the mental liberation of the oppressed and the intellectual expansion of humanity as a whole. Jerome Schiele has certainly incorporated, applied and expanded on more of my ideas in his brilliant and insightful writings than has any single young scholar that I know.

There is an array of people who keep my spirit alive by their love, support encouragement and just their presence on this planet. Rev. Dr. Barbara King is my very dear friend and spiritual mother whose frequent conversations and spiritual energy feed and heal me in multiple dimensions. I cannot imagine what my life would be like without the frequent or occasional conversations with Nashid Koleosa Fakhrid-Deen, Minister Louis Farrakhan, Lee Jones, Tavis Smiley, Susan Taylor, Lester Bentley, Jeanette Sabir-Holloway, Na'im Majied, Adib Shakir, Brent McPherson (a/k/a Omar Akbar,) Benson Cooke, Abdul Shakir, and Patrice Butler.

The people who work with me on my staff help to keep my life organized and productive: Dwayne Cole, Byron Thomas, Syiddah Mu'min and Kevin Brown are the posse of "Mind Productions and Associates."

Of course, my family constitutes the major wind beneath my wings. The love and support of my multi-talented, exuberant and nurturing daughter, Shaakira Akbar Anthony, my son-in-law, Derek Anthony; my wonderful and devoted sons Mutaqee and Tareeq Akbar, who keep me aloft with high expectations and regenerative love and the most recent additions to our clan, my grandchildren and insurance that tomorrow will be tended: Hassan Jhari Anthony and Niarra Jamillah Rena Anthony.

At this juncture in my life these are the names and spirits that tend the garden of my being. In varying ways and degrees they water, weed and feed my mind, body and spirit. I thank the Creator that these identified souls have all been placed in my life as well as the so many nameless ones who abide on the ancestral plane and those who constitute a multitude of supporters, students and friends who make it possible for me to do whatever I have been blessed to do. Thank you all for just being who you are.

Index

A

affirmative action 7
African
  i, iii, iv, v, vi, vii, viii, ix, x, xi,
  xii, xiii, xiv, xv, xvi, xviii, xix, 3,
  7, 8, 9, 10, 11, 14, 15, 16, 17,
  18, 19, 20, 21, 22, 23, 24, 25,
  26, 29, 30, 32, 33, 34, 35, 36,
  38, 39, 40, 41, 43, 44, 45, 46,
  47, 48, 49, 50, 51, 52, 53, 54,
  55, 56, 57, 58, 59, 60, 61, 62,
  63, 65, 66, 67, 68, 70, 71, 72,
  73, 74, 75, 76, 77, 79, 80, 81,
  83, 84, 85, 86, 87, 88, 91, 92,
  93, 96, 97, 98, 99, 100, 101,
  102, 103, 104, 105, 107, 108, 109,
  110, 111, 112, 113, 114, 115, 116,
  117, 118, 119, 120, 121, 122, 123,
  124, 125, 129, 130, 131, 132, 133,
  134, 135, 136, 137, 142, 148, 149,
  150, 151, 153, 154, 157, 158, 159,
  160, 161, 162, 163, 164, 165, 166,
  167, 168, 170, 171, 172, 174, 175,
  176, 177, 178, 179, 180, 181, 182,
  183, 184, 187, 188, 189, 190, 192,
  193, 197, 198, 199, 200, 202,
  203, 213, 215, 216, 219, 221,
  223, 231, 225, 226, 227, 228,
African Psychology
  ix, x, xi, xiv, xv, xvi, xviii, 3,
  7, 8, 9, 10, 11, 14, 15, 16, 17,
  18, 22, 25, 29, 30, 61, 62, 66,
  67, 73, 75, 76, 77, 80, 84, 85,
  91, 105, 121, 135, 154, 159, 197,
  198, 203, 216, 231, 228
Africanity 21
Africentric. *See* Afrocentric
Afrocentric xv, xvi, xviii,
29, 30, 92, 157, 158, 222, 223
Afrocentricity xv, 221
Akan 123, 137, 149, 151, 214
Akbar, Naim iii, xvi, xviii, xx, 3
Akhu 207, 211, 212, 214, 215
Alien-Self Disorder
  165, 166, 169, 181, 190
Ani, Marimba 231
Anti-life 164, 178
Anti-Self Disorder
  165, 169, 170, 176, 184, 185
Artificial Humanism 95
Asante, Molefi xv
Association of Black Psychologists
  106, 158, xi, xii, xiii
Atmu 207, 212, 213
Azibo, Daudi xix, 158
Azibo Nosology 158

B

Ba 207, 210, 211, 213, 215
Baldwin, James 5
Baldwin, Joseph xv, xviii, 79, 92
Behaviorists 94
Ben Jochannan, Yosef 198, 199, 200
Billingsley, Andrew 44
Biogenetic 166
Black, Harun xvi
Braithwaite, Harold xvi
Browder, Tony 231

C

Caldwell, Leon 231
Call-and-Response 116, 124
Carruthers, Jacob 63-65, 198
Christ 212, 213
Clairvoyance 16

Clark, Cedric. *See* Khatib, Syed
Clarke, John Henrik 198
Colonialism 96, 184
Colonized Mentality 169
Conscience 63, 151, 153
consciousness 14
Counseling 131, 183

D

Darwinian 95, 142
deconstruction ix, xii, 29, 30, 48
Democratic Sanity
   61, 160, 161, 169
depigmentation 11
Diop, Cheikh Anta
   iv, viii, 198, 199, 200, 202, 226,
   215, 219, 222
Dixon, Vernon xix, 75

E

Egypt 9
Egyptian 9
empirical xvii, 9, 11, 15, 16, 21,
   39, 49, 148, 213,
epistemology xiii, 38, 74,
   76, 78, 79, 81, 82,
Ethnographic research 49
Eurocentric v, vii, viii, xii, xix, 29,
   30, 34, 37, 45, 56, 57, 59, 92,
   222,
extended-self 20

F

Falsification research 49
Fanon, F. 80
Fardan, Anees xvi
Farrakhan, Minister Louis
   xvi, 232
Frankfort 226, 212, 215
Freudian
   60, 67, 81, 93, 94, 95, 110,
   139, 151, 162

G

Gary, Lawrence 29
Grills, Cheryl (Tawede) 231

H

Hare, Nathan xvi
Harper-Bolton (Brown), Charlyn xvi,
   231
Health
   16, 47, 72, 87, 142, 157, 158,
   159, 160, 161, 162, 163, 164,
   169, 177, 179, 180, 184, 185,
   188, 189, 191, 193
heuristic research 50
Hilliard, Asa xviii, 198, 231
Homosexuals 166, 168
Horus 212
Humanistic 94, 95
Hyperactivity 116

I

Initiation 206
initiation 19, 46, 206
integration 5, 6, 7
intelligence 225, 4, 7, 8, 10, 14,
   16, 17, 22, 41, 43, 44, 47, 74,
   75, 76, 78, 81, 82, 142, 144,
   145, 147, 152, 211, 212, 214,
   215
Intuition 76, 104, 117, 118

J

Jackson, Gerald xv, xviii, 71, 108
James, George. G.M. xviii, 5, 49,
   199, 200, 205, 216, 227

K

Ka 207, 209, 210, 211, 212,
   213, 214

Kambon, Kobi. *See* Baldwin,
 Joseph
Karenga, Maulana 198
Kemit 139, 197, 198, 199, 203,
 205, 207, 213, 215
Khaba 207, 211, 215
Khatib, Syed xi, xviii, 3, 82, 108,
King, Lewis xix
Kuhn, Thomas 4

L

Language 109, 122, 229, 230
Leakey, Louis 10
Leakey, Richard 10
liberation vii, xiii, 6, 33, 46,
 50, 52, 53, 78, 86, 92,
 169, 215, 225, 231

M

Ma'at x, 212
Massey 200, 207, 209, 210, 212,
 216, 227
McAdoo, Harriette 29
McAdoo, John 29
McCall, Nathan 231
McClelland, David 37
McGee, D. Phillip xi, xiv, xviii, 3,
 35, 38, 46-47, 108, 183, 231
Melanin xiv, 10, 11, 122, 228
melanin 11
melanocytes 11
Melting Pot 226, 107, 121
Mentacide 158
Mental 163
Mental Illness 164
Metaphysics 151
Metapsychology 135, 153
Microcosm 67, 150, 204, 205
Misorientation 158
Muhammad Elijah. *See* Muhammad
 Honorable Elijah

Muhammad, Honorable Elijah xvi,
 8, 25, 97
Myers, Linda James xviii
Mysteries 205, 206

N

Nation of Islam iii, xvi,
 xvii, xviii, 97, 127,
 128, 154, 185
Negro 18, 21, 35,
 41, 44, 50, 54, 68, 86, 99, 100,
 101, 102, 103, 131, 132, 162,
 178, 202, 227, 228, 229,
Neters 202, 204
Nichols, Edwin xix
Nigger 111, 172, 176
Nobles, Wade vii, xi, xiii,
 xviii, 3, 62, 68, 71, 92, 108, 200,
 203, 231,
Nommo 149
Nyama 149

O

Okra 123, 137, 149, 214
ontological xix, 14, 19, 20, 21, 45,
Oppression
 v, vi, vii, 22, 32, 40, 45, 65,
 66, 67, 68, 70, 71, 73, 79, 80,
 83, 86, 87, 91, 107, 153, 157,
 158, 160, 161, 162, 163, 164, 166,
 169, 171, 172, 175, 176, 180,
 184, 186, 188, 189, 191, 192,
 193
Organic Disorder 165, 174
Original Man 97, 98, 103, 104
Osiris 209, 212

P

Pan Africanist xx

paradigm
xi, xii, xiii, xiv, xv, xvi, xviii,
5, 6, 7, 29, 30, 32, 33, 34, 35,
38, 40, 42, 44, 45, 48, 49, 52,
53, 92, 157, 158, 198, 221,
222, 223
parapsychology 16
Parham, Thomas xix, 231
Pharaoh 204
Pluralism 121
precognition 16, 17
Psyche 200, 213
psychic ability 17
Psychogenic 166
psychokinesis 16, 17
Psychotherapy 70, 183
Psychotic 172, 173, 185
Putah 207, 212, 214
pyramid 9

R

Ramey, Louis xv
reconstruction x, 30, 48, 67,
69, 91, 92, 104
rhythm 18, 19, 69, 70, 71, 97,
99, 110, 115, 124, 125, 131,
132, 133

S

Sakhu 200
Schiele, Bernard xvi
Schiele, Jerome 231
Schwaller de Lubicz
201, 204, 206, 207
210, 211, 212, 216, 229
Seb 207, 212, 214
segregation 5, 6, 7, 108, 128
Self- Destructive Disorder 165, 172
self-knowledge xv, xvii, 15, 16, 17,
33, 52, 53, 77, 185, 186, 188,
189, 191, 192, 205,
Shakir, Adib. *See* Schiele, Bernard
Shockley, William 43

spirit x, xi, 14, 21, 38, 127, 131,
132, 137, 145, 148, 149, 150, 151,
188, 189, 191, 211, 212, 232
spiritual i, iv, x, xvi, 9, 14, 16, 20,
23, 24, 25, 37, 45, 48, 51, 53,
80, 92, 96, 97, 98, 99, 100,
104, 127, 129, 130, 137, 138,
140, 144, 148, 149, 150, 151,
152, 153, 154, 175, 187, 188,
192, 203, 205, 210, 211, 212,
214, 223, 232
spirituality 20, 45, 52
Spontaneity 119
Sunsum 151

T

Taylor, Kevin xvi
Turner, Alvin ii, 231

V

Van Sertima, Ivan 197, 198
Vanzant, Iyanla 231
vitalistic pneumaticism 19
Voodoo x, xv, 3, 17, 26, 29, 86,
91, 105, 121, 177, 226

W

Weems, Luther. *See* Akbar, Naim
Welsing, Frances Cress xiv, xvi,
65, 79
White, Joseph 60, 83
Williams, Robert xvi, 74, 200,
Wilson, Willie 231
Wright, Bobby xv, 158
Wright, Jeremiah 231

X

X, Cedric. *See* Khatib, Syed
X, Luther. *See* Akbar, Na'im
X, Malcolm vi

About the author

Na'im Akbar, Ph.D.

Noted scholar, lecturer and author, Dr. Na'im Akbar has established a highly respected reputation for his research in African-American Psychology. His scholarship in this area has led to numerous honors including the Distinguished Psychologist Award from the National Association of Black Psychologists; Honorary Doctorate of Human Letters from Edinboro University of Pennsylvania and Lincoln University as well as commemorative Days named in his honor in Atlantic City, New Jersey; Jackson, Mississippi; Cleveland, Ohio and Cincinnati, Ohio.

Dr. Akbar has served on the Boards of Directors of several important civic and professional organizations, including the Board of the National Association of Black Psychologists to which he was elected president in 1987.

Dr. Akbar is a graduate of the University of Michigan, where he earned the B.A., M.A., and Ph.D. degrees. He served as chairman of the Department of Psychology at Morehouse College and on the faculty at Norfolk State University. He currently is on the psychology faculty at Florida State University, as well as President of his private consulting company.

He has appeared on numerous national, television talk shows including The Oprah Winfrey Show, Tony Brown's Journal, and The Phil Donahue Show. Significant articles about him have appeared in many national newspapers and magazines, including The Washington Post, and Essence Magazine. Akbar has received scores of awards and plaques from all over the world and he is recognized as one of the great Thinkers and Orators of our time.

He is the very proud father of three adult children and two grand-children.

Other Publications by

Dr. Na'im Akbar

Breaking the Chains of Psychological Slavery

The Community of Self

Light from Ancient Africa

Natural Psychology and Human Transformation

Visions for Black Men

Know Thy Self

Audio, video cassettes, and CD's of Dr. Akbar's lectures as well as contact with Dr. Akbar for lectures and live presentations can be obtained from:

Mind Productions & Associates, Inc.
P.O. Box 11221
Tallahassee, FL 32302

Tel. (850) 222-1764
Toll free: (800) 662-6463
Fax: (850) 224-5331

Webpage address: www.mindpro.com
E-mail address: sales@mindpro.com